Photograph by Hugh Cecil

The Prince of Wales

THE KING'S FIRST AMBASSADOR

Other Works by Basil Maine

Biographies

ELGAR: HIS LIFE AND WORKS (2 Volumes)
CHOPIN
PADEREWSKI (in "GREAT CONTEMPORARIES")

Novels

RONDO
PLUMMER'S CUT

Essays

RECEIVE IT SO
BEHOLD THESE DANIELS
THE DIVISIONS OF MUSIC (Edited)
REFLECTED MUSIC

*A biographical study of
H.R.H. The Prince of Wales*

THE
KING'S FIRST
AMBASSADOR

by

BASIL MAINE

WITH 27 ILLUSTRATIONS

HUTCHINSON & CO.
(Publishers) Ltd.
LONDON

Made and Printed in Great Britain at
The Mayflower Press, Plymouth. William Brendon & Son, Ltd.
1935

PREFACE

AT the time when this book was being conceived and planned, I discussed the project with Sir Godfrey Thomas, Bt., Private Secretary to the Prince of Wales, and since then I have been in communication with him in connection with various details. I wish to thank him for the valuable advice and the always courteous assistance which he has given me. I desire also to acknowledge my indebtedness to the following works, authors and publishers : *The Biography of the Prince of Wales*, by W. and L. Townsend, published by Albert E. Marriott and Son; *H.R.H., a character study of the Prince of Wales*, by Major F. E. Verney, published by Hodder and Stoughton; *Speeches by the Prince of Wales*, published by Hodder and Stoughton; *H.R.H., a pictorial biography*, by E. C. Middleton, published by John Lane; and *Sport and Travel in East Africa*, compiled from the private diaries of the Prince of Wales by Patrick R. Chalmers, published by Philip Allan. The last of these volumes has been particularly helpful, not only as a record of the Prince's visits to East Africa, but also because of Mr. Chalmers' experience of big game hunting. Both author and publisher are to be congratulated on a very interesting publication. It is impossible to name all the newspapers over whose files I have continually pored for confirmation of facts, dates and spoken words. My most frequent guides were *The Times*, the *Times of India*, the *Daily Mail*, the *Morning Post*, the *Sunday Times*, the *Observer*, the *Daily Telegraph* and the *Sunday Graphic*. I am indebted, therefore, to the editors of these and of other journals, not to mention those anonymous experts, the reporters.

B. M.

CONTENTS

9

CONTENTS

CONTENTS

CONTENTS

Commons. How the Prince received this interference with his personal liberty. A broken collar-bone. Plays polo well. No great love for shooting or fishing. Squash-rackets, the best-liked game of all. Cards— almost an aversion. " Crown-and-Anchor " in the trenches. Active support of National Playing Fields Fund. The Prince and the post-War generation. His regularity. Fitness for service the dominating motive of his life. A tribute to the King which is no less applicable to the Prince.

CHAPTER 8

The Prince's example in dark and difficult times. British Legion nearest his heart. The fruits of war experience. Never forgetful of ex-service men. The Prince's resolve as strong and clear as ever. His warnings to the on-coming generation. His qualifications as a leader. His devotion to England. A day in Durham, as Patron of the National Council of Social Service. His example to the House of Commons. The Prince's public addresses. Analysis of his address to the Royal Institute of British Architects, 1934. The effects of the speech.

CHAPTER 9

A word to the idly curious. The Prince's wardrobe. No aspiration to be " the best-dressed man." His sense of humour. Cracking Scots jokes. The Prince on books and newspapers. A tribute from the Archbishop of Canterbury. The Prince among the farmers. The Albert Hall Speech, 27 January, 1932, and its three points : (1) A fresh response to national service. (2) Opportunity is at our own door. (3) " Away with depression and apathy : they are the Devil's own ! " Effects of the speech : a check to the tendency of making the State's increasing power an excuse for individual indifference.

CONTENTS

CHAPTER 10

CHAPTER 11

CHAPTER 12

CHAPTER 13

CONTENTS

CHAPTER 14

CHAPTER 15

APPENDICES

LIST OF ILLUSTRATIONS

The King's First Ambassador

CHAPTER 1

PROLOGUE

THERE is a photograph which, to the writer, has always seemed as apt a symbol of the dawn of the twentieth century in England as any consciously composed picture or official poem could be. It is a simple photograph, showing the present Prince of Wales, at the age of six, and one of his brothers, looking over the Palace wall to watch the Mounting of the Guard. The Prince is wearing a sailor suit. Already he was, without knowing it, a leader of fashion, for there was, of his generation, hardly a male child of us who did not follow him in that particular suit. With the accompanying knotted cord, whistle and large, round, flexible-brimmed straw hat, it was a part of our boyhood's charade. We did not take part in the game, however, with more glee than our parents. It was, in fact, more their show than ours. But if there was any spirit of revolt among us it was never encouraged, and if we began by being a little self-conscious in our fancy dress, the feeling in all but the most abnormal was soon displaced by a possessive pride. In that photograph, the young Prince seems already at ease in the white blouse and the great circle of a hat. Perhaps the assurance of his bearing was due, even then, to a realisation of the good fortune of being born an eldest son. In later years he surprised a fellow-cadet at Osborne with a piece of information as to the outstanding advantage of that accident of birth. "When you are the eldest," the Prince told him, "you have not got to wear any of your brother's clothes." The sailor suit was made for him and was his own. That explains at least some degree of his self-confidence as he stands there, head, and almost shoulders, above his brother.

Behind them the trees are in midsummer leaf; in front is the high wall, and below, people in their stiff, straight clothes are passing by or standing to watch the pageant. If for a moment we put the pageant out of mind, it calls for no great flight of fancy to see in that wall the dividing-line between the nineteenth and the twentieth centuries, and to see in the Prince's attentive gaze the looking out of a young child upon the future with its unknown responsibilities. Yes, already we can speak, with this photograph before us, of responsibilities, of burdens to be shouldered, for the sun's glare has caused the boy, in protecting his eyes, to force a frown. There is, too, in his expression a concentrated interest, and at an age when an open-eyed wonder might have appeared appropriate the features show instead more than a suggestion of practical observation.

But that, of course, is in relation to the Mounting of the Guard. In imagining the boy as looking towards the coming years, we need not pretend that there was anything for him to observe lest we end by attributing to him the qualities of a seer. Being a boy, six years old, he was doubtless as much a dreamer as most children of that age are. But that is our childhood's condition, to be walled in by the fantasy we create for ourselves. The Prince has since revealed that by nature he is not in the least a dreamer, if by that expression is understood one who is content to stay a-dreaming in a world of increasingly urgent change. When as a boy he looked over the Palace wall (and we may be grateful to that photographer either for his inspiration or his vigilance) it was, we may be sure, a military ceremony of a domestic nature that he saw. And we can be equally

18

sure that his elders in the staring crowd saw nothing more than that; were not aware, that is to say, of any prophetic significance in that smartly dressed, brightly coloured, well-produced enactment. In the pageant of everyday life this episode was, in people's minds, entitled " Homage to Loyalty and to Orderliness." And so simply it was regarded. How could anyone, living in the year 1900, have had prevision of the tragic Mounting of the Guard which was carried out, but then without leisure and orderliness, fourteen years later ?

So far from being a dreamer, the boy Prince at whom we have been looking in the photograph has been an unmistakable realist through the succeeding phases of his life. It so happens that the first pages of this study are being written on the Prince's fortieth birthday. The occasion has been celebrated by leading articles in the newspapers throughout the land. For the last twenty years the Press has always marked the 23rd of June as a day of tribute to the heir to the throne; but, whereas the early tributes were often stilted formalities, in later years a far more spontaneous enthusiasm can be read between the lines of these editorial pronouncements. They no longer have the air of a journalistic ritual. The reason is not far to seek. The Prince has proved himself. If it were not so this passage from a tribute in the *Observer* could not conceivably have been written : " The nation has long since felt itself assured that the Prince followed no mere path of obligation. He has shown an exploring mind, a quickness of sympathy and a touch with the vital growths of current history that the highest diplomatic ability could never have feigned. As he has become increasingly absorbed in the network of public life his individual bent and natural disposition have progressively declared themselves."

Those words are here quoted because they call to mind a figure, a type, with which the Prince has never at any time been identified, namely, the Feigning Diplomat. So ubiquitous is that figure, so obviously patterned is he, that he can be given capital letters without fear of exaggerating his numbers and influence. Diplomacy has its uses. It is more than useful in these years when all nations, and all classes within nations, are driven into conflict by a prevailing inferiority complex. But, in the nature of things, diplomacy must always be untrustworthy. It is the art of temporising, the fine art of cultivating insincerity to the finest degree. The Prince has never had any ambition to master that art. Since his coming of age he has shown a free and flexible mind, one that has impatiently cast off the shackles of diplomatic observances. Frequently in his speeches he has declared for that freedom and flexibility. He has made open war on the cant of official expression, and so far as he himself is concerned he has utterly defeated it. It is his belief that the sincere motive needs no more verbosity than good wine needs bush, that goodwill is best conveyed through straightforwardness. During the twenty years of his life which form the subject of this study, goodwill to all sorts and conditions of men has been the leading motive. The governing strength and the power of development which are unfolded by a central theme in a work of art can be discerned in this *idée fixe* of the Prince's manhood. So much so that, whatever his private problems and distractions have been, however threatening they have sometimes appeared, the resultant design of his career presents to the spectator (to this author, in fact) a unique and most satisfying aspect of the art of living.

This is not to say that a single motive has led the Prince, as it sometimes leads the zealots among us, along a narrow path. The range of his interests has saved him from becoming the bore that, alas, the man or woman of goodwill so often is. That and a capacity for hard work have given him at the age of forty the look of a man eight or ten years younger. Lest the reader should think this an idle, easy compliment, let him but look around among any of his friends who are between thirty-five and forty. The trim figure, the activity and the alert bearing of the Prince argue a rigorous self-discipline that, to judge by appearances, is not practised by the majority of his generation. If the reader's experience leads to a more favourable verdict than this he is happy in his acquaintances who, in all probability, have been influenced by the Prince's example. It was an example set and upheld when most it was needed—during that period of drifting and dis-illusion and bitterness which followed the Armistice. To this day that ideal of self-training and service has been maintained. So rare are the Prince's leisure days that the quiet spending even of a birthday at Fort Belvedere is by no means to be taken for granted. Only by making elaborately previous plans can that particular occasion be kept clear of public and official engage-ments. After that, his normal activities are immediately resumed, as this skeleton diary of the week following his fortieth anniversary testifies : Tuesday, Inspection of the Welsh Guards, as Colonel of the Regiment, at Wellington Barracks ; Wednesday, Visit to a Kent Social Service Display at Maidstone ; Thursday, at the Italian Embassy ; Saturday, at Hendon for the Royal Air Force Display. Then, the following week, to Ipswich for the Royal Agricultural Show.

To set forth a bare list of activities is always dan-gerously near to suggesting a dull existence, for such a schedule *looks* dull. But this short extract from a normal week in the Prince's life is given here to indicate the variety of his interests and but a few of his spheres of influence. And, in each case, the interest and influence are real. Even if he himself regards the programme as part of the common round, its importance is not thereby reduced. Indeed, it is a tribute to his democratic spirit that he is able to undertake such a miscellany of engage-ments as being all in the day's work. They are not carelessly accepted, these engagements. If they are to be part of his daily work he takes good care that they

represent some vital interest of his own. Were it otherwise, boredom would have aged him long ago. Of the
innumerable requests for his personal patronage, only
those are granted which can engage his full attention
and to which he can lend a whole-hearted advocacy.
To a high degree the spirit of adventure has always
animated his way of living. He has the gift of discovering adventure, whether he is touring the distant parts
of the Empire or merely going the round in the home
country. To interpret the Prince's activities as representing the life of an uncommonly busy district visitor,
is to overlook the peculiar charm of his personality.
There, in the writer's opinion, lay the weakness of that
film of the Prince's official life which was released not
long ago. The scenes had been unimaginatively compiled. Whereas formality had been unnecessarily stressed,
character was almost entirely suppressed. One hand-
shake is very much like another; and to show twenty
handshakes instead of one is not necessarily to make a
film twenty times as interesting.

It is the purpose of this study to catch a reflection of
its subject's personality. Especially in relation to his
conception of service will he be regarded. There could
hardly be a better angle of observation than this. Since
his coming of age the Prince of Wales has set himself
the task of carrying out a definite programme in connection with social reforms and endeavour in this country,
and yet another in encouraging loyalty and co-operation
among the peoples of the British Empire. In the succeeding chapters he will be followed along the various
paths to which that programme has led him, so that his
achievement and the extent of his influence can in some
measure be appraised. His active campaign has always
attracted the intense interest of his contemporaries,
whatever their nationality; and it is as a result of a
spontaneous admiration for his spirit and accomplishment that this book is being written. No one is more
acutely aware than the author of the pitfalls that threaten

him on the way. One at least he will do all in his power
to avoid : the pit called Ineptitude, which claims so
many who write about living Royal personages. The
Prince of Wales deserves a better fate in literature than
to be set up as a uniformed effigy in a waxwork show.

For all the affection which he has everywhere inspired,
the importance of the Prince's work, and the true nature
of it, have yet to be completely understood. We accept
his popularity as being greater than that of any other
figure of our time ; but what is the secret of it ? For
popularity cannot live by publicity alone. In the
Prince's case, it is true to say that publicity has lived on
his phenomenal popularity. No role in life is more
difficult, indeed more dangerous, than that of the popular young man. Few can play it to the end. Whether
in art, or sport, or politics, or society, an early success
has impeded the career of many a man. It weakens
resistance to adversity, undermines that sense of proportion without which no achievement can be of lasting
value, upsets the balance which should be the goal of
all education. The apparent power which suddenly
arrives with success often goes to the head like wine,
inducing a false security and a false superiority, so that
every action tends to be intolerant and contemptuous.
In such a mental condition criticism is resented and,
because it threatens security, is blindly resisted. There
is no reason to believe that the early popularity of the
Prince was unattended by these dangers. We do well
to think of him as being human like all the rest of us.
It is strange that, in this era of blatant realism, that
simple, obvious statement should need so much repe-
tition. But the truth is there are still many who forget
or cannot imagine that it is true ! The Prince himself
is forever attempting to defeat the attitude of mind
which the average Englishman still unconsciously shows
towards the Royal Family, an attitude which concedes
human emotions and habits to its members only with
the greatest reluctance. Let us, then, dare to make a

platitude our starting-point : the Prince is a human being. It is a poor compliment to one who has so freely mixed with his countrymen to cloud his personality with unreal attributes, stilted anecdotes and an obsequious narrative. Having enjoyed, from boyhood on, a generous portion of favour and goodwill, he has also contended with all the implied disadvantages. They were as real to him as to any other triumphant young hero walking along the primrose path. Conceit, selfishness, intolerance, worldliness, cynicism and all the other deadly enemies were lurking by the wayside. But as the Prince passed along he gradually gained a mastery over inimical forces. Had it not been so, had he fallen in any one of these encounters, popular esteem would have been quick to desert him. For if the crowd must always have an object of affection and worship it must never be deceived. That same instinct which leads mankind to set up idols also prompts it to cast them down if at any time a flaw be discovered. It needs but a moment for people who have been crying that Brutus should be Cæsar to change their tune to praise Antony as the noblest man in Rome.

There is, then, to be explained the inescapable fact of the Prince's abiding popularity. In a sense, he is now more firmly established than ever in public esteem, for that esteem depends no longer upon spectacular occasions such as his Investiture at Carnarvon or his world travels. The glamorous phase has ended and we see him at close quarters, so to speak, settled among his countrymen, living as an ordinary citizen, sharing the community's routine and hopes and anxieties, working as hard as any man, making the most of holiday intervals[1] and caring wisely for physical fitness. Proximity has increased our affection, since it has helped us to recognise many exemplary qualities in his approach to the little problems of day-to-day living. We are more

[1] An instance was his ski-ing holiday at Kitzbühel as a preparation for the arduous period of the King's Silver Jubilee.

grateful for such an example than for that of a saint, for it is precisely these minor matters that saintliness, with disdain, often ignores. Moreover, and the point may easily be overlooked, the Prince's personal problems have not decreased with the passing of twenty years. That his youthfulness and vitality make as great an appeal to public imagination as ever is a tribute to his strength of purpose. There would have been little cause for wonder had he since slackened the pace with which he set out upon his manhood's career, especially as good health has not invariably assisted him. Not for a moment has he done so. His impetus is as forceful now as at his coming of age. An examination of his engagements, activities and speeches during the past six months has been enough to convince the writer on that point; if it were necessary to confirm the conviction a perusal of his engagements for the next three months would be sufficient! England is a country of good causes. To be a public man in England is to be a continual supporter of all such causes as are deemed worthy; and no public man has given more direct, more effective support of this kind than the Prince. To be hymned by diffident British voices as a jolly good fellow would not appear to a foreign observer to be a very generous, or even an adequate reward. But the compliment is most apt, for it is in honest fellowship that the Prince excels.

Reward in the sense that the average man understands it, is denied to the King and Queen and their children. It is not necessarily in a spirit of adverse criticism that philosophers, theologians and doctors agree to single out the idea of personal advancement as being the motive of the greater part of life's endeavour. Nor need we be surprised that during the past three decades the motive has been reinforced by the allurement of the films, the distortion of individual qualities that broadcasting encourages, and the mingled fantasy and reality of air travel. Seemingly, there is nothing now that man cannot accomplish. By aeroplane he can look down upon all the kingdoms of the earth; by microphone he can give out his opinions to all people without fear of contradiction. Everything encourages him to seek self-advancement, and every step up the ladder, whether it is measured in terms of wealth or social prestige, gives him the gratification of being rewarded for his pains. This means that whenever we see an act of charity advertised or see a good deed made dazzling by limelight we are instinctively aware of an ulterior motive. On the other hand, the peculiar virtue of the " services rendered " by the King and Queen and their family is that they are, and in the nature of the case must be, utterly without worldly motive. In their public life is to be discerned the selflessness of the priesthood; and in that, they are being true to the origins of kingship, which is in essence a priestly office. The differentiation between priest and king in the earliest times is a matter of the finest distinction; and in our own time we in England are witnessing a convergence of the two ideas. Sovereignty has for its focal point the sacred representation of a people, of its life, history and aspirations. In that representation no section is too obscure, no interest too insignificant to be included; and the moral force of the smallest endeavour is enhanced. When the new Chartered Insurance Institute in Aldermanbury was opened by the King we read in the Press the simple statement that Mr. George Atkins, a bricklayer of Norbury, Mr. George Moss, a plumber of Walthamstow, and Mr. George Colman, a carpenter of Southwark, were presented to the King and Queen. We were also informed that the King told them how pleased he was to meet them, and returned their handshakes with a warmth that surprised them; that the Queen, too, made them unmistakably welcome. The surprise is that such incidents are singled out by editors for notice, that they are not taken for granted. For never has the Sovereignty in England been more closely identified with the ideals of national life than now. It was a happy thought to choose three of his namesakes among working men to greet the King. George Atkins, bricklayer, meeting King George. What better illustration of the idea that the Monarchy is the embodiment of the people, in all estates and callings?

But if the theory of sovereignty, with its implications of the priesthood, remains unaltered, in practice the role of Sovereign has become increasingly exacting in proportion with the complexity of contemporary existence. To that role and the high example it has for many years evinced the Prince is heir. And already he has shown all the qualities that are needed to sustain it. His youth has been devoted to self-equipment. It has been a time of preparation, during which he has quietly accumulated knowledge of men and affairs and applied it to a diversity of interests. Few men of his age are more wise; few are more humble-minded. His passion has always been for direct experience, to know the world—the whole world, nothing less—at first hand. As soon as the days of tutors, Oxford and circumscribed continental visits were over he began to satisfy that passion to an extent that no former Prince of Wales had ever equalled. He did so with a zest which was only increased by the attendant discomforts and dangers. The War was his first graduation, and, after all the gossip and rumours and yarns have been sifted, we can now be sure that he felt the full force of its brutal shock. Its immediate effect was to send him, soon after the Armistice, exploring the vast honeycomb of labour at home and throughout the Empire. A catalogue of his subsequent movements is of little use if we are to convey the spirit with which this campaign was carried out. To record that he descended coal mines, studied aviation and turned it to practical account, went out with the fishing fleets, made himself acquainted with slum conditions and, in face of the most disheartening resistance, has since led the movement towards their defeat; to record, on the one hand, his chain of carefully prepared speeches in the interest of Empire unity, and, on the other hand, the encouragement he has given to local government; and again, his ready consent to relieve the strain of his father's work in times of ill-health, his live interest in farming, in hospitals, in the Boy Scout movement, his devotion to the cause of ex-service men and their organisations, his real love of sport and, especially (after some alarming accidents) of the steeplechase; and then to add a conscientious list of his tours—barely to record all this would be too easy a submission to the letter that killeth.

The purpose of this study is to recapture some of that spirit which has made the Prince's personality and life so immediately appealing to people in every part of the world. He himself would never have permitted his work to be advertised as being a crusade. But no other description seems adequate; and from that angle the past twenty years of his life will be approached in the chapters that follow. Also, the approach will be made in the belief that his magnetism is dependent not so much upon the accident of birth as upon the balance of character he has developed, an alert mind, an always well-planned activity, insight and fidelity; in the belief, indeed, that these attributes, so far from being reflected by the Prince's position, have themselves turned a new light upon the title of " King's eldest son," revealing above all else that the principles of sovereignty and those of democracy can together be harmoniously resolved.

CHAPTER 2

SELF-DISCOVERY

At Oxford. The Prince's desire to serve at the Front. Lord
Kitchener's objections. The Prince gets his wish. A General
Staff Officer. Adventures " off-duty." Soccer with the
Tommies. Queen Mary and the Belgian refugee's story.
Lending a hand to the R.A.M.C. The Prince conducts the
King on a tour along the lines. A piece of bad luck. The
Prince at the Front for his coming-of-age. Works for relief
organisations. May 16—with the Egyptian Expeditionary
Force. On the Italian front. Accompanied by King Victor
Emmanuel's A.D.C., the Prince visits the whole Isonzo front
as far as Montenegro. Home at the beginning of 1918 to take
his seat in the House of Lords. Strange effect of that ritual
in time of war. A memorable visit to Rome. After the
Armistice the Prince immediately goes to Dover to welcome
men released from German internment camps.

AMONG the men of his generation the Prince is
not alone in declaring that his university days
were the happiest of his life. He, however,
has special reasons for the wistful, backward look which
most graduates occasionally turn on that little interim.
For him, it was in the truest sense a time of free development, a testing time. Its significance was not lost upon
him. Irresponsibility, well he knew it, could either be
indulged in or used to heighten a sense of responsibility.
The welcome he received when he first arrived at Oxford
station did not encourage him to expect much freedom
there ; indeed, he was annoyed that it had been made a
crowded, official occasion. But his very first night at
Magdalen reassured him. At dinner in Hall that night
he began an ordinary undergraduate's life in the simplest
possible manner. Three hundred years before, when
a Prince of Wales (James the First's son) began his
university terms, it was thought necessary to segregate

him and his servants in Hall and to make his dining-in a minor State function. Even in our own time, a manifestation of this attitude was seen in King Edward the Seventh's university life, for not only did he live in special apartments, but a private design was devised for his cap and gown, which, incidentally, were proudly displayed until recently in the maker's shop window.

The present Prince of Wales's life at Magdalen carried none of these distinguishing marks. Indeed, it was his own wish to be regarded as an ordinary student, a wish that was respected by dons and undergraduates as soon as they had satisfied an initial curiosity. Magdalen College, with its catholicity of schools, opinions and tastes, provided an immediate environment that well accorded with his desires to meet and know all sorts and conditions. Especially in the political field did he encounter a wide range of ideas. The free speech and attendant loose thought which seem to be almost a condition of an English undergraduate's brief career, were everywhere around him. If by chance he found himself in the company of an extreme Socialist, he usually found a way for both to escape embarrassment. If it was a question of avoiding politics in the conversation, that was easily arranged; if it was a question of meeting extremists half-way, that, too, could be tactfully done. On one occasion the Prince went the whole way by giving an impromptu performance of " The Red Flag " for the benefit of a Socialist undergraduate, singing it to his own accompaniment on the banjo. How good, bad or indifferent the performance was the writer has no way of discovering. But it proved to be a master-stroke of conciliation.

The formative influence of those Oxford days can hardly be exaggerated. The Prince led an active life. In games it was his wish to have a shot at everything, and if he brought to light no latent genius for any one of them, it can at least be said of his golf that by virtue of the serious application which that game ruthlessly demands, he has become a thoroughly sound exponent. At Oxford he played polo, hunted with three packs, and found time for tentative excursions into cricket and tennis. Not long ago the writer of a newspaper article, seeking to extend the list of the Prince's athletic accomplishments, paid him a doubtful compliment. "In addition," he wrote, "the Prince played soccer in the Magdalen second eleven, and was very fast." So curt a statement succeeds in conveying only the faintest of praise, and, in any case, there is always the danger of the latter part of it being removed from its context for the exercise of mischievous tongues. The same writer solemnly informs his readers that when the Prince began his Army career as a private in the Oxford University Training Corps, "he did his weekly drills and parades in exactly the same manner as any other member of the corps." To have done otherwise would hardly have been to the Prince's credit. Besides, there was always the risk that original ideas of drill would be discouraged by what grim humorists still call "the unsubtle criticism of sergeant instructors." There is, indeed, no cause for surprise in the fact that, as a member of the O.T.C., the Prince of Wales did as other privates did, went to camp with them as part of the Territorial Army, shared a tent with the usual number, used the squad wash-tub, and even developed another of the grim humorists' conventions, the "lurid vocabulary," which, of course, and conventionally enough, he used "in no uncertain fashion." These simple facts do but show him only too willing to follow a normal course, only too happy to form friendships with some of those he met. So far from being condescending, he gave evidence of the natural desire in him to escape the loneliness with which university life can overwhelm a man. It is true that this ordinary, unprivileged life was part of a deliberate plan to avoid anything like the mistaken formality of King Edward's career as an undergraduate. But it was one thing to come up to Oxford as an ordinary freshman, with full intentions of living and behaving ordinarily, and another to persuade fellow-students to respect his intentions. On occasions he found it necessary to rebuke those whose attentions were too exuberant. " I wish you fellows would not make such a fuss," he said at a small dinner-party where they called upon him for a speech. Admirable reproof! But almost pathetic, too, for he had come to the party on the strict understanding that there were to be no speeches.

After a term or two, however, the problem of mixing with the crowd became less burdensome. But still to be reckoned with were those who considered that Pragger Wagger and the Prince of Wales were incompatible descriptions, if not, indeed, incompatible persons. They forwarded the dignity of the Crown as their weightiest reason. To them the phrase had a static meaning. It did not occur to them that even a phrase must move with the times if it is to retain any meaning at all. At Oxford the Prince was beginning to find a new significance in the dignity which appertains to Royalty, and new ways of expressing it in fellowship. The Union debates brought him into touch with every shade of political opinion, and with every degree of thinking ability, from the reasoned essays of near-lawyers to the sheerest hot air. While these clamant views reverberated all around him he kept his own counsel. Without making any show of a private intellectual problem he had, nevertheless, to find a way of reconciling the claims of tradition with the progressive bias of his nature. Essentially he was a young man of his own time.

But if it was at Oxford that the beginnings of self-discovery were being made, it was the war period that completed the process. No incident in the whole of the Prince's life has led to so much apologetic verbosity as his decision to serve with the British Army in France. It is hard to see any good reason for this. Some of the wordy smoke-screens that surround this particular

A War-time picture

episode only lead the reader to suppose that there was
something to hide. The facts are plain. The Prince
could easily have taken the line of least resistance by
joining Kitchener's staff in London with a superior rank
in the Army. During those early months of upheaval
no questions would have been asked. But the Prince
had a genuine wish to be on active service. We need
not pretend that the false glamour which drew so many
young men to the trenches at the outset was not also a
factor in forming his ambition. This and the sense of
duty which had always been educated in him combined
to make his requests urgent and insistent. There were
many who, for a variety of reasons, raised objections.
Lord Kitchener was obstinate, and to the Prince's argument that he was one of five sons, replied : " If I were
certain you would be shot I do not know if I should be
right to restrain you. What I cannot permit is the
chance, which exists until we have a settled line, of the
enemy securing you as a prisoner. You have a lot to
learn about soldiering yet. When you have learnt a bit
more perhaps then you may go to France."

Bluntness is the prerogative of the soldier at any
time ; in time of war it acquires an added virtue. Kitchener's words were taken to heart and a period of intensive training was begun. The Prince joined the 1st
Battalion of the Grenadier Guards at Warley Barracks
on August 10, 1914. He had been gazetted as a second-
lieutenant. Like many another young officer in those
early days, he took pride in his appearance in uniform ;
nor was he alone in looking under age when he joined
his regiment. Those smart lieutenant outfits were worn
in the first stages with a half-serious, half-irresponsible
air. For many they were a novelty and so provided
a little distraction from the thought of the dreaded
unknown future. But it was not every second-lieutenant
who had been urged on by a home-truth straight from
Lord Kitchener himself. The Prince had good reason
to take his new job seriously. He took less time than

most to shed that half-irresponsible air. At first there were doubts about his ability to endure the physical strain of Army life, and it was his constant endeavour to allay all fears on that score. About five weeks after he had joined his regiment it was preparing to leave for France. The prospect of seeing the Front was brought nearer. But more objections were raised, and when the time came for his platoon to depart it was his Colonel's duty to tell him that his training was not yet advanced enough for active service in the front lines. He was not vain enough to dispute the judgment of his senior officers, but he knew well that there were young lieutenants, no better trained than himself, who were allowed to take platoons to France. He knew, in fact, that once again he was up against that eternal abstraction, "reasons of State." He began to kick against the pricks.

The "authorities" for their part were at their wits' end. There were all kinds of arguments to be taken into account. The heir to the throne must not be put in the way of unnecessary danger: that was the first consideration. If a referendum had been taken in August, 1914, a majority would probably have been found in support of that view. On the other hand, there was undoubtedly a section of public opinion which held that the Prince of Wales must take his chances with the rest, the opinion, indeed, which the Prince himself held. It was not long before the Prince discovered that, in the eyes of the "authorities," his personal wishes were the least factor in the situation. He was beginning to understand the implications of being regarded as a tradition and a title and not at all as a living person. It was not a very cheerful thought.

At length the problem was solved in a compromise. First of all he was informed that he was fit for active service; later, on the way to France, he learnt that he had been given the appointment of aide-de-camp to Sir John French at General Headquarters. He came to the conclusion that the only way to overcome the restrictions which were for ever being put upon him was to lie quiet and plan some private adventure. The "authorities" hoped to secure his safety by keeping him busy and by having him closely watched. But their vigilance did not prevent the off-duty escapades which had been in his mind. It was his fixed intention to make close acquaintance with the private soldier wherever and whenever he could find him. What better opportunity than an impromptu game of football! Some Tommies were having a pick-up game on a slushy bit of ground behind the line. If not fast, the game was sufficiently furious. They played on for some time, unaware that one of the sides had picked up a member of Magdalen second eleven. Nor was he easily recognised at the end, for like the rest he was covered in mud. He had had the time of his life, he said.

There was the story, too, which Queen Mary was told by a Belgian refugee whose son had seen the Prince take cover in a Flanders village. The Prince had been walking alone through the village when a German aeroplane took him by surprise. There was just time to think : the Prince made his steel helmet a little more secure and, as if he had been a diviner, found the cellar of the little post office. It had been converted into an advanced aid post. In the candle-light the Prince saw the R.A.M.C. and some nuns attending to some of the worst cases. They were waiting for ambulances. When eventually these arrived the drivers discovered the Prince in shirt-sleeves lending a hand with the bandaging. It was no more than most of us would have done. But incidents of that sort commended him to the troops. They appreciated his desire to be one of themselves and the difficulties he encountered in realising it. "We thought it was a good show," said one of the drivers.

More than at any other time of his career the Prince was living and learning. In that hard school he took many lessons to heart. Not the least valuable of his assets was an ability to take all chaff, however rough or coarse, in good humour. He was not the only young officer who had occasional difficulty in finding his war legs, and until he could be sure of his equilibrium he knew he must occasionally be a target for the old hands and their scornful jests. He was never allowed to forget the time he wore canary-coloured puttees. "I'll bet he can sing all right," the old hand said. Ready wit was exercised on many other occasions at his expense. Rarely was it resented. How have these yarns come down to us if they have not been handed on by the Prince himself? He enjoys telling them. A laugh against himself provides a welcome opportunity to unbend. In this we see him possessed of one of the most normal of English qualities.

During King George's visit to his Army in 1916 his son proudly enjoyed the privilege of accompanying him on a tour along the lines. Here was the Prince's opportunity to turn his experience to account. The King soon discovered that his son had not been content with knowledge of his immediate environment. Even if the Prince could not pretend to be an expert on strategy he was able to give his father a description of the various fronts and the movements in this and that sector of the field. Those who saw the King during that visit can never forget the ovation he received from the troops, for although the Kaiser had given express orders to the German Air Force to place none of the British Royal Family in danger it was recognised that the King was risking his life in order to learn the conditions under which his subjects were fighting. He was gratified to know that a member of his own family was fully acquainted with those conditions. It was natural that Earl Haig should be solicitous for the Prince's welfare and, as far as possible, for his comfort, but he found the Prince only too willing to accept hardship when it came his way. How completely he had sunk his position and title and had succeeded in allowing his personality to emerge is witnessed by the occasion when, after a long day's march, he slept, and slept soundly, on the floor. With a party of soldiers he had arrived at a village and found a shortage of billets. The senior officers took what they could find in the shape of beds, but in the fatigue and hurry, and also because he was never self-assertive, they left the Prince out of reckoning. When the oversight was noticed there were offers from the billet-holders, but the Prince refused them all. It was a case of bad luck and there was an end of the matter. With his knapsack for pillow and his British-warm for covering he thought he could manage quite well on the floor.

The development of his character was accelerated by these months of war service. In peace-time he could never have been brought so close to the average types of his countrymen, could never have seen and judged them for what they really were, could never have watched the free interplay of their temperaments. He was an eye-witness of the tremendous enactment, but a participator also. He could not stand aloof. Inevitably he was drawn into the playing of those grim scenes, drawn into the pattern which was being woven of men's lives. He felt the full shock of death's devastation. Personal tragedies were continually being brought home to him. One of the losses he felt most was the death of the chauffeur who had been in his service since those remote-seeming Oxford days. The Prince, on duty, had been driven to the fighting zone, had left the car and his chauffeur for a short period, and returned to find both blown to smithereens. What he could recover of the man's personal belongings he collected and carefully stored away, and when next he went to England he restored them himself to the chauffeur's family.

Such incidents as those which have been here set down serve to supplement the more general description of the Prince's duties which we read in the official despatches. This, for example, is an extract from an

Army Order: " H.R.H. Edward Prince of Wales, Staff Captain[1] in the 14th British Army Corps from July to October, 1917, in the region of Boesinghe-Langemarck, by ensuring liaisons up to the first lines under bombardment, contributed very effectively to the close co-operation in the battle of the 14th British Army Corps and the First French Army." A dispatch from Sir John French stated that reports from General Officers agreed in commending the thoroughness with which the Prince performed any work entrusted to him, and added : " H.R.H. did duty for a time in the trenches with a battalion to which he belongs."

His service throughout the War was almost continuous, for his periods of leave were spent in obtaining support for this or that emergency organisation. No leave was granted for his coming-of-age, nor did he desire it. He celebrated the event at the Front, and asked that an announcement should be sent out from Buckingham Palace expressing his wish for a postponement of public ceremonies in this connection until peace was declared. As soon as two years after the outbreak of hostilities he had started a fund, under his own name, for the relief of those whose near relations had been killed in action. He stressed the importance of having ready the means of relief. His motive was to go some way towards staying distress by alleviating anxiety. At the beginning of 1916 he was chairman of the first committee meeting in connection with the Naval and Military Pensions Act. By reason of his close association with the troops he was able to speak then not only convincingly but also effectively. In his speech there was one passage in particular which indicated that, in spite of the deadening pressure of immediate events, he was trying to take a long view and to urge others to do the same. " There is a class," he said, " to whom the whole sympathy of the nation will go out,

---

[1] His promotion to captaincy was gained after nearly two years of war.

and who may count upon the hearty consideration of this committee, those who in the prime of manhood and vigour of health have been permanently disabled. Although they will receive substantial pensions from the State, our special duties will be to initiate schemes of training and of finding employment, and thus enable them to feel that they are still active members of the community." The words carry no especial eloquence. They form the plainest of statements. But in the light of recent years their point is made sharper. Increase of crime, class antagonism and conflict, the nursing of social grievances, are not these and others of our present discontents due to the numbers who have lost that sense of being active members of the community ? The Prince was then referring only to the men who had been physically disabled for life. An even greater problem is presented by those who, having been wounded and having since recovered a measure of health and physical fitness, are nevertheless permanently disabled in mind and spirit. Nineteen years ago the Prince had dimly foreseen that problem and did his best to put into motion the machinery which might conceivably help to counteract it. He was wise enough to see that the State unaided could not possibly meet the case. He struck the note of voluntary service, and has continued to strike it ever since. Here is a passage from another speech he made in 1916 : " Any State grants which may be made from time to time—and already the Chancellor of the Exchequer has promised to ask Parliament to start us on our way—will, I hope, be used, in the wealthiest areas at all events, to support and stimulate, not to supplant and suffocate, local effort and local generosity." With a more mature outlook the Prince was able to express the same hope more forcibly and in more detail in his famous Albert Hall speech of January 27, 1932, wherein he warned his audience of the danger of making the State's increasing power an excuse for personal apathy.

There is no doubt that the Prince's varied experience
of the War gave power to his elbow whenever he
addressed emergency committees in England. He was
given the opportunity to see more than one area of the
great struggle. In 1916 the "authorities" decided to
attach him to the Mediterranean Expeditionary Force.
He spent an uncomfortable time in Egypt and then
proceeded to the Italian Military Headquarters. This
was an opportunity for the Italians to express their
warm regard for England and implicitly encourage the
hope of an Anglo-Italian royal marriage. Driving in
an open car with the King of Italy, the Prince was given
an eager and high-spirited ovation. The interlude was
not an unmixed blessing. It served to remind him that
inimical forces can lurk in pacific relations no less than
in the conflict of war. The enemy called Rumour
menacingly crossed his path. Stories were told in
England that the Italians' warm-heartedness and the
Prince's consent to be a guest of the Italian Royal Family
undoubtedly pointed to an imminent engagement
between him and the eldest daughter of that family, the
Princess Yolanda of Savoy. Official denials were un-
availing. They did but help the enemy to wax fat and
flourish. Even after the Armistice it was busy with that
particular item of news. And since then it has frequently
lifted its head and given tongue to all manner of false-
hoods and importunate wishes. The Prince perforce
has had to learn that, on such occasions, silence is his
most effective weapon. Few factors can have contributed so much to the forming of his character as
these encounters, for to be silent while the public makes
arbitrary decisions on the most vital and personal
details of one's life is to exercise self-discipline in its
extremest form.

The Prince, it is true, did become a cousin to the
King of Italy when the latter conferred upon him
the Order of the Annunziata ; but whatever hopes the
public idly entertained of a closer relationship were

At Dover for the unveiling of the Patrol Memorial

discouraged, as similar hopes have since been discouraged, by the Prince's fixed determination to lead at least a part of his own life and, in matters of private judgment, to be independent. The visit to the Italian area was marked throughout by the most cordial expressions of racial and personal friendship. In the company of the King of Italy's A.D.C. the Prince systematically visited the various fronts and was as anxious to make close acquaintance with the Italian troops as he had been to know the Tommies. The visit ended with a sea cruise to Grado.

If a graph were plotted of his movements during the rest of the War it would leave the impression of an erratic existence. It was an erratic period. Nerves were frayed. The first problem for every man was to keep a hold on himself. The Prince managed to keep going by plunging into all kinds of reconstruction movements. He developed a faculty for speech-making. It was against the grain, but he saw the necessity of training himself to overcome personal aversions. He did so successfully enough to receive a compliment from Mr. Balfour, who said : " He shows an admirable lucidity and restrained eloquence whenever he speaks of the War." That from a master of lucidity and restraint was praise indeed. At the beginning of 1917 we hear of the Prince on a flying visit to England and addressing his committee for the care of war graves. Then, soon after, we hear of him bringing over dispatches from Sir John French to the Secretary for War, and afterwards spending a few days' leave at Windsor and relating his experiences to his parents. Apart from signs of temporary fatigue, his appearance at this time gave no cause for anxiety. His complexion and the lighter colour of his hair witnessed an open-air life. Many who saw him in France remarked, as people will remark of young princes, that he did not look his age. And when, in February, 1918, he came over to take his seat in the House of Lords, the currency of the remark received a

new impetus. This was an occasion. A Prince of
Wales had not taken his seat in the House for over half
a century. More than ordinary care was taken to
ensure a smooth and impressive ceremony. Lest any
point had been overlooked, a rehearsal was held on the
previous day. Unreal and fantastic the whole thing
now seems when we look back upon it in its context.

Against the dull drabness of war-time dress and outlook, the pageantry appeared more dazzlingly bright,
and the robes, with their broad bands of gold, scarlet
and ermine, their intricate knottings of firm white silk
on the left shoulder, more gaudy. The multi-coloured
ritual with its customs, its curious wording, its rigid
bowing and bending, its awe and solemnity, was carried
out with a deliberation that was sharply in contrast with
the urgency and confusion of outside events. Who
were these almost allegorical figures—the Deputy Earl
Marshal, the Lord Chamberlain, the Lord Privy Seal,
the Lord President of the Councils, the sombre Deputy
Gentleman Usher of the Black Rod, the gay and magnificent Garter King-of-Arms, and that stiff and impassive
figure seated there on the Woolsack? What were they
doing parading through the strange enactment at such
a time as this? The questions can hardly be avoided.
Yet, to the present writer, the answer is clear. To care
for the preservation of such a custom is to do something towards confirming a belief in our race, is to
strengthen our hold on history and tradition. Upon
that strong hold the united action of a nation ultimately
depends. That ceremony called attention to the constitutional aspect of the Prince of Wales's position. At
that moment it was an admirable gesture to make.

A few months after this another opportunity came
to solidify Anglo-Italian friendship. To mark the
anniversary of Italy's entry into the War a ceremony in
Rome had been planned. It was the King of England's
intention to be present. He was prevented from going,
however, and called upon his son and first ambassador

to represent him. The Romans gave the Prince an unforgettable welcome. They were intent upon impressing that visit upon his memory. Next day, when the anniversary was being celebrated, their fervour and warm-heartedness precipitated them into a breach of etiquette, and instead of allowing the Prince to deliver his brief address without interruption they broke in with cheers at the end of every sentence. In view of the grave misgivings which then prevailed, one part of that speech is interesting in retrospect. It is this : " In the city of Rome, the ancient capital of the world, the source of social order and justice, I proudly proclaim my conviction that the great object for which our two nations are fighting against the forces of reaction is inevitably destined to triumph, owing to the union of which our meeting this evening is symbolic."

As in many other courageous declarations during those black weeks, the wish was father to the thought, for a review of the whole situation was anything but reassuring. Yet, unexpectedly, unbelievably, the struggle ended, and the Allies were left to make what they could of their victory. The sudden silence took soldiers and civilians alike by surprise, left them at a loss. If the Prince, too, was momentarily at a loss, and perhaps a little loth to take leave of men he would never know quite so intimately again, he was quick to rediscover the path of service. One of the first duties was to care for the returning prisoners of war. A week after the Armistice the Prince travelled to Dover to meet about eight hundred men who were coming back from internment in Germany. He waited for them for some time. Either the ship was late or in his zeal he had arrived too soon. But it was a moment worth waiting for. When at last that strange assortment of men landed, and a band blaringly exhorted them to pack up their troubles, the Prince did everything he could think of to make them feel that there was, indeed, reason to smile.

CHAPTER 3

ADVENTUROUS TRAVELLER

January, 1919—the Prince with the " Aussies." The immediate
effect of the War is to send the Prince adventuring among
working people of all kinds. Individual sacrifice is the key-
note of his activities. Visit to the Royal Duchy. Beginnings
of his zeal for housing reforms. Takes up residence at York
House. Five years after the outbreak of war (almost to the
day) the Prince sets forth, in the *Renown*, on an Empire tour.
Canada's almost too hearty welcome. The Prince's right
hand paralysed. An incident at Toronto. Lays the foundation stone of the new Parliament Building at Ottawa, and the
foundation stone of young Canadians' loyalty everywhere.
Takes immense trouble to get into touch with all sorts and
conditions as he passes on to Montreal, Fort William, Winnipeg, Calgary, Saskatoon. Canada and the Canadians greatly
appeal to him. Buys a ranch in Alberta as " a home from
home." Sends his English cattle there for breeding purposes.
In this and many other ways the Prince helps to promote
Anglo-Canadian friendship. On his return, visits United
States. First time a Prince of Wales had visited U.S.A. for
over fifty years. At Washington for the first anniversary of
the Armistice. Visits President Wilson in a sick-room. The
significance of the remarkable welcome at New York.
Rumours of a marriage alliance between England and
America.

FOR the duration of the War, the Prince's position
was an unenviable one. His private longings
pulled him one way, the " authorities " pulled
him another. It was a case of sinking his personality and
conforming as far as possible to expediency. As the
months dragged heavily on he began to recognise that
the " authorities " had a public duty to perform in con-
fining his movements to zones of reasonable safety.
There were times when, satisfying a natural curiosity,
he made excursions into dangerous areas. More than

once he narrowly escaped death. But the glory of memorable deeds was denied him. He could hope for nothing better than a grey, dull existence, in which duty meant ceaseless routine. In such circumstances his unforced, unbroken conscientiousness stands out as a sterling quality. In later years he habitually made reference to "the insignificant part" he played in the War. In that phrase we catch a hint of what he would have liked to do. It is not for him, but it is for us, to point out that the quality of courage was variously displayed during those years. Not always was it greatest in its most obvious manifestation. Some of the most courageous decisions of that period will never be known to us. In time of war there are few who are not called upon to show great bravery in one form or another.

Small service is done to the Prince by those writers who, striving to emphasise his democratic sympathies, make elaborate apology for his every action and its supposed motive. Unfortunately, many examples of this kind of writing exists, but for extreme ineptitude the following is difficult to surpass : " When the Prince asked for a light for his cigarette or asked for a cigarette it was not because he wished to be considered friendly, but because he really needed a light or a smoke, and in bringing his personal needs before the humblest soldier showed that even a prince is at best a man indeed." What is the effect of such an observation but to make the average reader suspect that some of the soldiers who casually met the Prince thought him patronising ? Does it not create the very impression it is unnecessarily attempting to remove ? What kind of information is this that reveals that the Prince asked for a light for his cigarette because he really needed a light ? So sadly misconceived an explanation is only too successful in making the Prince appear an utterly unreal person. It is an example of that kind of obsequiousness which he himself has always deprecated. If any proof is wanted

THE KING'S FIRST AMBASSADOR

that he was glad of the chance to enjoy the fellowship of officers and men alike his movements immediately after the Armistice can be cited. He arranged to spend the Christmas of 1918 with the troops abroad, and stayed in Brussels *incognito*. A few weeks later he was with the Australian troops and spent nearly a month of close association, living with their officers. What he had seen of the " Aussies " in war-time kindled in him the warmest regard for their hardihood and stolid characters. His one wish now was to know them better and to prepare the way for the visit to their country which one day he would surely make. His stay with them was a happy informal time. There was much give and take in the matter of story-telling. If the reader supposes that the Prince was required to make allowances for the blunt, rough-and-ready ways of the Australians he is forgetting the Prince's everyday experiences during the preceding years. He had met all sorts and conditions and callings and in every kind of circumstance. He had learnt to look past the incidents and accidents of a man's behaviour to his spirit and intention. Well enough did he know that for singleness of purpose and honest-to-goodness friendship there were no finer types anywhere than these men who had crossed the world to fight in a European war. Even now there are people living in England who apparently cannot bring home to themselves the magnitude of that sacrifice. The Prince was never in any doubt about it. Some have remarked that he visited Australian Headquarters to say "thank you for your services to England." That, no doubt, was the bare motive. But in effect the visit was more than an official recognition : it revealed the deep sincerity of his own gratitude and the pleasure he found in their company. The visit was so successful as to suggest that had the Prince been a member of the M.C.C. Committee the recent controversy on the rules of cricket would never have assumed such absurd proportions.

Coblenz was the Prince's next objective. There he visited the American Army occupying the Rhine and was received by General Dickman, whose guest he was. The occasion was marked by a dinner, followed by speeches and an impromptu concert by the soldiers. The Officers' Club gave a ball, at which the Prince danced with some of the American nurses. The ingenuous welcome he received from everybody persuaded him to change his plans and prolong his stay. To such occasions as these he owed the extraordinary harvest of hearty friendship which he was to gather later in the United States. He then went on to present colours to some of the Battalions of Guards Regiments which the War had brought forth. One of these engagements, near Cologne, brought him into touch again with the Grenadier Guards. He gave the New Zealanders a pleasant surprise by turning up at their Headquarters just before they were due to set sail. It was not without considerable difficulty that he managed to cover so much ground in so little time, for the roads were hardly of the best class. He had had some previous experience, however, of sudden encounters with shell-holes; now, impediments only increased his zest. He must visit not only Empire troops, but also Americans, Scots, Welsh, all who had played a part in that grim resistance. It was as if he were borne on a great wave of ceaseless energy after labouring so long under a sense of confinement and ineffectualness. Now, at least, he was free to be of utmost service.

But soon the voice of the British public reached his ears. For some time little had been heard or seen of him in his own country. After the excitement of peace celebrations that fact began slowly to emerge. Towards the spring of 1919 the Prince returned to England and was immediately flooded with engagements. Cities and towns intimated a wish to honour him in this way or that as a mark of devotion. The problem was to choose among so many urgent invitations, for it was impossible to accept all, or any number approaching all, of them. Moreover, on his return there were doctors at his elbow advising him not to call too exactingly upon his reserve of health.

Plymouth, where he was High Steward, desired also to make him a Freeman. Then, on May 29, followed his admission to the Freedom of the City of London. The right was his by patrimony and he became the City's youngest Freeman. Much was made of that ceremony. It was London's opportunity to greet the Prince who had graduated into manhood. A drive in an open landau from Buckingham Palace to the Guildhall was the very thing. The Lord Mayor met him at the Guildhall entrance. Then within the walls of that majestic structure the brief ritual was performed. It fell to the lot of the Fishmongers' Company to present him, for of that Company he was an Honorary Freeman—so much had better be explained for the benefit of those who might suspect the Prince of indulging in some curious form of humour when they read his words : " It is a special pleasure to me to be presented to you as a Fishmonger." In that same speech the Prince, with earnest tone and mien, spoke of the task which lay before him. The part he played in the War, he said, was " a very insignificant one," but he would never regret his period of service overseas. The War had permitted him to mix with men, to find his own manhood. When he thought of the future, he added, and of the heavy responsibilities which would be his, he was sure that those four years of experience would stand him in good stead. Then he spoke of his pride to be standing there as their youngest Freeman, and assured them he would ever be mindful of the duties now owing to his fellow-citizens, and that, with God's help, he would strive to follow the example of his distinguished predecessors on the long list of the Freemen of the City of London.

Another memorable ceremony was that which was

Central Press Photo

The Prince on his Ranch

carried out after he had been called to the Bar. He was a little frightened at first by its grave formality ; but when, surprisingly, the barristers gave voice to " He's a jolly good fellow," he was grateful for the concession and able to appear less awestruck than perhaps he felt. He made an especially happy speech. " The Master Treasurer asked me," he said, " if I had read the document I had signed ; I could not say that I had. He has also said that I have not eaten the number of dinners which are necessary. I am afraid I have not, nor have I done many other things which I should have done. I feel very embarrassed standing before you in this gown. I cannot pretend it makes me learned in the law ; in fact I feel rather magnificently camouflaged. But I do want you to treat it as a symbol of my desire to study and associate myself with the great legal institutions upon which the stability and welfare of our great country so largely depend." That was well said. No one seriously supposes that every organisation, faculty, municipality, trade or branch of learning which desires to honour itself by honouring the Prince can claim his specialised attention. If the honour is accepted it stands as a sign of his considered recognition of notable achievement. It is no more than that. Certainly the Prince never allows it to be less.

Where so many claims are made upon his time and interest the difficulty is to give room for the play of his own preferences and ambitions. His conscientiousness does not reduce the problem. It is possible that in those first hectic post-war days he was too conscientious. His parents thought so and advised him to spare himself. The doctors told him that a country holiday was absolutely necessary. He made that the excuse to visit his estates in the Duchy of Cornwall. Already, before the Armistice, he had devoted some time to these estates during a widespread tour of industrial areas. (He had started this tour in South Wales ; had gone on to Cornwall where he descended a mine and made himself

49

acquainted with the routine of a miner's life; had proceeded to Plymouth, to the East End of London, and finally to the Clyde shipyards.) His present purpose was to resume the work and inquiries he had then begun. This, then, was by no means an idle holiday. The Prince inclined to the view, which has since become more and more recognised, that a complete change of occupation makes a more beneficial holiday than enforced inaction. The Royal Duchy—Cornwall had been this since the fourteenth century—provided a test for the knowledge and opinions he had lately been gathering. Farming, fishing, mining—each presented its peculiar problem, and he set to work on an experimental basis to work out a solution. In Flanders he had observed that the country-folk favoured an intensive system of land cultivation. There was no reason to believe that small-holdings were indigenous to that region. Circumstances sometimes alter cases, but at other times show them to be parallels. No conservatism is stronger than that of the worker of land. Many of the Prince's tenants were Independents. That capitalised description gives a better idea of them than the label of any political creed, just as it truly represents the country people around the borders of Norfolk, Cambridgeshire and Suffolk. Small-holdings fitted in very well with their ideas. The Prince also experimented with co-operative ideas in farming and gave some time to the study of that movement. Not so readily as others have done did he dismiss the ideas which had prompted that little band of early pioneers in Rochdale to whom the movement owes its being. He made every effort, too, to encourage the fisheries, which as a result of war-time exigencies had been saved from almost total extinction. The ancient tin mines had also been in a bad way, but the grievous question of unemployed miners made it imperative that considerable capital should be spent upon up-to-date machinery and conditions of labour.

That, however, was meeting less than half the problem.

To improve machinery without improving the houses of those who worked it was a short-sighted policy which could commend itself only to profiteering minds. To that fallacy the Prince was fully alive, and it was at this time that he can be said to have begun that whole-hearted drive for slum clearance which has been one of his chief preoccupations during the last few years. Even then he appreciated the pitfalls which lay in the path of any who set out upon a housing reform, however limited its scope. His experience in Cornwall and also on his Kennington estate made it only too plain that slums could not be knocked down merely by breathing goodwill into the air. So many people, even of this present year of grace, believe that to solve the housing question you have simply to pull down the foul and build up the fair. They take no account of the most important factor in the case, the inhabitants themselves. The present writer believes that it was because the Prince had observed in war-time what men and women were like essentially and out of their home environment that he avoided the error of judging their homes apart from themselves. Undesirable as some of the Kennington property had become, he did not impetuously condemn it until he had taken immense trouble to know his tenants and their own wishes. In this he was helped by his sister, Princess Mary (now the Princess Royal), and together they entertained some of the tenants to tea at a hostel. Much virtue in a cup of tea! If its outpouring is conducive to similar outpouring of loquacious tales of weal and woe it is equally encouraging to frankness. Tea was the password, too, when the Prince followed up this party with surprise visits to his tenants' homes. He was received with mingled perturbation and delight. That they should freely speak their mind was his one wish, and he knew that the surest way was to call when the tea-pot was on the hob. Since then the work of reconstruction on all his estates has been begun and is being carried out according to carefully considered

plans. At Kennington, which is the source of a great part of his revenue, the housing problem has demanded more than ordinary sagacity and foresight. For some time surveyors and builders have been busy there, and last summer many a bricklayer was indebted to the Prince of Wales for a first-class view of the Test Match at the Oval.

After giving so much of his time and interest to the homes of other people it was meet that he should now take steps towards the establishment of his own. Since his coming-of-age, the War and the possible eventuality of marriage made it unnecessary to consider the setting up of a household apart from his family. With his approaching tour of North America in mind he might have considered it still unnecessary, at least until his return. But various other considerations—precedence, for example, and a care for the dignity of his position—brought the King to the conclusion that his eldest son should have his own house and his own Court Circular. On July 1, 1919, the Prince began residence at York House with a staff which included the Honourable Piers Legh and Lord Claud Nigel Hamilton as equerries, Sir Godfrey Thomas as Private Secretary and Sir Sidney Greville as Comptroller and Treasurer of the Household. Lord Claud Hamilton had been a close companion of the Prince during the War.

No sooner had his home been established than preparations for the Canadian-American tour were begun. Not that any rigid plans were made. Indeed, the Prince was anxious that his programme should permit as much flexibility and informality as possible; anxious, too, that the staff accompanying him should be strictly limited. It was exactly five years and one day after the outbreak of the War when he embarked on H.M.S. *Renown* for Canada. On August 11 he arrived in Newfoundland and, through the people's acclamation, received a reward for his special interest in the regiment which that island had sent to the War. Only the weather failed him. It was as bad as could be. But it did not deter the crowds. At Saint John, New Brunswick, the heavy rains seemed to contribute to the rising tide of enthusiasm. There was no way of keeping the people under control. They just walked through the ropes and insisted on knowing the Prince " personally." This was a surprise for those who, when they first heard of the Prince's project, shook their heads and prophesied a poor reception from the hard-headed people of the dominion. Perhaps the Prince himself had not been too sure. It is easy to be glib about his charm and diffidence and modesty. Indeed, so much has been garrulously written about these characteristics, so much picture post-card capital has been made from his smile that sceptics have had no difficulty in denying their existence, in declaring them to be manufactured for public consumption. All who lead a public life must pay that penalty of seeming to be unreal. Yet no one who has met and talked with the Prince for five minutes could possibly miss the reality of his charm. To say that it is dependent upon the glamour of his position is a complete misunderstanding, for it is that very glamour, real or supposed, which he has always striven to shed. If ever there was an absolute proof of direct personal appeal Canada's welcome to the Prince was one. Even now the words of one of his speeches there reflect something of its spirit. " This is a red-letter day for me," he said, " a day to which I have eagerly looked forward and which I can never forget. At the same time I do not feel that I come to this great dominion as a stranger, since I have been so closely associated with the dominion troops throughout the War. . . . I want Canada to look on me as a Canadian, if not actually by birth, yet certainly in mind and spirit, for this, as the eldest son of the Ruler of the great British Empire, I can assure you that I am."

The Prince was later to prove how deeply felt was that declaration. Canada and the Canadians attracted him. For a real holiday—the kind which means " getting away from it all "—Canada would be his first choice. That country has never had a better friend than the Prince. He has never ceased to sing its praises, and many have been infected by his enthusiasm. The recent suggestions in the English Press that the Duke of Kent should be appointed Governor-General of Canada however unauthorised are probably based upon memories of his brother's success with the people of that land.

It is not the writer's purpose to record every detail of that memorable tour. The very fact that it was accompanied by such a continuously high pitch of acclamation would tend to monotony in an attempted reproduction in narrative form. It is enough to say that the Prince's reception everywhere silenced those who had doubted the wisdom of the project. For the first time the Prince was putting to a real test the character which the war years had helped to fashion ; he was drawing upon compound interest. And upon himself the visit had a beneficent effect. It gave him self-confidence when most he needed it. The first post-war years found him, with thousands of others, unsettled in mind, unsure of his direction. He had plunged into a maze of activities without discovering any single path for specialised self-development, without resolving his private thoughts. Any satisfaction he enjoyed was due to his unquestioning fulfilment of the duties nearest at hand. To pretend that it was a complete satisfaction is to ignore the inner conflict of nature, the preferences, aversions and forming tastes which constitute the personal life of any young man. In Canada the Prince was happy not only in carrying out a duty as the King's ambassador but also in realising some of his own natural inclinations. Canada helped to confirm and give point to his character. Not every man in the middle twenties could have maintained a balance in the face of such an onslaught of popularity. At few other junctures in his life has the Prince proved so conclusively his absolute reliability in a dangerous situation. For sitting on top of the world *is* dangerous. Whether attained by act or accident, what position is more perilous ? Few can hold it for any length of time or with any degree of grace. In the Prince's life that Canadian tour was a time of crisis, no less. We know now how well he came through. The outstanding effect of it all upon himself was not to produce conceit or a false sense of proportion but to induce a true and deep affection for Canada and its people.

We left the Prince at Saint John, New Brunswick. He went from there to Halifax on his way to Quebec, where he was greeted with equal warmth by the French and English elements of the population. Thence he travelled to Toronto and to Ottawa, where he was compelled to seek respite from the already great strain of the tour. Then he made his way to that beautiful St. Lawrence city, Montreal ; to Port Arthur, Fort William and Winnipeg ; then through the prairies to Edmonton, Saskatoon and Calgary ; then to Vancouver. Canadians everywhere gave him almost too hearty a welcome. He soon found that he had not developed a sufficiently strong technique of handshaking. Every man who could get near him insisted on seizing his right hand, with the result that once, after meeting about two thousand Canadian soldiers, it was put out of action. There was still his left hand, of course, and it was not long before this, too, was being threatened by paralysing grips. During the whole of the tour there was hardly a stopping-place where some little unrehearsed incident did not mark the occasion. Some of these will be longer remembered than the official welcomes—the incident of the war veteran for example, who fought the police to establish his right to meet the Prince and, at the Prince's own request, was at length rewarded ; the windy day at Toronto when a wounded soldier's cap was blown off and the Prince, with forty thousand people looking on, sprinted after it, brought it back and put it on the man's head; the day when the Prince was perched on the back of his car for a drive through the streets, because people had been complaining that they could not see him; the stopping of the royal train at the most unexpected places to give the Prince a few minutes' conversation with people in remote parts. But Canadians will tell you that the crowning incident took place at a rodeo in Saskatoon. That was an inspiration. The Prince had been watching the cow-punchers in exhibitions of steer throwing and all manner of outlandish horsemanship. To be a mere spectator did not altogether satisfy him. At the end of the pro-gramme the crowd, which was waiting for him to leave, was surprised to see him jump on to a broncho's back. To jump there was one thing, to stay there was quite another performance. And it was one which was thoroughly enjoyed by the cowboys as they followed him round, yelling like madmen. He took their shouts to mean encouragement and, almost unbroken though the mount was, kept his seat. What would have hap-pened and what would have been thought had he been thrown is not easy to surmise. As it turned out, he could not have chosen a quicker or surer way to lasting popularity. Saskatoon was not long in spreading the news.

As the tour progressed the Prince was more and more impressed by Canada's great diversity of scene, of resources and of opportunity. He perceived, too, that its numerous communities were separated not only by big distances but also by disparate interests. The photographs which he brought back give some idea of the variety of types and occupations which he met. One shows him taking part in a round-up on a ranch; in another he is camping at Qu'Appelle Lake and is accompanied by two guides whose expressions clearly show that they consider posing for a photograph a wicked waste of time; one of the happiest is of the Prince paddling an Indian canoe on the Nipigon River

—the guides are there again and this time have managed to raise something nearly like a smile ; in another the Prince's face is just visible under his magnificent head-dress as an Indian chief, by name " Morning Star " ; yet another presents him in the free-and-easy mood and dress of a rancher. It might be supposed from these pictures that he had an irrepressible liking for dressing-up, whereas the truth is that it was the people themselves who forced these investitures upon him. Wherever he went it pleased them to see him dressed in the habits proper to the various callings or climates or races. They wanted to visualise him as one of themselves. He saw the wisdom of complying. On such simplicities does far-flung imperialism ultimately depend. Even if the Prince could hardly think of himself as an Indian star of the morning except in metaphorical terms, he had the fullest intentions of becoming a rancher. These were carried out when he purchased a ranch for himself in Alberta—let us call it a Canadian home from home. Civilisation's present headlong course permits but few of us to enjoy what is called the " simple " life—that dream, that tantalising abstraction. To the Prince, with the responsibilities of his public and private life, that ideal must appear impossibly remote and therefore so much the more desirable. Almost the only occasions when he has been able to realise it have been his visits to that ranch. One of the results of the acquisition has been the transference of some of his fine English cattle to Alberta for breeding.

The tour as a whole was one of the most brilliant successes of the Prince's career. When, on September 1, he laid the corner-stone of the new Parliament building at Ottawa he can be said to have laid also the corner-stone of the loyalty of Canada's youth. Trouble had been anticipated that day. It coincided with a great Labour procession, and there was a possibility of its getting out of hand. The Prince turned the occasion into an opportunity. Greatly daring, he took a leading part in the procession. His action might have been resented by Labour's supporters as well as by its opponents. It could so easily have been misunderstood. The issue depended entirely on the way it was done. Well, it was done with such obvious sincerity that the crowd could not but welcome him to the fold. Incompatibility of creed was overleapt.

On the return journey from Vancouver to Montreal the Prince stopped again at Winnipeg and assured the people of the West that he would be soon among them again as a rancher. A new vein in the Cobalt silver mines was named after him, and he spared some time to stop there and descend the mine. Montreal was reached for the second time two and a half months after the arrival in Quebec, but, of course, not without a short stay at Niagara. During the tour the Prince had managed to visit more than fifty towns as well as numerous settlements and nameless places by the wayside. When, all too soon for the Prince, the time of parting came, Sir Robert Borden said in a public speech: "In the Dominion of Canada we notice constantly the need of a better understanding with each other, to be followed by more co-operation. How much more do we comprehend the need for such in the world-wide community of nations who owe allegiance to Great Britain! It is also true of an understanding between the Sovereign and the people that there should be that mutual service so needful in the preservation of institutions. That has been given by the visit of His Royal Highness."

Very much more than that was given. This was full-blooded service, given lavishly and given humanly. Had the Prince merely devoted himself to the reinforcement of phrases and formulæ his accomplishment would have been so much the less important. A better understanding was indeed his aim. He achieved it by giving always just that little amount more than he was expected to give.

The original plans had not included the United

States in the itinerary. Probably it had been anticipated that ten weeks of public appearance in Canada would prove too exhausting to permit any extension of the Prince's travels, especially into the States where he was certain to encounter more democratic, high-spirited welcomes. But the invigorating North American air makes a man ready for any venture. Here was an opportunity, one that it might seem ungracious to miss. Permission from the King was hastily obtained, and the Prince felicitously timed his arrival at Washington to coincide with the first anniversary of Armistice Day. More than half a century had gone by since a Prince of Wales had been received in the United States. It was unfortunate that President Wilson was too ill to be present at the official welcome. Mr. Lansing, acting Secretary of State, was his deputy. The President's wife and daughter also entertained him. The American Press surpassed itself. Journals tumbled over each other in the frenzy of featuring the event and—need it be added?—in the devising of those tortuous word-patterns called headlines. The Prince was anxious not to leave Washington without seeing the President if a meeting was in the least possible. It gave him great satisfaction, therefore, when a call on the sick man in his bedroom was arranged. No more than the briefest incident, it yet served as a symbol of the real purpose of this descent upon Washington.

So to New York where, of course, the ovation reached its culminating point. That great city, a fantasy built upon hard-headed realism, saw nothing paradoxical in taking a Prince to its democratic heart ; or, if it did, " Aw, never mind," was its attitude. " What's a paradox, anyway ? Isn't all life just one big paradox ? " In New York it is, indeed. Live there in a heat-wave and you will wonder how a liberty-loving people could ever be persuaded to build for itself a towering, stifling, frightening prison. See it on the sky-line in an autumnal dawn or, on an early summer's night, look upon its flood-lit enchantment from the roof of a Fifth Avenue hotel, and you will marvel that out of so many parallel straight lines so much beauty could be evolved. Or, again, go to Wall Street and from the gallery watch the crazy scene which is daily enacted there and you will scarcely believe that it can have any bearing upon a nation's, not to say a world's, financial system.

New York's business men and their wives and daughters (especially these) gave the King of England's heir an ovation of that concerted kind which is second nature in the land of baseball crowds. It was the Prince himself who was aware of the contradictory situation, at least so it appears from the remark he made when looking back upon his experiences among the Americans. " They ' Princed ' me so much I expected at any minute to bark." His lasting affection for America and its people has often been strongly and clearly expressed. The country and its life appealed to him. If the exuberance of a few individuals sometimes became a nuisance it was never very difficult to bear in mind their motive, however ingenuous, of utter friendliness. One topic did develop into a nuisance—the inevitable subject of marriage. Once again the Prince found Rumour, the monster, in his path. He had come to the United States, of course, to seek a bride. (So did Rumour begin the attack.) Or, if not, the hint must be dropped, no matter how tactlessly, that he should forthwith set about the business. America was not lacking in beauties, if beauty was his desire ; nor in wealthy beauties, if so be his eye was fixed upon that fortuitous combination. And what a great day for the English-speaking peoples, could such a union be brought to pass ! So, like wildfire the word went round. The word, with its several versions and interpretations. As for example, that the union *must* be brought to pass. Or, in a mood of desperation, the union *will* take place, and suggested names and dates following to bear out the fable. We cannot be surprised that they " Princed " him until he was ready to bark.

The surprise is that they did not " Prince " him into a marriage of self-defence.

It is in situations of this kind that we can observe the peculiar problems of the Prince's life. Self-determination is assailed on every hand. In a sense, it is true to say that no man's life is his own. Let that be so, and yet the majority of mankind can create and exist in the safe illusion that it is living its own life. Even that illusion is denied the Prince. Far too many claims upon his time are made for that to be entertained for a moment. From those early ambassador years until now he has always accepted that fact. And that very attitude has helped him to discover, after all, a way to lead a life which he can call his own. By identifying with his own will and purpose the interests he is required to serve he has found a solution to the formidable problem of being a twentieth-century Prince of Wales.

If the War brought his personal problems to a head, the North American tour did much to resolve them. He was more sure of people, more sure of himself. He had felt the warmth and strength of Canada's handgrip; he had seen their country at the height of its glowing autumn loveliness. He had been acclaimed by the democrats of the United States, welcomed among them as a man, but still more as a Prince. When at last he was ready to set sail from Canada in H.M.S. *Renown* and heard again the people's entreaties for his speedy return, the Prince was filled with regrets as sharp as if in truth that land had been his own home.

CHAPTER 4

ADVENTUROUS TRAVELLER (*continued*)

Spring, 1920—aboard the *Renown* again for the second Empire tour.
To the Antipodes by way of Panama Canal. A tragic incident
and its effect on the Prince. An effective rebuke to the busybodies at Panama. While his free-and-easy manner offends
some, it endears him to the younger generation. The Prince's
ability to reconcile spontaneous behaviour with dignity. His
social manners are exemplary. He is at one with his generation
in being highly strung and, on some public occasions, restless;
but no one has given a better lead to young English people.
The painful custom of " crossing the line." A Maori serenade.
Finds a railway strike in New Zealand. The strikers make
an exception for the Prince's train. In Australia, disappears
from a ball given in his honour and is found later at a reunion
dinner of ex-service men. " Ex-service men always have a
claim on my time." Far from idle words. That cause has
been the leading motive of the past fifteen years of his life.
Nothing in the way of adventure denied him—not even a
railway accident. When this comes his way (in Western
Australia), his presence of mind turns it into a not unpleasant
diversion.

H.M.S. *Renown* herself has claim to be considered
one of the Prince's homes. For a fair proportion of his life during this period was spent
aboard her. Those who write about the Prince's life at
sea usually take immense pains to show that his presence
makes no difference at all to the ordinary routine of
officers and crew. They assume that their readers start
by visualising these voyages as an unending succession
of ceremonials, in brief that they have never seen the
sea and know nothing of what sailors are. Then they
blandly proceed to spring the surprise. They vouchsafe
the information that the Prince dines with the Captain
or else invites the officers to dinner in his private suite;

that he takes part in the usual deck-games; that he devotes the mornings to reading in his cabin; that, as one writer in a superb phrase puts it, " he would never think of upsetting the common round of duty in a peace-time battleship." It is as if these authors had almost expected the Prince to turn life on the ocean wave into an unending whoopee, after the manner of a Jack Hulbert film. They appear not to have taken too seriously the fact that there was once a Cadet Edward of Wales at the Royal Naval College, Dartmouth.

Soon after his return from North America the Prince began to form his plans for a tour of Australasia, and it was decided that he should again be carried by H.M.S. *Renown* and via the Panama Canal. During a cold spell at the beginning of Spring, 1920, he set sail from Portsmouth for Bridgetown, Barbados, the first port of call. These days at sea were of great benefit to his health of body and mind. The rush of social engagements which met him on his return to England had drained his energy, and if Australia's hand-grip was to be as forcible and insistent as Canada's had been it would be necessary to go into training. The beneficent effects of a sea voyage, however, are not unconditional. Too many doctors airily dismiss the most important condition as being of no account. After all, it *is* necessary to be not merely a good sailor but one of the very best if a trip round the world is to be remedial. The Prince has the comfort—more to be esteemed than the comfort of wealth or learning—of being a very good sailor. On the way to the West Indies recuperation was fast. Moreover, he now had the time for a little healthy introspection and for arranging the amorphous mass of recent experiences into some kind of significant order. For, unless we are to regard him as an automaton, as a mechanism designed for taking people's hands and saying a few well-chosen words, we must credit him with the power of turning his impressions into constructive thought and the forming of opinion. What a richness of experience had already been his, to be sure! How much of the world and its inhabitants had this young man seen! It is easy to say: "What luck! What privilege!" without remembering the implied responsibilities. The Prince has never been oppressively introspective. But he is a man of sensibility, of keen observation and quick judgment. There was never any danger of his taking responsibility too lightly.

Before H.M.S. *Renown* arrived at Barbados tragedy's shadow passed over her life. She had run into a stormy sea and one of the crew fell overboard. They strove to the utmost to save him but, hindered by the storm, they failed. It is hardly necessary to stress how much this death saddened the Prince. He attended the simple funeral service and sent a message of sympathy by radio to the dead man's family.

Bridgetown was reached soon after. Here was a reception which triumphed over the colour bar. The inhabitants could hardly be expected to sort themselves into separate crowds of black and white. Negroes and negresses were if anything even more demonstrative than the rest, and found a way of expressing themselves by improvising head-dresses from Union Jacks. The Prince responded to this handsome gesture by taking more than ordinary trouble to learn the conditions of life in this part of the West Indies and something of the inhabitants' minds and natures. In set and impromptu speeches he was careful to use simple phrases and to express well-defined opinions and sentiments. He took the chance of denying that negotiations were afoot to sell some of the West Indies to America. In brief, he made it his business to be tactful. But soon he was to find out that, even in those parts, there were many watching for an opportunity to criticise. And, of course, the opportunity came. Wherever in the world you go you will always find members of the Society for Keeping Up Appearances. Over the whole face of the earth they are sprinkled as salt is sprinkled. For, in

The Prince visits his College at Dartmouth

their own estimation, they *are* the salt of the earth. Where society is remote from the centre and inclined, therefore, to be slack, they come to stiffen it. The more remote their dwelling-place the higher the Appearances are Kept Up ; the slacker their fellows, the stiffer they. Take Panama, for example. Some of these worthies, it seems, were lurking there when the Prince arrived. A ball was given in his honour. How they peered, these members of the S.K.U.A., to see that everything was *comme il faut*. (Heaven knows why they go so far as to use French, with its associated abominations, to explain their standards of conduct !) Everything was not *comme il faut*. Indeed, the most important thing of all was awry—the matter of the Prince's dancing partners. Now, since the city of Panama had made this a holiday occasion, the Prince saw no harm in complying with the spirit. He would dance to his heart's content. But to dance contentedly a man must have an harmonious partner. The Prince found one so harmonious in beauty and movement that it was in his mind to dance with her through the night. Then began the conspiring tongues o wag. Did the Prince not realise that he was devoting his attentions to an assistant in a drug store ; that there were mothers and daughters of society vainly waiting their turn ; that, to put the matter bluntly, Appearances were being badly Let Down ? The tide of indignant murmurings rose and rose until it reached members of the Prince's staff, and afterwards the Prince himself. " An assistant in a drug store," he heard them say. And variations of the theme were many. " Only an assistant in a drug store," and, with a note of final condemnation, " Just a little drug store assistant, that's all." And the Prince replied, as if he had been caught up in a fairy-tale, " An assistant in a drug store, did you say ? What a jolly good drug store it must be ! " So, after the Prince had dutifully danced with her peering ugly-minded sisters, he came back to Cinderella ; and they danced many more foxtrots together.

THE KING'S FIRST AMBASSADOR

The story, of course, could be told from the S.K.U.A.'s standpoint. The present writer, however, cannot disguise his pleasure in that rebuke to busybodies. Once again the Prince had shown that he possessed that precious gift, the ability "to bend so far and never break." We need not ignore the fact that during these years of adventurous travelling his free-and-easy manner offended some who met or saw or read about him; but this very characteristic endeared him to the younger generation who were aware that he, no less than themselves, must pass through the phase of relaxation which is inevitable in an after-war period. Now, as then, one of the Prince's accomplishments is the reconciling of self-possession with spontaneous behaviour. Whether in this country or abroad, his social manners are exemplary as regards lack of ostentation and unforced dignity. He is a normal example of his own generation in being highly strung and in giving signs of restlessness when he is carrying out some of his more tedious public duties or when he is tired; but no one has given a better lead to young English people in rejecting pompousness in favour of simple good manners.

In the Panama Canal H.M.S. *Renown* encountered difficulties and, because of a recent landslide, was required to perform a nice feat of navigation. It all helped to make the voyage memorable. So, too, did the welcome given by three American aeroplanes (how meagre, though, the number seems in this present air-minded period!) and the forming of a guard of American soldiers and, later at San Diego, the sending of six American destroyers to escort the *Renown* into harbour. The people of San Diego did their best to upset the Prince's plans. In the shape of festivity they stopped at nothing. Through their gaiety and lavishness they attempted to lure the Prince into a prolonged stay in California. The crew of the *Renown* were not forgotten; they, too, were generously entertained by the residents. Perhaps the most singular evidence of San Diego's ambition to overtop all previous welcomes was the mammoth organ which was built to be played in the open air. Magnificently careless gesture! Fine weather had set in: they would have organ music out of doors (as lesser mortals take tea out of doors), and with it would shake the earth and rend the heavens. After all, the instrument could be easily dismantled when the rainy season set in. For big thinking the Babylonians could hardly have beaten that.

The Prince was now living in a world of fantasy, passing from one tremendous exhibition of high spirits to another. But he had probably never been so far from reality as when he was greeted by the Hawaiian islanders. After seeing the commercialisation of those islands, with their grass-skirted maidens and their languorous guitars, by the dance-music racket, it is difficult for any who have not been there to conceive the poetry of native custom and environment. To the Prince the girls brought fruit offerings; they decked him with garlands of flowers. The air was filled with the playing of little fountains of music. For a young man who was carrying out the sternly realistic duties of imperial ambassador this was a dangerously idyllic interlude.

Before leaving the islands the Prince took advantage of the surf riding which the Bay of Waikiki offers, and enjoyed the sport all the more for a few accidents and immersions. On the way to Fiji he was required to suffer the ordeal of "crossing the line." Ordeal is not too strong a word for this curious ritual. Its rigours make the accolade by which a man was dubbed Knight seem like a pleasant nursery game. The Companionship of the Royal Order of the Equatorial Bath cannot be conferred until the subject consents to be lathered "in the traditional manner," traditional meaning rough, and manner meaning just anyhow. A photograph of the ceremony shows the Prince facing it like a man. The ode to King Neptune which was specially composed for this occasion is apparently undiscoverable in its entirety.

Either because of its simple, unvarnished old-world language or because it was too obviously an impromptu invention the ode has never seen the light of day. But the final couplet gives sufficient clue to its (one might say) open-air style. Here it is:

> I know I'm for it, King—so, boys,
> Don't let me keep the party waiting.

There exists, too, a document which bears witness to the awe with which the ritual was anticipated. It is a letter written by one of the Prince's staff to the captain of the *Renown*. Selected passages from this revealing communication are given here:

"His Royal Highness the Prince of Wales has not yet crossed the Line. I am desired by H.R.H. to say that he is looking forward with interest to his meeting with His Majesty King Neptune and Amphitrite his wife, and also to his initiation as a Freeman of His Majesty's domains." Then follow the names of those of the Prince's staff upon whom the Order of the Bath had been bestowed on former occasions. "Rear-Admiral Sir Lionel Halsey having crossed the Line more than two hundred times, has been strongly recommended for the order of Old Sea Dog. But Lieut.-Colonel Grigg and Lord Claud Hamilton, who have also crossed a few times, state that owing possibly to some special favour, or else to some serious preoccupation on the part of His Majesty, they were not privileged to undergo the full ceremony of initiation. They are all the more anxious, therefore, on this account to pay every respect to His Majesty and not to presume on his former graciousness. In expressing their duty to His Majesty they await with great humility the verdict of his most excellent Court as to whether they will be required to be initiated or not."

In substance and manner, is not this letter illuminating, showing how necessary it is for those who are hedged in by the etiquette of Court life to find occasional relief in parody ? Showing, too, the kind of diversion people at sea, voyaging across the world, must perforce invent. Another diversion awaited the Prince at Fiji, where the native chiefs brought him tributes and offerings after their peculiar kind. Then, on March 24, he entered the splendid harbour of Auckland and was met by a scene of quite extraordinary animation. Ships of every size surrounded the *Renown*, their flying flags giving sign of the fluttering excitement which was everywhere to be heard and seen. Stream upon stream of welcome flowed towards the ship—from bands blowing gaily, from children singing as they had never sung before, from the crowds on shore. The Governor-General came on board the *Renown* to greet the Prince. Then, on shore, representatives of the Government extended their welcome. Many looked through tears upon the scene. The Prince himself, after long days at sea, was overwhelmed by the emotional stress of the event.

New Zealand very soon produced a list of strenuous engagements. So, when a serenade was begun one night outside the Prince's bedroom window, one can understand that at first he did not find the compliment altogether acceptable. Besides, the music was queer, yet not unattractive. Certainly, in comparison with his own instrumental essays at Oxford, he could admire its technical assurance. The music made him curious. He got up, went out and found some Maoris playing and singing. He joined them, and for a long time listened to the strange articulations of their melody. He had not forgotten that this intelligent, vigorous race had volunteered for service in the European war, and at Gallipoli and other places had shown great bravery. On another occasion the Maoris assembled in great numbers to show the Prince some of their native dances and afterwards to present to him through one of their chiefs an address of loyalty to the King of England. Among scores of similar addresses from groups and societies in New Zealand this one was something to remember. From a people that had enjoyed parliamentary representation for more than ten years, it could be accepted as something more than lip service.

At that time Labour feeling was running strong in New Zealand, and a railway crisis impeded the progress of the tour. A strike was called. The Prince was held up at Auckland. This was unfortunate because, of course, there were some who hastily concluded that the two incidents were connected. Then the strikers sent to the Prince a message—which, surely, can be interpreted as a very remarkable tribute—saying that they would make an exception of the Royal train and ensure its punctual running. But the strike was short-lived. New Zealand had in its Prime Minister (the Rt. Hon. William Massey) a mediator whose counsel prevailed. Later, the railway workers took the trouble to express through a delegation their regret that the Prince had been held up. He for his part wanted them to know that he was not above trying his hand at driving an engine; nor, as it turned out, was he unequal to the job. On one of his journeys, after receiving instruction from the engine-driver, he was able to deputise for part of the way and to drive the train at between fifty and sixty miles an hour.[1]

As the tour progressed, supporters of the Labour Party discerned how unaffected were the democratic sympathies of the Prince, and before he left New Zealand, in spite of the outbreaks of political conflict, he was able to give his decided opinion that nowhere in the world was there a people more faithful to British traditions and ideals. From end to end of the dominion he had found the strength of their loyalty " as keen and bracing as mountain air." " Mere diplomacy," some will be inclined to say. The answer to that are the great bursts

[1] The Prince revealed the same desire to become acquainted with jobs which the average man takes for granted when, during one of his voyages, he took a turn at stoking and, according to a witness, "put all his weight into it."

of spontaneous enthusiasm which surprised him every-where. The scenes of welcome were not confined to the centres where he stopped. One of his train journeys by night, for example, was illuminated by a line of bon-fires which remote villagers had kindled as flares of welcome and in the hope of catching a glimpse of the Prince by drawing him from his compartment.

The Prince will not easily forget his first visit to Australia. Rough seas on the voyage from New Zealand, fogs, grey days and torrential rains after a spell of drought, these were the accompaniment to his first impressions. Before reaching Melbourne the *Renown* was held up in a fog which in density challenged London's reputation. On the one hand the captain was being urged on by the Prince who was anxious to land in time, on the other he was made to pause by the risks he would be taking. The *Renown* stopped dead, sent wireless messages to the Australian fleet and waited for guidance. The answer was the arrival of H.M.A.S. *Anzac*, destroyer, and soon afterwards the Prince and his staff were in Melbourne, where the people, in their first shout of welcome, dispelled the impressions made by the weather's contrariness. The wonder is that, during the days that followed, the Prince was able to endure so long the physical strain which must always result from acknowledging the acclamations of crowds, replying to innumerable addresses of welcome, inspect-ing processions and parades and shaking endless rows of hands in such a way as to convince the owner of each hand that the meeting has been a personal one.

There came a time when the Prince's doctor inter-vened. A week's rest from the glare of the public eye was ordered. Golf, riding and dancing were to be his tonic, with a little iron added in the shape of an early morning run. The aid of the Press was solicited to help him secure a reasonable amount of privacy for these few days. How much he had been in need of relaxation was made clear by the way he planned his own arrangements on one occasion without telling any of his staff. The official programme required him to attend a reception and after that a ball. He was present at the reception, but, apprehending perhaps a possible reappearance of the S.K.U.A., decided the ball had less claim upon his time than another function he had heard of. He disappeared. But if there was a shadow over the gaiety of that ballroom there was a happy surprise at a dinner and concert which were being given for a reunion of ex-service men. The Prince turned up and thoroughly enjoyed their company. When at length he was tracked down his explanation was given in the form of a rebuke. " Why was I told nothing of this reunion ? Ex-service men always have a claim on my time." Far from being a formula vainly repeated, those words bear witness to one of the strongest of his purposes. That cause has been one of the leading motives of the past fifteen years of his life.

Ballarat has reason to remember the Prince's visit, for it was there he made a speech in a downpour of rain. At the end he looked as if he had pulled himself out of a river. Perhaps for a moment he wished he had been standing on Ararat instead of in Ballarat. But when he heard what blessed relief the torrents had brought to a sun-baked, thirsty land he was only too glad to have been baptised at the initial ceremony. After a tour of Western Victoria he went on to Labour's stronghold, Sydney. There was good reason to believe that a *decrescendo* would mark the reception here. With Test Matches so rarely occurring, there was even the possibility of a little barracking exercise. The English team would soon be appearing there and the crowd on the Hill might be glad of a little practice. The Prince did not underestimate the difficulties of taking this stronghold, and was particularly careful in preparing the details of personal tactics. So far from seeing signs of fashion-leading in dress, the citizens of Sydney saw him for most

Photograph by Hugh Cecil

The Prince was made Admiral in 1935

of the time in a plain grey suit and a brown felt hat. A natural desire to slacken the ties of public appearance could, of course, be given as an explanation; but in the circumstances the costume appears to have been the result of a studied carelessness. The record of this visit gives plenty of evidence of its success. Twenty thousand demobilised men stopped work, not for a strike, but to dress again in their war uniforms for an inspection by the Prince. The crowd watching this scene was estimated at thirty thousand, and the disabled men, with each of whom the Prince shook hands, numbered many hundreds.

The remainder of the tour—to Brisbane, a rough sea-passage to Western Australia, to Adelaide, to Tasmania and to Sydney again—developed in the Prince an increasing affection for Australia, an affection which, in all likelihood, was the firmer for the uncertainty attending some of his visits. Bidding the Australians farewell, he was able to tell them how much he regretted that the tour had ended. He told them, too, that everywhere in the Commonwealth he had been impressed by their free and splendid spirit, that spirit which the " Diggers " had already displayed so convincingly during the War. And this was the simple conclusion of the speech: " I refuse to say good-bye. I have become so fond of Australia now that she can never be far from my thoughts wherever I may be, and I look forward most keenly to the time when I shall be able to return. My affectionate best wishes to her people, one and all." At no time since then can Australia have been nearer the Prince's thoughts than during the recent visit of his brother, the Duke of Gloucester. England's grey November days must have increased the longing to be there with him, especially since the other side of the world had just then been brought so fantastically near by the almost superhuman flights of C. W. A. Scott and Campbell Black, and of Cathcart Jones and K. F. H. Waller.

Nothing in the form of adventure had been denied

the Prince in Australia, not even a railway accident. This happened near Bridgetown. The Prince had a most fortunate escape. Cattle wandering on the line had caused the train (consisting of sleeping-coaches) to slow down. A single track ran through this part of the swampy forest-lands and the recent rains had undermined its foundations. The rails gave way and two coaches were overturned. When the news was first released in Australia, there was great consternation and exaggerated versions, born of acute anxiety, were in temporary circulation. Happily, only one person, the Prince's surgeon, was injured as a result of the accident, and he no more than slightly.

The Prince himself was jolted and thrown about, and was unable to escape from his sleeper until some assistance was brought. His first thoughts were for his diaries and private papers. Then, when he discovered that nothing serious had resulted, he perceived an opportunity for a pleasant diversion. He packed some hampers and, with some of his staff, went for a tramp and a picnic until the breakdown gang arrived. But if he was inclined to make light of the incident, he soon discovered that the Australians took a more serious view. Indeed, there is a singular contrast between the thought of thanksgiving services in the cathedrals and churches of the Commonwealth and a photograph of the Prince standing by the overturned coaches. In this picture he appears to be wearing the grey suit which was a factor in Sydney's capitulation, and, although he is wearing a cap, he has also taken care to rescue that soft brown hat which also played a part in the tour. Not for the world would he be losing that shapeless thing. No great urgency is apparent at any point in the scene. On everyone's face can be read, only too plainly: " Well, nothing can be done about it."

But to the reader of this narrative the accident serves to bring home once again the immense physical stress of these Empire journeys. Canada's welcome had put the

Prince's right hand out of action ; Australia's took toll of his voice, and in Tasmania he could only whisper his replies to the welcoming address. He whispered, too, when prominent citizens were being presented to him. One of them, thinking that whispering was part of the formality of such presentations, carefully enunciated his reply to the Prince in the most genteel of whispers.

The return voyage was an opportunity for recuperation. Still, it was far from being without incident. The route was through Samon, Honolulu, Mexico, Panama, Trinidad and the Bermudas. The Prince saw England again on a dull, cheerless October day, but since his first glimpse of Melbourne had been through a fog, Australia perhaps did not seem so distant after all. As a result of his tour, it is certain that the Australians and New Zealanders, for their part, felt themselves drawn nearer home.

CHAPTER 5

ADVENTUROUS TRAVELLER (*continued*)

October, 1921—to India in the *Renown*. Opening of the new
Maltese Parliament at Valetta *en route*. Received by the Viceroy, Lord Reading, at Bombay. Serious disturbances. Critical situation and its causes. The Prince's anxiety to help win
back allegiance to the British Raj. Opportunities for sport.
This tour is accompanied by an undercurrent of ugly rumour,
especially at Lucknow and Allahabad. At Benares, where he
opens the Hindu University, there is a change of atmosphere.
Big game expedition in Nepal brings his first tiger. Visits to
Calcutta, Burma, Lahore. Brief digression on Indian government reform. Desire to see Japan. Greeted by the Prince
Regent at Tokyo. Our war-time allies create the Prince a
General. An earthquake.

IN so massive and intricate an idea as the British
Empire, the invention of phrases becomes a necessity. The constant danger is that the life of the idea
will become phrase-ridden. In every corner of the earth
men's minds are deadened by the weight of phrases that
no longer hold a meaning. From time to time they
discover the flaw, rebel and throw off the burden, only
to find themselves gradually pressed down by the
heaviness of new phrases. One immediate result of the
Prince's voyages was the re-vivifying of the idea called
British Empire with all its attendant ideas, not least the
idea that England was a sister country. If ever there
was one, that is an idea worth keeping alive in every
aspect of its implication. For it represents a relationship
which is far more appropriate to Imperial government
than that of distant cousin on the one hand or of heavy
father on the other.

When the Prince began to draw up the programme for
his visit to India, he was fully alive to the probability

that this would prove more difficult than all previous undertakings. Its importance, therefore, was so much the greater. For one thing, it would be necessary to hide his flexible, easy manner behind a façade of stateliness and circumstance. He must put his democratic feelings in his pocket and assume a role in keeping with Oriental imagery. Whatever else he packed he could leave behind that grey suit and old brown hat.

A year after H.M.S. *Renown* had brought the Prince home from Australia, she was carrying him to India. On the way the Prince stopped at Gibraltar, then at Valetta, where they had arranged that he should open Malta's new Parliament. Before he left the Mediterranean he was able to rejoin his brother Prince George (now the Duke of Kent) who was then serving as a midshipman on H.M.S. *Iron Duke*. We need not be surprised that both seized the chance of being thoroughly off duty. The Prince was invited to dinner in the gun-room. One record of the occasion states : " The young Prince George did the honours with true nautical hospitality." It is one of those expressions—nautical expressions— which wear an appearance of eloquent information, yet are wholly cryptic. Let it stand, however, for the reader to make therewith what imaginative play he will.

When the Prince arrived at Bombay he took part in an enactment which for pomp, ceremonial and symbolism was as elaborate as any he had previously appeared in. The crowds first saw him dressed in white naval uniform. He saluted them and their land. After being received by Lord Reading, Viceroy of India, His Royal Highness himself received the Princes of India, chiefs and holders of important offices. Then, at a point of climax, he read the King's greeting. Following this, in the company of the Viceroy he drove in procession through the streets. This drive was by no means lightly considered by the police and the Prince's staff. Nor was the Prince himself unaware of the dangers which were created by so prolonged a public appearance. Rebellious feeling was known to be running high among the natives of Bombay, and the police were redoubling their vigilance to prevent an outbreak.

As for the Prince, he was willing to take chances and, as in former situations, relied upon the sounding of a personal note. It was one that he could always be trusted to sound without a trace of harshness, insistence or aggression—clearly, that is to say, and appealingly. In Bombay he sounded it with harmonious effect, to the great relief of all who were in charge of the proceedings. It was immediately obvious that he had not embarked upon this tour of India without forethought and careful study. He had perceived that India was not only a problem in itself but also a special problem in relation to himself as an ambassador from England.

Two incidents can here be cited to show how careful he was in seeking a right-minded attitude towards the people of India. During one of his drives through a throng of natives, he saw a group of people whose despairing eyes at once told of the tragedy of their existence. They were the " untouchables." As the car was passing the crowd was surprised to see the Prince spring to his feet. Every eye was upon him now, expectant and curious : the action had appeared so impulsive. A questioning look was on every face. Then the people saw him facing that forlorn, half alive, group, and standing at the salute.

The other incident was a passage in one of the later speeches of the tour. " There are, I believe," said the Prince, " some persons who come from England, and after spending even fewer weeks than I have in this country give their valuable views and impressions about India to the public. You must not expect me to-night to disturb their monopoly ; I am content for the present to remain a reverent student of the many wonderful things which the book of India has to unfold."

If the reader has ever been audience (as the writer

often has been) to the recital of a tourist who has " done " India—bazaars, polo, temples, pig-sticking, native dances, the rope-trick and all—in three weeks, he will agree that those words of the Prince were especially well said. And they did more than carry a timely criticism : they threw light upon the Prince's commendably diplomatic way of approaching a civilisation whose unpredictable subtlety has always been an ineradicable element of its grandeur and awe-fulness. He took the only possible path towards an understanding of the things which were to be unfolded, humility's path. In a speech to one of the crowds he expressed a desire to *know* them all, and it was towards this understanding of India's people that he continually directed his steps, remote and unapproachable though that people often seemed.

One of the most brilliant scenes of the tour was at Poona, where the Prince laid the foundation-stone of the Shivaji Memorial. Three days at Lucknow held more engagements than would be considered normal in a week. Here the Prince found himself facing a more difficult, because less overt, situation than that at Sydney ; one, moreover, that could not be overcome by the same ingenuous methods. Merely to be a good " mixer " was not a sufficient recommendation here ; in many places it was not a recommendation at all. Far more successful was an attitude of reverent watchfulness. It was necessary for the Prince to learn that lesson, for his natural impulse has always been to meet a crowd on equal terms, and there were occasions in India when, by acting upon it, he caused more than a little anxiety to the police.

At Lucknow there were natives who had openly declared their intention to do their utmost to end the tour. To the relief of the Prince's staff and the police authorities alike, the threatened trouble was averted. It is foolish, however, to encourage the belief, as some writers have done, that a hotbed of disloyalty was suddenly turned, as if by a magic wand, into a bed of roses. Rebellious feeling was expressed in the silence of some quarters of the city when the Prince arrived, and by the enforced closing of the bazaars. At Allahabad the native city was deserted for the duration of the Prince's visit there. The implicit ugliness of these silences and withdrawals could not be ignored. Those who were responsible for the arrangements of the tour rightly took a very serious view of these developments.

Another misapprehension, which has been fostered by some of the accounts of this journey, is that the Prince himself made light of these manifestations. He took risks, it is true, and had to be advised against taking any that were unnecessary. Sometimes in the excess of his desire to conciliate the refractory elements, his judgment was mistaken. In that respect he was in good and honourable company, for there is hardly another country in the world where the Englishman has gained so much experience through so much error as in India. But those who have been in continual and immediate touch with the Prince, have always borne testimony to his readiness to admit an oversight or a too sanguine opinion in the forming of his projects. Part of his wisdom has always been the willingness to learn, and even if this is a natural trait, being inherited from each of his parents, credit can also be given to the early training he received at the hands of his tutor, Mr. H. P. Hansell.

The Prince, of course, was continually being shown examples of the Indian arts and crafts, the skill and beauty of which have been a source of abiding wonder to the world. In all the heated discussions which have recently been centred round the subject of India's future, it is strange to find so little reference to the work and products of artists and craftsmen, whose activities, after all, are an integral part of the country's life. That much-vaunted book *Mother India*, reveals a fatal flaw in giving no attention to this all-important aspect of the mind of India. Nor is any evidence of its importance to be found in the Simon Commission's report, which it has pleased many people to describe as comprehensive. Perhaps this is not so surprising after all, seeing how miserable is the treatment of the fine arts in England.

We do not feel the force of Fletcher of Saltoun's famous saying which, in effect, was that so long as a country had good song-writers, its law-makers could go hang. To the majority that opinion is sheer nonsense. The majority is wrong, hopelessly wrong. It is not too much to say that in a country of India's magnitude and complexity, no satisfactory political solution can ever be found which does not take full account of the creative force of her arts. Yet, at the present moment, little is done to further their development or even to encourage their continuance. If there is a demand for the products of Indian arts and crafts in the world, it can create no corresponding supply in the present state of affairs. How many people realise the range of those arts and crafts? To the average Englishman the very term " arts and crafts " is an invitation to make fun. It means a piece of sackcloth with painted stripes.

Here is a list of only a few of those Indian crafts which have managed to survive in spite of apathy and lack of proper control : carving of ivory, carving of wood, cutting of stone, weaving of silk by hand, working in metals, in lacquer and in lace, embroidery, weaving of carpets, the numerous branches of pottery and of jewellery. As for drawing and painting, the innate talent of the people of India can never be hidden. Taste in colour arrangement is displayed by poor as well as rich women. In Bombay the decorative instinct is clearly apparent in the *Rangoli*. At festival times these are executed by boys and women in coloured powders on the thresholds of their houses. Lamps are lit at night so that passers-by can see the pictures. A casual survey of the *Rangoli* would perhaps suggest that they offered no stronger evidence of artistic instinct than the exhibits of our Western pavement-artists. It is in the villages of Western India that these domestic drawings still reveal how pure is the feeling for simple design and composition, how strong the need for its exercise.

India has many things to show as a rebuke to those who regard folk-art as a curiosity and pay it regard merely because it belongs to the past. Mohammedans, Parsees, Christians, Hindus, all have a living tradition of artistic creation, each group being marked by idiomatic qualities which can be related to its beliefs and culture. No political or economic system which ignores or makes little of the passionate and necessary devotion of India's people to the manifold sub-divisions of creative art, can ever bring harmony to the life of that unhappy land.

If he has never made any claim to be considered a connoisseur of the arts, or anything more than an average observer knowing very well what he liked and still more definitely what he disliked, the Prince has never been in need of a prompter in giving the artist his due. When he spoke of India being a book which he was just beginning to read, he was not forgetting, perhaps was thinking chiefly of, the marvels of imaginative creation which were continually before his eyes, marvels of building, of carving, of filigree, of painting. But he never committed himself to second-hand appreciation of what he saw. Only in the most general terms did he describe his impressions, whether in public or private. In this respect, his example has always been especially salutary. The arts, in whatever civilisation, in whatever period, have never benefited from the attachment of those who, with an eye only on their own glorification, apply themselves to the wooing with the help of parrot-phrases and random, high-flung epithets. With such snobbery the Prince has no sympathy. It is not sufficiently realised how much the genuine followers of the arts owe to him for this complete absence of pose.

But, if he was inarticulate in the face of India's multiform art, he was able to express with enthusiasm his appreciation of that country's no less various sport. As the guest of the Maharajah Sir Chandra Shumshere Jung he enjoyed the thrills of a big game expedition, and there came the momentous experience of shooting his first tiger. At other times he entered whole-heartedly into the various manners of contest provided by duck-shooting, pig-sticking, polo, paper-chasing and horse-racing.

The big-game hunt was in Nepal. The Prince had come there for a holiday after he had opened the Hindu University at Benares, where he was given the degree of Doctor of Letters and where the crowd's reception served to reassure him after his experiences at Lucknow and Allahabad. From Nepal he went to Patna, then, for a quiet Christmas to Calcutta where he also attended the Indian New Year procession. Happily, the rumours of a possible show of disloyalty at Calcutta were followed by an unmistakable atmosphere of welcome. Then the R.I.M.S. *Dufferin* took him to Burma where he was greeted in carnival spirit. So soon after his big game expedition a mock pageant of wild beasts was a much appreciated show. In Burma the Prince's staff found relief from the tense anxiety from which they could rarely escape in India. The Prince himself was no less relieved. How pleasant an interlude the people of Burma provided is reflected in the Prince's message to the Governor when the time came to go. He assured them of his gratitude and affection and expressed a deep regret that he was leaving them. Madras, Bangalore, Mysore and Hyderabad were next on the route. It was at the last of these places that the Prince, as the Nizam's guest, experienced " Oriental splendour," that so threadbare phrase, in its fullest, richest meaning.

Just as the North American tour would have been incomplete without an inspection of the Niagara Falls so would the Indian tour have been an imperfect accomplishment, indeed, a thing of naught, had the great Taj Mahal been omitted from the programme. At Delhi, Rumour crossed the path once more, and in shape more than ever formidable. On the road between Delhi and Patiala, it was said, the Prince's car had been hit by a bullet. An official explanation was given, but not before the tale, like wild-fire, had traversed the land. It was carefully pointed out that, whereas the arrangements were that the Prince was to travel by train, no one outside his own staff knew that these had been cancelled in favour of a road journey. Moreover, an examination of the mark (on one of the staff cars) on which the rumour was based, revealed that it could not have been the result of a bullet. Possibly it had been made by a stone. Even so, it could not be proved that it had been thrown, since it could easily have been a loose stone in the roadway which had been knocked up by the car itself.

One can understand the care with which this explanation was prepared and worded. Had the rumoured tale met with no resistance, it might have led to the conceiving of plots in earnest. In spite of the Prince's continuous concentration upon strengthening allegiance to the British Raj, there remained recalcitrant sections of the population which no amount of personal charm and goodwill could touch. The police authorities were only too conscious of the implicit danger which accompanied the Prince's every appearance. Not the least of the inimical forces was false rumour.

Lahore was the next place to be visited. As a result of the effects of the Delhi story, and also of the Prince's obvious fatigue, great pressure was brought to persuade him to cut out the engagements at Lahore. If he paid any heed to the advice, he did not finally take it, and his reward was a remarkable ovation when he arrived there. The undercurrent of discontent and protest was nowhere stronger in its running than at Lahore, so that there was greater consternation than usual when the Prince was seen to be moving unrestrainedly among the natives

The Prince in Japan

at a nearby fair. The attendance at that fair was estimated at twenty thousand. Many had journeyed forty, fifty, sixty miles for the occasion. Acrobatic feats, tugs-of-war, wrestling contests, exhibitions of animal training were given in the Prince's honour. And, of course, many native dances. In some of these, choreographic tradition required the dancers to perform barefooted upon red-hot cinders. At the finish they came before the Prince and offered their feet for inspection, to show that the cinders had left no mark of burning upon the flesh.

Neither during the tour nor on his return to England did the Prince indulge in theories on the subject of Indian Government in any of his public addresses. He was content to admit it was too hard a knot for him to untie. Since it has also proved too hard for specialists, has he not shown common sense in this? Yet, on more than one occasion, instinct led him to point to one of the surest roads to conciliation. At the fair near Lahore, for example, he persisted in his habit of moving among the people and attempting to know and be known by the common man. Without pretending to be an expert, or indeed anything more than an outside observer, the present writer believes that in that persistence, the Prince was right. Far too heavy reliance has been put upon the intelligentsia in the attempts to solve India's problems. The peasantry has been almost ignored in their paper schemes of government.

Almost as important as the Hindu-Moslem question is the conflict between the needs and claims of urban and rural populations. In the present state of affairs, the urban population is entering into a monopoly of power in spite of being greatly outnumbered. By what right? By right of its fight for political freedom and by right of its Western education? Yes, both can be admitted as strong claims, even if the first is far stronger than the second. Yet neither of these reasons is weighty enough to support the argument that out of a hundred people, twenty should have all power and eighty should have none; especially in India where the eighty rurals have nothing whatever to hope for from the twenty urbans, unless it be heavier taxation. There are those who go so far as to declare that the idea of the Crown as Paramount Power in India must ultimately rest upon the village council, and they give as their reason a firm belief in the peasantry and land-owners as the political and economic foundation of Indian life.

To the assertion that the Lothian report has made full provision for the peasant to voice his needs, they have many objections : that the peasants have no form of political organisation, for example; that, even if they could find candidates, they could not prevail against those of the powerful Congress; that Congress, in any case, would be supported by the shop-keeper class of the rural population. The reforms these critics demand amount to the establishment of rural constituencies and the grant of a full voting power to the peasant. As for the retort that the peasant lacks political education and is unable or unwilling to realise his responsibility as a voter, the reformers believe that it will cease to hold in future years; and they look to radio as their ally. Some go so far as to visualise the appointment of a neutral-minded radio authority which would act as a guide for the peasants in matters connected with the new constitution. In any case, there is no reason to believe that radio will fail to extend its influence to India's rural life.

The reformers, moreover, have one particularly strong reason to advance in support of their contention. It is this : hatred of British rule has not been systematically fostered among the peasants. It is this which gives force to their argument that the balance of power should be in the hands of the peasantry and the landowners, from whom the police and soldiers of India are largely drawn. Without this reform, they are convinced that good government can never be secured; nor can we ever hope that India, without it, will completely attain the status of a Dominion.

These notions have been briefly set down here, not because the writer believes they hold the final solution, but because he sees in them a measure of rational observation and opinion. The humanist dream of a united civilisation—with religion, language and culture all made one, and all past contentions forgotten—that, in the case of India, can only be entertained by dreamers of the most quixotic dreams. But the ideal of an harmoniously working government need never be abandoned. With that end in view, we should perhaps be working, not on humanist lines towards the abolition of all divisions and boundaries, but rather towards a re-making of India's provinces into more compact and manageable units.

Let no one suppose for a moment that the Prince of Wales entered India believing that he could pour such oil upon the waters that they would never again be troubled. He was only too aware of the political problems which continually threatened to mar his tour. Like Victoria when, nearly a century ago, she became Queen of England at eighteen, he faced the task relying upon his honesty of purpose and not at all upon doubtful subtleties of intellect. Indeed, without putting too big a strain on the genealogical table, we can perceive some of that young Queen's qualities in this young Prince of Wales, notably her diligence, her fervent conscientiousness and that precious thing which, in English, can only be defined by means of a variation of print—*sense*. That she was also honest and thoroughly capable will not escape those who are on the look-out for family traits. In India it was the Prince's honesty of purpose which won for him so much affection, sometimes in unexpected quarters. During the Gaekwar of Baroda's reception in his honour, for instance, Hindus of every caste assembled to give him welcome. And even in the unrestful districts, he frequently overcame opposition to the extent of bringing home to the people that, however great and just their grievances, they had no personal quarrel with himself. This success must have been in Prince Ranjitsinhji's thoughts when that chivalrous ruler and sportsman paid tribute to the Prince of Wales's lovable characteristics, not least his supreme tact as an ambassador.

Now that the end of the tour was approaching, and the desire came to re-live the experience in retrospect, tributes such as this were a source of inspiration. For it must not be thought that the Prince is not alive to the difference between polite formality and the expression of genuine feeling. In India he had heard and seen much that was purely ceremonious—in that land of ritual it was inevitable—but there were moments when a spontaneous burst of good feeling broke through the heavily ornate façade. The thought of India was sweetened by those memories.

It had been arranged that the *Renown* should meet the Prince at Karachi, and he arrived there by way of Peshawar, the Khyber Pass and Kapurthala. From Karachi he sailed to Colombo where energy was let loose in some hard games of polo. But the Oriental Grand Tour was not yet ended. An epilogue was added. The Prince's great desire to visit Japan was now to be gratified. He landed at Yokohama, went on to Tokyo and there was greeted by the Prince Regent. By creating him, not a Doctor of Letters or of Law, but a General, our war-time allies were perhaps giving sign of their persisting war-like mentality. A rich variety of experience has marked each of the Prince's tours. His list of untoward happenings include some of the most extreme nature. For his visit to Japan an earthquake was staged. It was not one of the grandest, but we shall not impute to Japan a lack of courtesy on that account.

CHAPTER 6

LANDOWNER

Organises his Cornish estate. Favours small-holdings. Develops tin mines. Encourages oyster fisheries. Plans for afforestation. Unemployed work at tree-planting on Dartmoor. Improvements on the Kennington estate. Learning his tenants' ways and wishes. Rebuilding in the London Duchy estates. The Prince a good landlord. Gives a lead by exporting cattle from Cornwall to his Canadian ranch. His advice to young men who are thinking of going to Canada. An unofficial visit to the ranch. Financial affairs. The Prince not a super-wealthy man.

IN a preceding chapter various references have been made to the Prince's supervision of his estates. At this point there arrives an opportunity of discussing this aspect of his activities in more detail. Although plans for the development of his property have frequently been interrupted by his tours, they have been among his first thoughts on each occasion of his return. The large estates he owns in Cornwall claim a continually active interest. When he is resident in London he is in touch with the Duchy through his comptroller, and many of the improvements there have been directly due to the sums of money he has devoted to its greater prosperity. An object of particular enthusiasm has been the encouragement of well-run small-holdings. We have already seen him using his eyes in France and Flanders when he was on active service there. He was not slow to observe the benefits of intensive land-cultivation. With the problems of peace-time pressing so urgently for solution, the system commended itself even more insistently.

Before the War a steady movement had begun in

favour of increasing the number of occupying cultivators of the soil, a movement which was consolidated by legislation. After 1918 the problem of the ex-service men gave further impetus to the movement, and it has been chiefly on their account that the Prince has advocated its support. A succession of Land Settlement Acts provided special facilities for ex-service men and others who desired to own small farms or crofts, with the result that increasing areas of land have been claimed for market gardening, fruit-growing, dairying and on the larger holdings, sheep grazing and general farming.

Another direct result of the War and the threat of food scarcity which accompanied those years, was an enormous increase in the number of allotments. Local authorities were empowered to utilise waste areas and even public parks for the supplementing of food supplies. The claiming of the land, however, whether for allotments or small-holdings, was less difficult than to ensure its successful working.

In Cornwall the peculiarities of the soil were such that it could not be subjected by a stranger except after considerable experience, that is to say, after several trials by error. So the Prince made it a condition that none but those who knew the soil and its nature should be allowed to work the small-holdings on his Cornish estates. To make a special point of his keen interest in these holdings is unnecessary, for in this he displays no more than the ordinary instinct of a business man. He is, to use an expression more commonly used than deserved, a good business man. Whenever he visits the Duchy he makes it part of his duty to visit the farms and holdings, to enquire of the farmers and their families what success they have had and their prospects, and to look for himself into the state of the property and the conditions of living. Housing reforms were started there as soon as he returned from the War. No one should be given a chance of answering his subsequent appeals for wholesale slum clearance by pointing out his omission to put his own house in order. After all, when this county was made a Royal Duchy in the early fourteenth century, it was constituted so in order to be a source of income to the King's eldest son.

The present Prince of Wales has not been unmindful of that fact. In encouraging the Cornish people to make the very most of their resources and industries he was acting as any sensible landlord would act. Those who have interpreted his attentions to Cornwall and the Cornish in the light of charitable deeds, do him little credit. He himself would not say " Thank you " for such a poor compliment.

Falmouth's oyster fisheries, like the allotments movement, were given a push by the food shortage of wartime. The Prince came along and gave them a little extra push on his own account. The small-holdings and the big co-operative farm he began, were further witness to his determination to make land and labour profitable. Worthy of his hire is every labourer; but *how* worthy he can realise only by being part of a going concern. The tin mines, too, had been in a bad way for years. The reader will recall the reference to these in an earlier chapter, and to the outlay of capital the Prince wisely made for their mechanical modernisation. This was another sound investment. Indeed, any scheme which helped towards the relief of unemployment, could, as an investment, be pronounced sound. The Prince's plans for afforestation, for example. These provided for the annual planting of trees over large areas of East Dartmoor.

The sound of the name at once brings before the mind's eye that grim and terrible fortress set in the midst of a naked landscape, Dartmoor Prison. The dreadful building, even when seen from a distance, overwhelms a man and fills his heart with heaviness. The Prince looked upon that place and visited it. They took him to see the bakehouse and some of the cells. The depression which filled him as he left can be imagined without much difficulty ; for whatever he might be able to do to help men in the world outside, face to face with *that*, he was helpless, as we all are helpless.

During his inspection of the prison he recognised a man he had met a few years before on the battlefield. The man was now a warder. The Prince talked with him of past times and of present times and then discovered that the man was anxious about his wife who was ill. The Prince suggested that he should go to see her, and a little later the sick woman, taken by surprise, was entertaining the Prince to the best of her ability in one of the little houses in a row set apart for the prison officers.

When the extent of the Duchy estates is considered, it cannot be said that the Prince lacks either opportunities or responsibilities as a landlord. Parts of them are in Devon, in Dorset, Berkshire, Wiltshire, the Scilly Isles and London. From the London property at Kennington a considerable part of the Prince's revenue is derived. (It was as a result of the Prince Consort's administration that this property's value increased. In 1841 the estates were bringing in £16,000 a year. Eighteen years later they were yielding an annual income of £60,000, and out of the capital which had been saved, the Sandringham estate was bought.) How careful and prudent were the Prince of Wales's enquiries before he embarked upon any schemes for reconstructing the Kennington property has been exemplified at an earlier stage of this study. There he was dealing with people of a subtly conservative nature—hawkers, carters, porters and " chars," who for ages have epitomised the Cockney spirit. We sometimes forget how important a factor that spirit is in English life. It is obvious enough to practised observers from other countries.

In M. Paul Morand's opinion, English character is found at its most typical in the Cockney. Touring the Cockney haunts of London he met what he judged to be the true old English types, and he added, let us suppose and hope as a corollary, that " the character of the Londoner seems to be astonishingly stable." It *is* stable as well as horsey. His is an open-air spirit, which partly accounts for his shrewd good humour, and also accounts for the flourishing of open-air markets in London. As it happens, the present writer recently encountered a description of an earlier generation of the very people with whom the Prince of Wales was dealing in Kennington—a description set down at the beginning of the present century, and, in this case, by a native. Kindliness, affability, good nature and free, but not low, morals are among the attributes he discerns; also a preference for an uncertain life with alternate plenty and poverty.

" Easy come, easy go " is the motto of these people, who, he writes, " do a good deal of singing before they go to bed," and " have money enough for amusement but nothing for their homes." In that last appraisement we see the problem which faced the Prince when he was considering his housing reforms in Kennington. The extent of his success in finding a solution can be measured by the fact that the local Labour Party considers the Prince to be one of the best landowners south of the Thames, and has placed that opinion on record. He has been no supporter of the die-hard argument which has become the bad landlord's parrot-cry: " What's the good of giving 'em bathrooms? They only use the bath for storing coal."

Still, there is no gainsaying the problem of rehousing people who love a market-stall and a " good place of amusement " better than their own homes, and the Prince has recognised that fact. Tenement buildings and modern houses are not in themselves a remedy. Without some form of house-pride they will degenerate in a very short time into slums worse than the first. Not very far from Kennington, the writer once heard a woman announcing from her doorway to the neighbours: " If

my 'usband was to 'ave a bath, 'e'd drown 'isself, I know
'e would." And " So would mine" came from the
neighbours in chorus. There's evidence for the bad landlord ! It almost bears out that article of his creed concerning the inevitability of the bathroom being turned
into the coal-house. The Prince has never subscribed
to that belief. Even if a reversion to slum conditions is a
constant danger to reform, he holds, with numbers of
other people, that the tendency can be overcome by tactful education, the tact consisting of a total avoidance of
anything in the nature of uplift. Since the conditions of
slum-life are evil, it follows that human beings who have
been subjected to those conditions will temporarily
carry their influence into any environment to which they
are brought. Paradise Row cannot be turned into Paradise merely by pulling down the Row.

To this question of housing reform the Prince has
devoted much earnest thought. Whether on his London
or country estates, he has never plunged into reckless
schemes for the mere satisfaction of " doing good."
It appears to him to be nothing more than common
sense to try and learn something of the inhabitants' own
ways and wishes. " It's his own neck, isn't it ? " he
once said to a farmer who, showing no sign of recognising him, had informed him that the Prince of Wales had
had too many falls from his horse and would be breaking
his neck one of these days. So also with the slum-
dwellers. Had they not to live in the newly-planned
tenements and houses ? Let them, therefore, be heard in
the matter. In the case of the Kennington Cockneys, at
any rate, they would not be slow to give tongue.

The Prince has not failed in his determination to be a
good landlord. Although his activities in this direction
are, except for Kennington, mostly confined to the West,
a tribute which can be appropriately applied to his efforts
is one paid in the Norfolk dialect to another landlord
about a century ago, one familiarly known as Coke of
Norfolk. (Later he was created Earl of Leicester.) The

incident is related in Mr. R. H. Mottram's *East Anglia*:
" The scene is the great annual audit dinner at Holkham.
. . . Dinner is over and the old chief tenant rises, mug in
hand. This is what he is reported to have said : ' Here's
to Mister Cewk an' his tenan's. And, if they du as he du,
they 'on't du as they du du.' "

For he's a jolly good farmer, in plainer English. Many
a tenant in Cornwall would, in his own idiom, say the
same of the Prince. Consistently he has kept before him
the idea of combining progressive development with
increased employment. He has been sufficiently modern
in outlook without rushing into any of the noisy madcap
schemes which have been so prominent a feature of
post-War life. Heredity and position give him a measure
of healthy conservatism just enough to balance his
natural leanings towards democratic ways of thinking.
Such a balance of sympathy is rare in our time, and was
never more needed than now.

Some of the Princes he met in India, when we allow
for the pomp and extravagance that are indigenous to
that land, have it in greater or less degree. And, incidentally, in spite of all the vilification the Indian Princes,
whether good or bad overlords, have suffered, it may be
that the more balanced among them will yet prove a
stumbling-block to the clever young demagogues who
are waiting for power. The very dearth of balanced minds
in this age gives them everywhere a peculiar and unsus-
pected strength. In the landlord that quality of sanity is
a virtue especially welcome. For, by his wise dispensation
of capital, he has the opportunity of being business man
and philanthropist in one. And the very best kind of
philanthropist moreover ; one who knows well enough
that by looking after his tenants' interests he is looking
after his own. How much healthier is that spirit than
that which prompted the " good people " of the early
nineteenth century to pour forth their consolations !

Hannah More, and the social workers she typified, did
their conscientious best to assuage the evil plight of the

people, but always their words were intended as a reinforcement of social distinctions, always their effect was to make the crowd stand at a respectful distance and to cry " God bless you, lady." Such philanthropists, being the poor's complementary part, are always with us. They have been called to mind here to indicate a type which is the very antithesis of the Prince of Wales. The immense publicity which he enjoys (or silently suffers) does not invariably assist towards a clear conception of him in this connection. There are those who, reading of his visits to tenants, his friendly chats and his requests for a bite of food, are quick to conclude that these are no more than incidents of play-acting, that they are harmless, necessary details in the enactment of the role of King's eldest son. They probably visualise the Prince sitting down gingerly in a Kennington kitchen and then hurrying back home for disinfectants and something to take away the taste of disgustingly strong tea.

In this he pays the penalty of having been for the last twenty years the most published personality in England and, in spite of the magnification of film-stars, one of the most published in the world. Part of that penalty has been to be at the mercy of the childish mentality of contemporary publicists. One of the objects of this present study is to correct the impression that the Prince leads the life of a matinée idol. The part he plays and must in the future play, has little in common with the stage. It is real and important. Most of the glamour with which it is associated exists only in the minds of spectators, especially in the minds of those who find allurement in any life outside their own, provided it can carry a headline.

It is certain that the people of Canada had no doubts about the Prince as a real man. They are not given to star-gazing in that country. If the Prince had been the type who relies upon a picture-postcard reputation to ensure him an ovation everywhere, the Canadians would have brought him to earth with a minimum of

Central Press Photo

A visit to a China Clay Pit. (Duchy of Cornwall)

ceremony. But before he had been there very long, they took him at face-value, as one of themselves. One of themselves : that was not just a phrase, a formula. How true it was he made plain when he invested in that Alberta ranch. His visits to the farm have been all too few for his liking. But, as we have already noted, he has established a practical connection with the ranch by occasionally transporting some of his English cattle for breeding. To the Canadians that was a transaction which spoke louder than any set speech. It was a sign of encouragement to Canada's trade, a sign that the fifty thousand United Empire Loyalists of long ago and what in their pioneering spirit they strove for, had not been entirely forgotten. When we think of the magnitude of Canada and the major importance of her trade problems, we may perhaps be inclined to acknowledge it as a sign, but no more than that. But the Prince has never made any pretence of being able to remove mountains merely by saying the word. He can do no more than give a lead. But by timing it well, he has frequently given that lead with excellent effect.

On his Canadian ranch the Prince of course created as many openings for employment as possible. The Educational section of the British Association raised this matter with him at one time. They found that he had already discussed the question with Sir Walter Peacock, Secretary of the Duchy of Cornwall, and with Mr. Carlyle, who was managing the ranch. There was then no accommodation for boys on the ranch, and sufficient work for no more than three or four men. But the Prince had approved of two or three extra rooms being provided when the new bunk-house was complete. To the British Association he passed on his ranch manager's opinion that, with the exception of boys who go to a Colony Farm at an early age, the best age for young men to start life in Canada was twenty. Those who were at a public school, Mr. Carlyle thought, ought to spend a year on an English Pedigree Stock Farm before setting

out for Canada. "They will then discover for themselves whether they are suited to a farmer's life, and they
will also know something about stock. So many young
men who go out to Canada drift into the towns and
eventually return to England." The Prince commended
these views to the Association as being thoroughly
sound.

During his 1927 visit to the E.P. ranch he was gratified to learn that his venture into cattle-breeding was
having so much success that he had no difficulty in
selling to Canadian farmers. One commentator sees fit
to remark that on no account must we suppose the
farmers to have been influenced by the idea of doing a
deal with the King of England's son. As if those astute,
hard-headed folk would have been so influenced! They
were buying stock, not keepsakes. We may be quite
sure that those who bought from the Prince had had a
close inspection of other cattle in the market before
deciding. They were paying him, in other words, the
kind of compliment he liked best. There are always
those who are eager to emphasize that, when a member
of the Royal Family enjoys a success of this kind, chief
credit should go to the immediate manager of the concern. In doing so they are only troubling themselves
to point out what the Prince already knows and fully
acknowledges. But is he himself to receive no portion
of the credit for the choice of a good administrator—
such choices, for example, as Mr. Carlyle for the E.P.
ranch and Sir Walter Peacock for the Duchy—and for
securing good administration through the tact of his
supervision? In this he follows the example set by the
King, who takes the greatest pains over the management
of his livestock and is always keen to enter into competition with other breeders at the shows. Great was the
disappointment on the Royal farms at Windsor when it
was learnt that the King's entries for Smithfield Fat
Stock Show in December, 1934, could not be exhibited
owing to outbreaks of foot-and-mouth disease in the

neighbourhood, and much sympathy was expressed by other breeders for those who had been managing the animals.

Thanks to Mr. Carlyle's expert knowledge, the Prince has won his share of prizes by exhibiting cattle from the E.P. ranch. " King of the Prairies " has a claim to be named in this chapter as the winner of the Grand Championship at Calgary Exhibition on two occasions, and also for masquerading in one account of the Exhibition as " King of the Fairies," a strange title for a shorthorn bull. How much hardier than the fairies the Prince's cattle are appears in the fact that they are out of doors all through the year. As for the ranch itself, there is little to distinguish it from others in Alberta. The land, which is situated at Pekisko High River, seventy miles to the south of Calgary, extends to thousands of acres, with magnificent pastures. The ranch-house itself, as the reader will have inferred from the Prince's reply to the British Association's enquiry, is far from being large or specially comfortable. Were it otherwise it would hardly be in keeping with its purpose. The ranch was not purchased, as some caustic critics were at first inclined to believe, to enable the Prince to dress up as a cowboy.

If Wild West films had ever created that longing in him—and in view of its prevalence we must admit the possibility—he could have satisfied it far less expensively at a fancy dress ball. An indulgence is precisely what an investment in a ranch could not be in any circumstances. If possible, the Prince's was to be a profit-making concern. Mr. Carlyle would be doing his best to make it so. At the end of the summer of 1923 the Prince, during an unofficial visit to Canada, looked in to see what progress his manager was making, and was well satisfied. Here was a rare chance of leading what is so mistakenly called the simple life. Eagerly he took it, lending a hand at everything from the common round of hay-making to the not so trivial task of rounding up the cattle. The simple life ! Not a few of the items comprising that kind of existence in Canada represent acts of the greatest skill and tests of humanity's utmost wit. The bronco's one obsession is to make man's life anything but simple.

Before the Prince left he invited to his ranch a large gathering of ranchers—neighbours let us call them, though the distance they travelled changes the complexion of the word. His greeting to these men reveals how earnestly he desired to be taken seriously in this venture of his. "Fellow-Albertans" was his way of addressing them. "Fellow-Albertans, you are welcome and I hope you will enjoy your outing. My ranch is open to you to-day." For their part, they availed themselves of the opportunity of having a keen look round, at stock, pastures and buildings ; for his, the Prince lost no time in talking freely with men who lived entirely by their wits and their senses.

Canada is not the only place to which the Prince sends his cattle from Cornwall. Official engagements take him to all parts of England, and having acquired the habit of looking at country with a farmer's eye, he is not backward in watching for openings for speculation. A Trent-side estate called Grove Farm, for example, attracted him during a visit to Nottinghamshire ; as a result of his enquiries the farm was run later in conjunction with the Duchy estates and took in from there several transferred head of cattle.

Nor is livestock the only interest on the Prince's estates. Flowers from his farms in Cornwall and the Scilly Isles are sent to London for sale. At the beginning of January, 1935, the Queen was being supplied daily with narcissi, jonquils and other spring blooms from these lands. It was a season of great activity on the bulb farms in the Isles and West Cornwall. Many tons of flowers were dispatched every day. If early-morning buyers at Covent Garden had some way of knowing which were the flowers from the Duchy they would doubtless excuse themselves for marking them with special retail prices. But there is no way. Blooms from the Duchy estates come up to London with the rest, and smell no less sweet for that.

Since the Duchy estates are the source of the greater part of the Prince's personal income, he takes trouble to derive from the lands their maximum yield. The lands and the workers receive a direct benefit from this efficiency, for the Prince devotes large sums to their continual development. It is interesting to note incidentally that by remaining a bachelor the Prince has forgone the £10,000 per annum which in England is set aside against the day when the King's eldest son marries. The increase, no doubt, would not be frowned upon, for, with the rest of us, the Prince's expenditure grows yearly heavier. The upkeep of his houses,[1] with staff salaries and wages, his subscriptions to charities and institutions, and, over and above these, his list of voluntary donations—these have not grown less during

[1] Although Marlborough House was chosen as one of the Prince of Wales's residences as long ago as 1927, he has never shown any desire to leave that modest wing of St. James's Palace which is known as York House. When the decision in favour of Marlborough House was made, various alterations were carried out in that early eighteenth-century palace, which was King Edward's residence when he was Prince of Wales. The present Prince knows Marlborough House well, for he frequently visited his grandfather there, and lived there when his father was Prince of Wales. York House faces Ambassador's Court and backs on to Cleveland Row. The Prince's private quarters are on the first floor, and consist of two sitting-rooms, a bedroom and a bathroom, all of normal size. One of the sitting-rooms is used for informal calls ; the other, which is almost filled by a large writing-desk, is for work. From the neatness and severity of the bedroom you would think that it was occupied by an army officer. No valuable works of art, curios or trophies are to be seen. The ground-floor consists of a small entrance-hall, an unimposing reception-room and two or three similar rooms for secretaries or equerries. The dining-room adjoins the reception-room. A Comptroller, a Private Secretary, an Assistant Private Secretary, a Groom-in-Waiting and three Equerries form the Prince's staff. All are very busy men.

the past ten years. And since he himself has so forcibly struck the note of personal service it is not to be supposed that he has left any loop-hole for criticism of his example. Nor are his Comptroller and the Inland Revenue authorities unacquainted. The sums which these mathematicians collect are calculated upon the Prince's net resources, and cause as much wagging of heads at York House as similar verdicts do in other houses.

In the most grandiloquent sense of the phrase, the Prince is not a wealthy man. But, in his financial affairs, he is content and he " manages." That in itself is an achievement. Compared with the past, it is an outstanding achievement, for not every Prince of Wales has reconciled position and economy, upkeep and outlay, " appearance " and real estate with so much success. Some, we recall, walked carelessly along a primrose way only to return by a path of thorny reckoning. In the context of the Prince's own time his achievement in this respect is notable in that his was a generation which first of all was subjected to the laxity of an after-war period, then was sharply pulled up by the strictures of economic adjustment. For how many wealthy men of that generation have these conditions proved too sore a trial !

CHAPTER 7

SPORTSMAN

Golf—not excellent, not bad. The " awful job " of playing himself in as Captain at St. Andrews. Horsemanship. The Prince's hunters. Miss Muffit's claim to fame. The spick-and-span stables at Melton Mowbray. Spills on the hunting-field. The point raised in the House of Commons. How the Prince received this interference with his personal liberty. A broken collar-bone. Plays polo well. No great love for shooting or fishing. Squash-rackets, the best-liked game of all. Cards— almost an aversion. " Crown-and-Anchor " in the trenches. Active support of National Playing Fields Fund. The Prince and the post-War generation. His regularity. Fitness for service the dominating motive of his life. A tribute to the King which is no less applicable to the Prince.

ASSIDUOUS though the Prince has been in applying himself to games of many kinds, he has never aspired to the role of champion. For this we may be grateful. In a sense, he can be said to have administered, by his attitude, an implicit rebuke to an age which tends to mechanise sport as well as everything else. At no other time has the very efficiency of athletes militated so fiercely against the spirit which, ideally, should animate their contests. From one point of view this seems an unaccountable paradox. From another the reason is plain enough. The true spirit of contest includes discipline of mind no less than of body. Only too often has it been proved that our efficient athletes of the present age have left mental discipline wholly out of reckoning.

The oldest and simplest of reasons have prompted the Prince's essays in sports and games—the desire to keep fit (with the attendant desire to avoid putting on weight). Those who, standing on æsthetic grounds, condemn that simple wish as being too painfully primitive, should pause to reflect what a world it would be if all grounds were æsthetic—if there were none, for example, for cricket, and no enclosures for that supremely subtle test of human character, golf. The Prince has shown himself only too willing to submit to that last test whenever time, place and mood concur. His opinion of the game is that there is none which offers so many chances of making a fool of one's self. For that reason he prefers to play a round with his intimate friends, and with men rather than women.

In the members' house of the Royal and Ancient Golf Club at St. Andrews there hangs a painting of the Prince carrying out the awful job of playing himself in as captain. " Awful job " was his own description of the ordeal to old Andrew Kircaldy when they came out, Andrew as caddy, to face the crowd. Never was a first drive so imprinted upon a golfer's memory as that was upon the Prince's. The most hardened professional would have been forgiven for a little shakiness in performing that solemn ritual and with the dignity of that ancient club at stake. Andrew, tactful and sympathetic, advised the Prince to pay no attention to the crowd. Counsel of perfection! As well tell an outfielder in a Test Match, waiting for a skyer, to ignore the breathless multitude! Relief came at length, however, no less to Andrew than to the playing-in captain. The drive was good enough to get a round of cheering from the crowd. Incidentally, it was approached with more deliberation than the Prince shows on less austere occasions. His casual preparation for a drive leaves him open to the criticism of those to whom golf is a religion. Salvation he can never know, in their sense of the word, until he gives more reverent heed to the articles of faith by which the initial act is hedged round about. That was made clear enough by the septuagenarian, Bob Lake, after a game with the Prince at the Royal West Norfolk Club. Lake, after winning the game on the last green, was, of course,

The Prince playing himself in as Captain of St. Andrews Golf Club

expected to narrate the epic feat to an inquisitive gathering of friends ; and when the tale was told there were still many questions to be asked and answered, and most important of all : " What sort of a player is he, Bob ? " To that Bob Lake, according to report, replied : " The Prince is a rare good golfer, but he needs a bit more practice. He has a fine long drive, but I don't like the way he walks straight up to the ball and hits it. I told him he should have a little more patience, and take a little more time over his putts, and I think he took my advice kindly. Leastways, when the game had ended and I had won he stood me a beer in the club-house."

The ring of this blunt speech is true enough to give it an air of credibility. In any case, we can be certain that the advice, howsoever it was worded, was kindly taken. In none of his activities has the Prince been handicapped by the inability to apply self-criticism. Had it been otherwise, it is scarcely believable that he would ever have delivered himself up to that merciless exposure which is golf's chief commendation as a human activity. How easily he can laugh at himself as an exponent of the game is borne out by the story of one of his golf experiences in New Zealand. During the course of the game he found, and appropriated, a ball discarded by another player, and later on, a second ball. This was a new experience. " Something splendid must be going to happen," he remarked. " Never before have I gone a round without losing a ball."

But we must beware of falling back into that soft bed of anecdotes upon which the devotees of golf all too readily and frequently recline, lest our resolve to keep these pages innocent of dubious tales be broken. The reader shall be spared the string of doughty deeds and quaint happenings which he apprehended the moment the word " golf " was mentioned. We shall be content to remark only this : that, for all the discouragements and setbacks which have come his way on the golf-course, the Prince still takes pleasure in a round, provided he is free to approach his drives as nonchalantly as he likes. Among the English clubs which are expecting to see him on their links in the near future is the Royal Eastbourne; at least, so much can be supposed from the members' emphasis of the fact that from one of the garden gates of Compton Place House, which the King and Queen have recently bought, the Prince will be able to walk straight on to the course. But the thought of an excessive public curiosity may deter him, as it has deterred him from playing on many another course.

Not the least of the reasons for his keenness on flying is that it is a form of escape. Another is that flying often provides an agreeable blend of business and pleasure. An official visit to a provincial town is frequently made the excuse for a journey there and back by air. Before and after facing the crowd, this way of travelling affords a recreative means of withdrawal, a safe retreat. If flying conditions prove contrary, they do but let an element of sport into the venture. A punctual keeping of the engagement becomes so much the more urgent, becomes an excuse for contest. In such a case, the Prince is rarely on the losing side. After a rough passage to Worcester, when he went there to open the new bridge over the Severn, he was ill after landing, but insisted, nevertheless, in carrying out all his appointments there.

The Prince himself once referred to the occasional relief of escaping from the crowd into the air and went so far as to place that among the principal advantages of flying. He mentioned others: how clean it was as a way of travelling, for instance, and—a more debatable point, so far as England is concerned—how much finer the country looks from the air. His enthusiasm for air travel was born, or at least became active, during his Oxford days. While he was at camp with the Officers' Training Corps he went over to Farnborough to see the *Beta*, one of the earliest of our airships, and was taken for a short cruise. This was an experience all the sweeter for his disappointment a little earlier in Germany. He had been to Friedrichshafen to inspect the airship works, where he was received by Count Zeppelin. The Count arranged for the Prince to take a flight in the latest completed Zeppelin, Z 4, but that touch of irony was prevented by adverse weather.

The well-known pilot, Cunningham-Reid, was another who, in early days, helped to develop the Prince's air-mindedness, although his methods were drastic rather than coaxing. Soon after the Armistice, Cunningham-Reid was flying the Prince over the Rhine. The Prince thought this a good place to indulge in the luxury of a stunt in the air. The pilot was only too ready. First he performed several convolutions known as "upward rolls"; then a "falling roll," then a series of "half rolls," then, immediately above Cologne Cathedral, a spin. Then began the pilot to ascend again to essay perhaps an even more ambitious set of variations. But a tap on the shoulder called attention to the passenger who had just enough sense of his whereabouts to point to the earth in earnest entreaty.

After that the Prince took a more strictly utilitarian view of aviation. He now owns two aeroplanes, both designed to suit his needs and tastes. A mile or so from Fort Belvedere, his country house, is Smith's Lawn in Windsor Great Park, which he uses as an aerodrome. For engagements which can be carried out with an equerry only in attendance, he uses a D.H. Dragon bi-plane. To carry himself and his suite he uses a twin-engined Vickers Viastra. Within this shell of scarlet, silver and gold, he can change his clothes on a day of many and various engagements, and, at will, discuss plans, make tea, prepare a speech or play a gramophone record. The interior has been made almost sound-proof. The question of the Prince's safety in the air has, of course, been raised by all sorts of people, from those who are genuinely concerned to those who regard the Prince not so much as an individual as a Perennial Topic for Busybodies. When he was asked by a duchess (who, evidently, decided that an indirect angle of approach was advisable) whether the Queen had shown any anxiety about his predilection for air travel, he informed her that the Queen was never agitated without just cause. For the duchess's benefit he recalled the time when he used to ride in steeplechases, and reminded her that only after he had had a succession of spills did the Queen reveal her anxious thoughts by asking him to avoid serious risks.

His enthusiasm for point-to-point riding, during the early post-War years, was a more reasonable cause for public concern than is his love of flying. So hard was his riding both in races and on the hunting field that a full share of accidents came his way and attracted more attention to his private pursuits than he wished for. During November, 1922, he was forced to cancel all engagements and to walk on crutches as the result of a fall while hunting. An ankle was badly injured. Before the year was out, however, he was mounted again and riding the harder for the energy that had been checked. Those who saw him hunting at that period were never given cause to think him a half-hearted rider. Rather did his zest lead him to try his strength ill-advisedly on occasions. He was almost too keen, even judged by the standard of those in whose eyes the whole of life is contained within the flesh and frame of a horse. He would never give up. A complete somersault over a gate did but incite him to try more gates ; and once when he took a toss and landed on his face, he remounted and finished among the first four.

An unhappy situation arose at the beginning of 1924. He was riding in the Army point-to-point races at Arbor-field Cross and had a bad fall. Those who saw it speak of it as a narrow escape. Even so, the Prince had presence of mind enough to telephone the King and Queen lest they should receive exaggerated news through other channels. The interaction of Press opinion and public opinion now began to have effect. Newspaper proprietors took it upon themselves to appeal to the Prince to give up the dangerous sports of point-to-point racing and steeple-chasing. But a few weeks later he was riding in the High Peak point-to-point races at Buxton, and, partly out of admiration, partly out of critical interest, unprecedented crowds came to the meeting. Here was a further danger, for if the crowds gathering round the fences became unmanageable and frightened the horses, possibility of accidents was increased to probability. Many thousands saw the Prince ride an exciting race that day. His horse fell at the second fence ; he remounted, made so much ground that before long he was challenging the leader ; then, at the very last fence, his mount fell again. The race was lost, but no winner was ever given a greater reception. Covered in mud, he was also covered in glory.

But these adventures led to a further wave of criticism, one which gathered enough impetus to break finally upon the floor of the House of Commons. Some thought the King should give his son a straight talk ; others held that the Prince ought of his own free will to give up these sports and allay the general uneasiness ; others again—perhaps a curtailment of their own freedom at some time had made them sympathetic— urged that he should be allowed to follow his own inclinations. There is no doubt that the controversy brought a crisis into the Prince's private life. At first he was dismayed that so much heated criticism should be focussed upon his recreations, which, when all was said, constituted the best part of his leisure. In some respects the situation resembled the crisis which Sir Robert Peel precipitated in the young life of Queen Victoria, when he made it a condition of his taking office that she should dismiss her Ladies of the Household. The Queen insisted that this was her own purely private affair ; Peel insisted, no less stubbornly, that these appointments had political significance.

The conflict became one between the official and the

unofficial aspects of the Queen's life. So, too, did this question of the Prince's riding become a conflict between his private wishes and what the House of Commons called an Affair of State. But, unlike that obdurate nineteen-year-old girl, Queen Victoria, the Prince did not create an *impasse*. However regretfully, he dropped the more dangerous forms of riding. He would give the public no more cause to think that he was wilfully taking risks. And no more opportunities of judging him a poor horseman ; for naturally, that was the verdict accepted by all who had no knowledge of horsemanship. It is a rider's courage, and not merely his skill, which, in many cases, is to be inferred from the number of his falls. If a spill invariably meant a bad mark, some of the most accomplished of horsemen would be showing a very poor record. Not that the Prince has ever claimed to be a perfect rider ; but it is certain that his reputation as a horseman is, so far as the general public is concerned, less than his actual achievements deserve, and chiefly because his accidents have seemed more glaring under the bright, narrow beam of publicity.

The fact that the Prince does not own a racing stud qualifies his interest in flat-racing. At any time and in any sport, he would rather be in action than a spectator. And, if possible, in speedy action. The *adagio* movement of cricket has never made any great appeal to him either as watcher or player, and when in 1930 the Oval Test Match between England and Australia gave him a chance of greeting the Australian players and of visiting his Kennington tenants on the same day, the match itself did not hold him for long. It is again the question of *tempo* which probably explains his lukewarm response to fishing. Of the various kinds of shooting he prefers that in which the target is a clay-pigeon.

As much as any young man of his age the Prince was attracted for a time by the idea of sheer speed. The phase involved the purchase of a speed-boat which a few years ago was often to be seen churning up the placid calm of

Virginia Water. When the Prince had acquired full control of the craft, he took the keenest pleasure in speed-boat racing with Prince George and other friends.

Among the happiest of his out-of-door memories are the polo games the Prince played in India. In conversation he has often recalled them and declared his intention of going back to India some day for more polo. He has described India as one vast polo ground— a country where you can get a game outside your door at almost any time, without bothering to fix it up days before. Seeing that his opportunities for continuous practice at polo are few, it is not surprising that he cannot be credited with a level standard of play. He has been known to play an indifferent game and also a very good one. In general, it can be said that he has a good eye, very fair stroke judgment, and that he plays with team-sense. As a judge of a horse he has frequently received compliments from the inhabitants of that separate world, but in buying he is wise enough to rely upon the judgment of one of those inhabitants who, as often as not, appear to have received something like a divine communication in the matter. The Prince's care for his hunters before he gave up the stud at Melton Mowbray is further evidence that he is a genuine lover of horses. Even the christenings were too important to delegate to another. He named them all. Who will say there is no such thing as horse-sense when he learns that Miss Muffit gave the Prince many of his falls? That horse, surely, was out to show just how much there is in a name. Moreover, she probably knew how great a favourite she remained in spite of her delinquencies. For good manners, the horse called Just an Idea surpassed them all and had a clean record so far as falls were concerned. Among others of the Prince's favourite horses were Son and Heir, Miss Gris, How's That, Hard to Find, Tarzan, March Maid, Pikeman, Lady Doon and—another delinquent—Degomme. With the help of Mr. Russell, his stud groom, the Prince set a standard in the comfort and cleanliness of his Melton stables. All who saw those spick and span quarters with their bright red walls are in agreement that nothing was wanting there in the way of example. Their commendation gives us leave to entertain an even poorer opinion of Miss Muffit as a lady.

The Prince did not face the risks of hard riding without taking the precaution of learning the elements of first aid ; and so well had he assimilated them that he was able to do much to relieve the pain of an opponent who, in the Royal Naval Hunt Club Race, fell and broke his collar-bone. On the occasion, too, when he broke his own collar-bone, he passed on very precise instructions to those who were giving him attention before the arrival of a doctor.

The hunting world still keeps alive that story of the Prince, the Master and the Farmer. It is worth repeating for the sake of readers who, being outside that inner circle, may not have heard it. Those who relate it usually resort to the opening formula, "Once upon a time." Even if the story be true, the formula is not inappropriate. For, like other stories about Princes, this one has a moral. Know then that while the Prince of Wales was hunting in a favourite district, the Master told him of the trouble he had had with a spoil-sport Farmer whose practice was to fence off his fields with wire. The Master had often asked the Farmer to substitute less dangerous fencing and was especially importunate in view of the Prince's visit. He argued in vain. It was a war between the Hunt and the Land. The Prince, listening to the Master's story, decided to try his own method of coming to an understanding. He called on the Farmer, talked with him, talked of local conditions, crops, horse-racing and, not too pointedly, of sport. But not of wire fencing. The farmer enjoyed the talk. So much so that his heart was changed, and without waiting for any further requests from the Master, he took down every one of those wire fences.

As a horseman

Games of chance, in the narrower sense of the term, make little appeal to the Prince, and in that fact there is, perhaps, further evidence of his predilection for action and speed. There is no need, in this connection, to drag in a comparison with the tastes of his grandfather, as is so commonly done. One writer, fearful lest the Prince should be misunderstood, goes to the length of remarking that the Prince's dislike of card games must on no account be taken as casting a reflection upon King Edward the Seventh. To be sure, it must not! Why, that would be making the Prince appear a kind of puritan! Whatever else he is, he is not *that*, and has never shown the slightest sign that there is a particle of puritanism in his make-up. The same writer informs his readers that they will never hear of the Prince of Wales being dogmatic about games involving a limited amount of gambling. As if we had not all heard of his games of crown-and-anchor with the Tommies in a dug-out! Those of us who contend that it is more blessed to adapt one's self to circumstances than, in any circumstances, to lay down the law, can find much to support the contention in the Prince's life.

The sporting world of England is an intricate honeycomb of tastes, interests and investments. For the unwary it is as full of traps and pitfalls as the political world. Few are aware of the amount of thought that a man in the Prince's position must give before he states an opinion or makes an appearance in connection with any form of contest. Those who are keen followers of the lesser blood sports have reason to believe that the Prince does not share their zeal. But he avoids public pronouncements on the subject, and knows when he must make exceptions.

For instance, since the King has given up shooting at Windsor, the Prince has undertaken the invitations for the opening shoot. There is now more shooting over the Windsor coverts than in past seasons (for breeding has been resumed there on a large scale), and both the

Prince of Wales and the Duke of York give parties. But these occasions can hardly be said to be red-letter days in the Prince's sport calendar. For those we must look to big game hunting, where the odds in favour of the hunted animal are greater. Boxing, too, has won his support, and those who see him at the ring-side know that they have with them a whole-hearted, if (as he himself would say) amateurish, exponent of the sport which claims, also, to be a not ignoble art.

Towards sports of all kinds, the Prince's attitude is fundamentally simple and sane. He values games for the opportunities they offer of measuring skill with fellow men and of maintaining physical and mental strength. Simply that. And these are the reasons that actuate his earnest support of all organisations having for their object the bodily health and fitness of boys and girls, young men and women. With his brother, the Duke of York, the Prince has been actively and specially interested in the National Playing Fields Fund, the chief object of which is to remove children from the dangers of street-playing in industrial areas and provide them with spacious recreation grounds in healthy surroundings. Being one of the aspects of the slum problem, it is no matter for surprise that this question should engage the Prince's attention. But we have lived long enough to see conditions in which the problem of children's recreation is no longer confined to the slums of large towns. We have lived to see the curse of ribbon development. That red rash of habitations which has broken out wherever a main road is leading to or from a town is called development. Eruption is its true and proper name. What the escaping townsfolk have sought, they, seeking, have destroyed. And they have brought their children from the dangers of town streets to the worse dangers of arterial roads. The National Playing Fields Fund was never more needed than now.

Love of speed has never led the Prince to cause danger on the roads. He is not keen enough on speedy driving

for that. After the first excitement of being an owner-
driver had passed, he willingly took back seat as a passenger, and in that respect his taste has not since changed.
Moreover, flying has robbed him of his early interest in
motoring. In the air, at least for the present, the
experience of speed can be indulged in without danger
to others. That, we can safely say, is one of the reasons
for his preference. Some of the other reasons have
already been quoted, the advantages of wider views,
cleaner travel and time-saving, for example.

The Prince's physical appearance at the age of forty
bears witness to a careful, almost an austere regard for
fitness. He did not begin with the asset of robust
health. He could not afford to take the risks that most
men in the twenties and thirties allow themselves. The
strain imposed by the routine of official visits, speeches
and functions, has sometimes been too great, and whenever that has happened, the Prince has been wise enough
to obey doctor's orders. Often his doctor's intervention
has set up a conflict between desire and expediency, but
such conflicts have only served to throw into relief a
quality of essential common sense. The Prince is neither
head-strong nor a hypochondriac, and in this we catch a
reflection of the King, his father. Since the King's
illness his doctors have been compelled to consider most
carefully each of his engagements and the advisability
of fulfilling it. The King himself dislikes to cancel a
State ceremony, and on these occasions doctors have
sometimes to apply tactful, but firm pressure.

Before the State opening of the new Session of Parliament in November, 1934, for instance, they were
required to be especially diplomatic. On the day before
the event a fog descended. The situation was not easy,
for the King insisted that he was prepared to disregard
the fog and carry out the ceremony. His medical
advisers did not want him to take this risk, and as late as
midnight were in consultation. They urged resort to
a Royal Commission such as Queen Victoria frequently

adopted and such as King George himself found necessary during his illness. In the end a compromise was made : the King abandoned the ceremonial journey in state coach, with its escort of Household Cavalry, and instead travelled slowly to Parliament in a closed motor-car.

Similar situations have sometimes checked the Prince in carrying out a heavy programme, notably during his Empire tours. It is easy to fall into the error of supposing these tours of England and the Empire to be smooth ways of unending pleasure; easy to overlook the fatiguing effect of continually meeting crowds excited to the highest pitch. The Prince is not of cynical mould. He cannot witness a crowd's elation without himself being filled with its influence. No man of his generation has been acclaimed with more spontaneity, with more genuine and immediate affection. Had he been in the least a cynic, or had he slowly become so with the passing of years, such acclamation would have proved excessive and gone to his head. Unfailingly it has gone to his heart ; and in that we see more clearly than anywhere else the stuff of which he is made. His nature is of the kind which not only shares the happiness of the crowds he meets, but also suffers the inevitable reaction. In his private life he must for ever be on guard against the possibility of things falling flat.

The possibility must always accompany the life of any Prince living at any time. The Prince of Wales, living in these present years of discontent, faces the danger every day. His very privileges can make for monotony; his very popularity can induce loneliness. There is only one way of escape, and that he has found for himself, the way of incessant service. But such service as is required of him cannot be rendered if the health account is overdrawn. Yes, the whole matter comes down to that prosaic level. And not the least of the Prince's services has been to show a generation which, because of the shock of war, has been prone to let physical resources run to waste and to make experimental havoc of their bodily selves, to show that generation how to avoid so steep and violent a descent. Only those who are contemporary with the Prince and have lived with him through those tendencies can fully know the value of the example he has quietly and unconsciously set. Only they can realise what peculiar courage was required of any young man of the 1920's who proposed to do anything so disgustingly hearty as to run for an hour each morning before breakfast.

For some time this was part of the daily routine of the Prince who, in a sweater and flannels, used to taxi to Buckingham Palace grounds for the purpose. Nowadays he begins the day in his gymnasium where he carries out a whole system of exercises. But there is hardly anything he prefers to a game of squash racquets, and most commonly this is his way of ending a day of strenuous engagements. He finds the game a perfect means of releasing energy and at the same time of relieving mental stress ; and at the Bath Club, which he uses as much as any of his clubs, he is frequently to be seen in the courts. All this points to what is known as a regular life and gives unexpected meaning to the compliment which an American engine-driver once paid when, in his idiom, he called him a regular fellow. In the Prince this quality of regularity is not strained. It is second nature. There are those who, apprehending the fact, automatically exclaim : " How dull ! " These are they who, running after strange fashions, of literature, of painting, dress, music, or behaviour, have themselves contributed liberally to the dullness of our world and time. *Faut être dans le mouvement.* So shrill and persistent has been that cry that many have lost all sense of direction. They have no sooner girded up their loins in response to a " Lo here ! " than they hear an equally urgent and strident " Lo there ! " Is there anything more dull for a man than not to know the way ?

The Prince's "regularity" has saved him from following

the dubious hues and cries which have filled the air since the day the Armistice was signed ; and those who complain that he has rarely given any direct encouragement to the arts forget how much the arts have been impeded by those who follow, not out of love but snobbery. The Prince is not an art snob. On the rare occasions when he attends a concert it is, as a rule, in support of a favourite charity. We have seen that his taste in music led him in early days to aspire to the mastery of bagpipes and guitar. What should such an one be doing in the Queen's Hall or Covent Garden ? That, perhaps, is his own attitude, although any sensible music lover would hold that the aspiring piper and guitarist had a far better right of entry to those places than many who dutifully take up their station there. If that is so, the Prince is quite content to neglect his rights. Nor has he ever itched to join any of the satellite sets attending on literature, painting or ballet. This, his attitude, has been dwelt upon here because it is closely bound up with that in him which we have been pleased to call " regularity." In an age which has made a virtue of irregularity his very normality has shone like a good deed.

But we must beware of emphasising this normality as if it were intended so to shine. Being a natural quality, it has never been flaunted for example's sake, as, for instance, were the virtues of Queen Victoria's Consort. In that age of precepts and inhuman respectability the public expected of Royalty a full-dress exhibition of all the virtues ; and what was expected was in good measure supplied. Imagine a member of the present Royal Family spreading virtuous plumes before the public of the Lax Twenties ! More than a little wisdom will be discerned, by future students of our social conditions, in the quiet, self-possessed conduct of the King and Queen of England during that nightmare decade. Through those years they were anxiously watching, but with no sign of panic, the development of their children and, through them, the interaction of character and the inimical forces which were then let loose. The post-war years of any period have invariably made life dangerous for the individual and for society alike. After *that* war it was a marvel that the oncoming generation did not sink irretrievably into the slough of cynical passivity. A marvel, indeed! In some countries the new generation has saved itself, temporarily at least, by yielding unconditionally to a wave of unreasoning patriotism; in England it has been saved by the sudden unaccountable emergence of Edwardian sentiment in a modified form. Whence it came and how are mysteries; but at least one young man had premonition of its arrival and, coming most carefully upon the hour, wrote a play which could not help but enjoy a long run at Drury Lane.

Through that decade (which in retrospect appears as one long, continuous and disreputable night-club) the Prince of Wales passed with the rest of us. He was no more sheltered from its insidious influence than any others of our generation. It was a testing-time of such intensity that many have failed to come through. They have lost their hold on life. The odds against them were too great. (The Lax Twenties! That we should be alive to tell the tale is something to be wondered at! But perhaps we speak too soon. We have yet to learn what the Thirties have in store.) It is not merely because we have lived through those years that we believe them to be unprecedented as regards the havoc they have wrought and the hopelessness they have bequeathed. After so tremendous an upheaval temporary chaos was inevitable. And what has been its effect upon the Prince? When so many have been chilled by disillusion's icy finger it would be pointless to pretend that he has escaped untouched. Pointless, too, to pretend that the dangers of the post-War years were any less real to him than to others.

The writer is not thinking here of those abstractions

which are conveniently grouped under the name of Temptations, nor of any specific items in the long catalogue issued periodically by the old firm of World, Flesh and Devil. In brief, he does not propose to hold an enquiry upon the exact nature of the Prince's wild oats. If that is what the reader is hankering after this author is not his man. By " dangers " is meant all that conspiracy which, under the cloak of sham prosperity, false security and lassitude was formed against mankind on November 11, 1918, at the very moment when the House of Commons was comforting itself with the words, " we have now entered upon a new chapter in international history in which war will be recognised as an obsolete anachronism, never to be revived."

We know the results of the conspiracy. It has not altogether succeeded. Subverted standards of living are giving way to a more determined insistence upon the normal course. In brief, " regularity " is finding its place again. The present writer has claimed that this is a quality to be admired. Some there are who contend that in the Prince of Wales it is less admirable since it has been imposed upon him by the duties of his position. Is this not saying that he has performed his duties well ? Is it to be assumed that every Prince has been willing to follow that path or, being willing, has been capable of doing so ? Must we belittle the Prince's achievement by referring to duty in almost a disparaging sense ?

It is the fashion to ridicule the type known as British Sportsman. He is an easy target, especially for those whose business is to manufacture humour for people who have none of their own. The commonest charge these humorists bring against the British Sportsman is that he is stupid. That is merely a roundabout method of confessing that he is clever in ways which the humorist fails to understand. Not the least of the Sportsman's attributes is that, generally speaking, he is of all fellows the most regular. The Prince is a true type of British Sportsman, and at the same time is

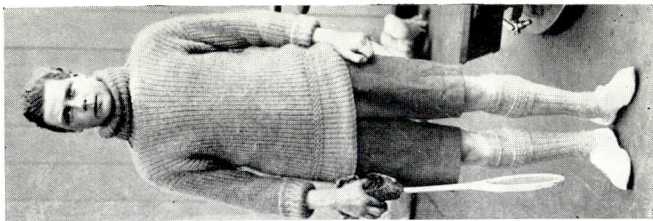

In a Squash Racquets Court

In Flying Kit

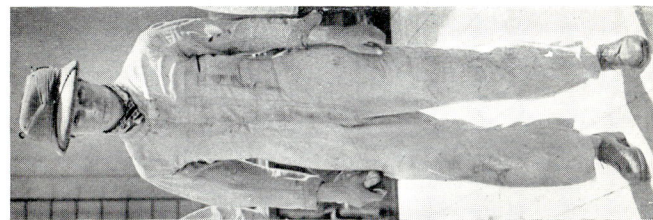

After a visit to the engine-rooms
of H.M.S. " Repulse "

marked off by many an idiosyncrasy. Enthusiast he has
always been, but never a narrow fanatic. When, for
private and public reasons, it was necessary to consider
giving up his stud at Melton, he went to Craven Lodge
to take one last wistful look at his hunters and then
decided as he knew he must decide. A few days later
the hunters were on their way to Leicester for sale by
auction. (All except Just an Idea. For services rendered, she was allowed to enjoy retirement on the
Prince's farm in Cornwall.) That is an instance of how
the Prince's private interests are always subservient to
service, not merely in deference to his own motto,[1] but
because from that state of things he derives most
satisfaction.

The reader will have gathered as much if he has ever
heard the talk on sportsmanship which the Prince
recorded for the gramophone in 1924. The very simplicity of the talk gives new force to ideas which were
in danger of becoming unheeded platitudes. Service is
the underlying thought of the speech. As long as any
form of sport can be said to make for equipment in
wider spheres of activity on the community's behalf, so
long can it be regarded as a beneficent influence. That
is the substance of the little talk. Surely there is nothing
to find fault with in that. The idea could easily be dove-
tailed into H. G. Wells's programme for Utopia.

This continual striking of the note of service has been
the distinctive feature of the last twenty years of the
Prince's career. Since his return from the second East
African tour it has been sounded with special urgency.
His crusading spirit has never been more intense than
during the past few years when the call to national unity
has been so insistent. Looking back over the Prince's
activities through that period, the writer is reminded of
a tribute paid by Lord Oxford (then Mr. Asquith) to
the King at the conclusion of the War. It was spoken
in the House of Commons and, in its elegant and formal

[1] *Ich Dien* (I serve).

way, can be as aptly addressed to the Prince of Wales in this jubilee year of 1935.

"There is no one," the speaker said, "that can bear testimony—first-hand testimony—more authentic or more heart-felt than I do to the splendid example which His Majesty has set in time of peace, as well as in time of war, in the discharge of every one, day by day, of the responsible duties which fall to the Sovereign of this Empire. . . . The Throne of this country stands unshaken, broad-based on the people's will. It has been reinforced to a degree which it is impossible to measure, by the living example of our Sovereign and his gracious Consort, who have always felt and shown by their life and by their conduct that they are there not to be ministered unto but to minister. As the right honourable gentleman said, monarchies in these days are held, if they continue to be held, not by the shadowy claim of any so-called Divine Right, not . . . by any power of dividing and dominating popular forces and popular will, not by pedigree and not by tradition: they are held, and can only be held, by the highest form of public service, by understanding, by sympathy with the common lot and by devotion to the common weal."

CHAPTER 8

GOOD NEIGHBOUR

The Prince's example in dark and difficult times. British Legion
nearest his heart. The fruits of war experience. Never
forgetful of ex-service men. The Prince's resolve as strong
and clear as ever. His warnings to the oncoming generation.
His qualifications as a leader. His devotion to England. A
day in Durham, as Patron of the National Council of Social
Service. His example to the House of Commons. The
Prince's public addresses. Analysis of his address to the Royal
Institute of British Architects, 1934. The effects of the speech.

IN a world where charitable impulse is in danger
of being stifled by the very universality of distress,
we welcome every effort to keep it alive, from whatever source it may come. The steep path from distress
to despair, from despair to apathy, is easily taken by those
of generous disposition. Even those who are in a position to lead are too often intimidated in such a world as
this, too often retire to an observation-post of com-
parative security. Soft tongues are everywhere heard
persuading men to shirk responsibilities, persuading
them that responsibilities in any case are illusive, and
they speak with an effectiveness that is alarming. The
isolation policy which makes men of international affairs
exceedingly wrathful, is overlooked as a motive in
individual lives, or else encouraged.

We welcome then, or should welcome, each point of
light we discern in this so dark and disjointed world. In
the writer's judgment, such a point of light is to be seen
in the Prince's steadfast devotion to the causes he has
chosen to support. Of these the nearest to his heart has
always been the British Legion. The office he holds as
President of that organisation has claimed more of his

time and activity than any other. However bitterly the ex-service man may complain that the community at large, jostled and put out of step by the arrival of a new and clamorous generation, has forgotten him, however just that complaint may seem to be, it is not likely that he will ever forget the Prince's loyalty to his cause. For there are few alive who can claim to have worked as faithfully and consistently as the Prince has worked for that great company of men. Ex-service men we call them; and it has been the Prince's sustained purpose that, not in irony should they so be called, but in pride.

At one point in the narrative the reader's attention has been claimed to mark how the Prince broke, or rather curtailed, an engagement in order to visit a group of ex-service men on an occasion of reunion; and how he said that these men had a claim on him at any time and whatever the circumstances. In this he has shown an imagination which has not been too common during the past two decades of English life—an imagination that outshines facile sentiment and outlasts the promptings of ceremonious occasions, an imagination that touches the truth of what the ex-service man stands for in the after-War world. They are not many who have touched that truth or who, having touched it, have firmly grasped it. Now that the War has been nearly exhausted as a theme for literature, now that the screaming hysteria has passed, we see that the phase had little connection with the organic processes of art, and a direct connection with the processes of Big Business. And nothing less than a work of art could have directed that inferno of human experience into an ordered and comprehensive expression. Literature, painting, the theatre, the film, each provided an outlet for public feeling in works which were no more than faded photographic reproductions of the chaos, and each, punctual to the day, administered an opiate when that was asked for. Even the poets and the composers were not above injecting their drugs the moment they heard the faintest call for them. (Happily

A Yorkshire Tour

Photographic News Agency

there were exceptions among these, instances which give us the right still to regard music and verse as being among the finest of the arts.)

Politicians are common; artists are rare. Never has the world swarmed with politicians—would-be, pseudo- and, alas, practising politicians—as it has swarmed during recent years; and that at a time when, by all the laws of probability and expectation, they should have been discredited. For, what we have been most in need of all this time is imagination's touch; and, because the politician cannot " afford " to be imaginative, that is the very thing which we have been most rigorously denied. Not every man with imagination, it is true, can be called an artist, even in the broadest sense of the word. But those who have discovered that quality in themselves and, unashamedly, have fostered and employed it, have shown, in doing so, that they are related, however distantly, to the family of visionaries. It is on that family, and not on the headstrong, weak-kneed, multitudinous Politics family, that we must pin any hopes we have for the years to come.

In his independence of judgment, in his clear and long-distance thinking and, especially, in his staunch but undemonstrative fidelity, the Prince for many years has shown himself to be related to that family. It is not easy for the ordinary observer to look beyond the official exterior of the Prince's career to form an idea of his mind and character. These will be discussed more fully at a later stage of this study, but we may remark here that even between the lines of daily newspapers, reflections of his outlook and spirit can frequently be caught. Consider as an example the plea he made in 1934 for Earl Haig's British Legion Appeal and which was reported in part in many English journals. (The talk was given for the special purpose of making a gramophone record to be sold in aid of the appeal fund.)

" A new generation fills the world with hopes and fears of its own," he said on that occasion, " but where should we all be to-day if those whose memory we cherish and whose needs we now seek to serve, had failed in their duty when the call came to them? This is our opportunity to salute the dead and to bestir ourselves to help the living. We who were their comrades can look back to famous days of trenches, marches, camps and songs, but what of the young men and women who were spared the supreme ordeal? They have got to look around. We have kept alive and intact those individual rights of citizenship and manhood which our forebears gained for us in bygone days. That is what we owe to those who bore the brunt of victorious war, and they must never be forgotten while we are safe and free."

Rhetorical appeal is nowhere to be heard in that passage or in any part of the speech. To some its directness will perhaps leave the impression of being no more than is proper to any statement of the obvious. But it is precisely these obvious truths and principles that nations and individuals have lost sight of in the scramble of post-War life. Fundamental as they are, they cannot be too often or too plainly reiterated. It is worth remarking that the passage quoted above is entirely free from aggression, bitterness and scorn. But warning is there, and perhaps an undercurrent of misgiving. The new-come generation with its fears and hopes must take its bearings; must be quite sure of what it desires and of the road it means to take; must avoid the elementary error of attempting to build up the future with no relation to the past; must beware of the dangers involved in the amenities of science; must ever be mindful of the axiom that added wealth means added responsibility. These eager importunate men and women must give themselves time, must pause and look around.

The Prince has not hesitated to admonish them. He has shown no desire to curry favour, as some of the older generation have done, by falling in unconditionally with their ideas. Yet it is possible that his sober words will make deeper impression upon them than the insipid flirtations of the elders. For they know him to be, in spirit, a young man still, and in no sense a cynic or a pessimist. Had he been either, some undertone of disillusion or hostility or partisanship would have betrayed him long before now. You will read his public speeches in vain if you are searching for an instance in which that note can be detected. To those who find all speeches dull in which no hated enemy is pilloried, we shall not commend the Prince's public utterances, for hatred and sarcasm and despising find no place in his armoury. Rather does he rely upon shrewdness, honesty and a certain plain humour.

Moreover, the earnestness of his speeches, especially of those delivered in support of the British Legion and of social welfare, increases with the passing of time. His appeals have never been stronger, more eloquent or more mature than now. The confusion and bewilderment of present-day life have not blurred the vision of service which, in the early days of " the Peace," he vowed to follow. The cool, peaceful air which wondering, returning soldiers were hoping to regain when once they had settled down, has not been their reward. It has eluded them and all mankind. Some, in despair, have fallen low; some, broken in spirit, none the less have struggled on after a fashion; some, in disgust and defiance, have run after strange gods. Where shall they look for help? In what shall they put their trust? Not in tyranny, if we are reading Europe's book aright. Yet some form of leadership is necessary. And leadership is our chief lack. For several years the Prince has displayed many of the essential qualities of a leader. But where leadership in the full sense is concerned, he is debarred. For in that sense, some form of politics is included. Again, it is possible that the circumstances and environment of the Prince's life preclude the complete coordination of his several talents.

Enough has been related here by way of narrative to

justify our setting down the following as being among his obvious qualifications : breadth and flexibility of mind; genuine sympathy; a keen business sense; strong convictions; straightforward expression in speech; a talent for hard work; tact, thoroughness, regularity. At the risk of leaving the impression of writing out the Prince's testimonial, we set down these attributes in order to note first, their rarity, second, their obvious advantage in conjunction. The peculiar problem of the Prince's career has always lain in the canalising of those attributes. Once he was heard to confess that much he would like to do in the shape of service was denied him; and "I have had my failures," he remarked on another occasion. There we perceive humble-mindedness, which, even at a time when the standards of life are all awry, still can be reckoned a desirable attribute in a leader. Yet it is probable that these qualifications in the Prince will never be allowed full and free play.

Leadership, however, is not invariably in the hands of politicians in office. The right man, using what influence he may have in the right way, can sometimes turn the tide of events, whatever his calling may be. In his own country the Prince will always be recognised as the "right" man. And for one reason above all others, namely, that his love for England is genuine. Can we say as much for every one of his predecessors ? The Prince is that typically English traveller who roams the world with zest and comes home more in love than ever with the English town and country-side. He loves the English people too, because there are none in the world he understands so well. This devotion has been the motive of the many tours he has undertaken through all parts of England. He is as anxious now as ever he was to become acquainted with every type of inhabitant and occupation, more especially the types and industries that have suffered most depression. If he has once promised to visit a district, he can never be satisfied until the promise has been kept. An engagement may sometimes be postponed, through illness or strain, but is never struck off the list. Even when the pressure of many occasions could be given as a reason, and perhaps the doctor is advising that it should be given, the Prince rarely avails himself of the excuse.

The days immediately following the wedding of the Duke of Kent and Princess Marina found him attending the *première* of a film,[1] paying a five-hour visit to the factories of the Gramophone Company, and renewing his acquaintance with the mining areas of Durham. A few details of the Durham tour will bear witness to the intensity with which the Prince follows his programmes. The items on that occasion included visits to the Voluntary Nursing Centre and afterwards the Occupation Centre in Sunderland, to social centres at New Washington, Usworth and Stanley, to Spennymoor Settlement, to the Escombe Playing Fields, to a poultry centre at Bishop Auckland and to the depot of the Durham Personal Service League. These involved a fog-beset road tour of 120 miles, which was everywhere the occasion of an extraordinary demonstration from the unemployed.

It is interesting to read the summary of this visit which was afterwards given by Alderman W. N. Smith, the Socialist Chairman of the Durham County Council. " Throughout the day," said the alderman, " the Prince insistently asked for details of our plans to regain lost prosperity. He admits that social welfare centres are invaluable, but he told me and every official he met that these must be augmented by plans to employ those who have proved that they are skilled craftsmen. He believes, and can quote facts and figures for his belief, that the County of Durham and the north-east coast generally can replace old industries with new manufactories, and

---

[1] " The Iron Duke," a laudable attempt to improve the prestige of British films—to win Waterloo again, in fact, upon the playing-floors of Shepherd's Bush.

it is his wish that all should struggle onward with this object in view."

Even in that sorry part of England where pits are deserted and the people are just living from day to day, the Prince's encouragement was eagerly accepted. The tour was carried out under the auspices of the National Council of Social Service in Unemployed Centres—a title which, in its unwieldiness, reflects the difficulties which are being faced, and the augmentations of service which, as the Prince remarked to Alderman Smith, are continually demanded. Darkness and heavy rain accompanied the last three hours of the visit, conspiring to show the plight of the county in its rawest aspect; yet the inhabitants waited everywhere along the roads, and in Durham and Stockton-on-Tees there were dense crowds. They were there, not because they believed the Prince to be arriving from the pages of a fairy-tale, with power to charm away their misfortunes, but because they recognised in him a good neighbour.

Throughout the day he was alert and observant. He studied the county's plans for slum clearance and at some of the centres found much to admire in the schemes for helping the unemployed to spend their time profitably. He went to Hardwick Hall, Sedgefield, which is a centre for training men and women in the management of occupational centres. There, with the unemployed, he had lunch—cold meat pie and vegetables, bread and cheese. In Sunderland he saw evidence of progress in slum clearance—a nursery school standing on a site which was formerly occupied by derelict disease-harbouring houses. He congratulated the Mayor and the inhabitants on their exemplary achievement and encouraged them always to look forward to "the great occasion when the whole country is clear of slums." At Stanley, too, he turned his eyes to the future. Occupational work for the unemployed was being carried on there in a small hut, but the Prince's visit was made the occasion of the laying of a foundation stone for a new brick building, on which the men have since been working. Perhaps the deepest of all the Prince's impressions was made by the people of Escombe. In that village, four out of every hundred men are fortunate enough to be in employment. The ninety and six unfortunates, seeking a way of escape from the despair of idleness, found it in a voluntary undertaking. Out of a slag heap they made a fine recreation ground, embodying a football pitch and tennis courts. The cost of this was borne by members of the Ministry of Labour's staff, who, in less than a year, raised over £700.

The part that music plays in relieving the distress of these districts was brought home to the Prince at Bishop Auckland, where a prize-winning male voice choir (entirely composed of unemployed) proudly sang to him some of their test pieces. A similar choir sang to the Prince at a centre which carries the name of " Framwellgate Moor and Pity Me," a name which has moved one of the Post Office departments to adopt the centre. No one who has heard the fervour and unanimity of one of these unsophisticated choirs could deny the plain fact that the music of their own voices has been the stay of these men and, in many cases, has saved them from utter despair.

At Bishop Auckland the Prince spent some time talking with twenty men who had been out of employment and had joined together in a poultry scheme. " I do hope that things are going to turn out well for you," he said to them. " You must be fine fellows to take on work like this, and you deserve a better lot than you have at present." Many beside that little group of pioneers were grateful for the encouragement ; for it revealed that the Prince realised what the unemployed of these and other areas are up against. In a word, Politics. Which, being further interpreted, is Lack of Imagination. To be convinced on that point it is only necessary to read an account of the House of Commons' work on the Committee stage of the Depressed Areas Bill. Some of the younger members had made no secret of their contemptuous regard for the Government's devices for lifting the fog from miserably depressed areas ; but when an amendment was proposed " to make a thorough survey of the possibilities of the depressed areas as a basis for their economic and social improvement," they indulged, quite naturally, in some playful sarcasm. But natural as the banter was, it was, in truth, no more excusable than the amendment itself. The whole attitude of the House, in fact, was both insensible and amateurish. Where there should have been a leavening lump, we found instead a lump of lead. For what did this amendment amount to ? Just this : that the £2,000,000 of the Depressed Areas Fund should be spent on preparing, on an experimental basis, a further series of reports before the actual fog-lifting was begun. In such circumstances it was difficult to understand what were the precise functions of the appointed Commissioner for the areas, and of his District Commissioners. Nothing of any great importance had been allocated to them by the Government.

It seems that we still must suffer gladly those members of the House of Commons who are inclined to use the subject of unemployment as a means of retaining the schoolboy complexion of their humour. Perhaps if they took a leaf from the Prince's book and visited some of the distressed counties and towns of England, with a view to discovering, not a palliative, but a lasting remedy, they would see this to be a matter for immediate action and not for point-scoring debates. In this connection we can hardly overestimate the value of the Prince's example. It is that which chiefly counts. He has never entertained the belief that by his own efforts he can solve this problem of distress. Only too often has he been aware of its overwhelming proportions in comparison with his own single endeavours. But he has at least led the way along a path which, if it were generally followed, would arrive at more substantial

At Bedford School

results than can ever be gained by bureaucratic commissioners.

He who has studied the Prince's career to any extent
will be struck by the number of occasions on which
people have been surprised at his knowledge. The
surprise is rather that this should be so unexpected.
Much of this air of being taken unawares is of course
the result of an excessive obsequiousness. But there are
times when it is genuine. The Durham alderman,
for instance, whose impression of the Prince has just been
quoted, was apparently expecting him to show no more
than a surface knowledge of local conditions. Great
was the surprise, too, at the factories of " His Master's
Voice" during the visit referred to above. The publicity
department of the Gramophone Company sent out the
information that the experts were amazed at the Prince's
technical knowledge of engineering and radio. As an
example, the department naïvely cited the fact that in
the mechanism for the automatic changing of records
he recognised an escutcheon plate, and the further fact
that he had no difficulty in recognising certain everyday sounds which had been produced by the High
Fidelity method. Now, for these amazements, two
among other reasons can be suggested : first, the
alderman and the gramophone experts (and others who
have been similarly dumbfounded) appear to have
forgotten that twenty years of the Prince's manhood have
passed and that during that period he has been living
fully and learning most eagerly and extensively ; second,
they have completely overlooked the fact that before each
of his visits he devotes time to a thorough preparation
of the subject involved and, if possible, consults those who
have special knowledge in that field. The surprised ones
almost persuade us that they had been expecting the
Prince to trip or commit himself to a howler.

Incidentally, that visit to the gramophone factories at
Hayes supplies an example of the informal way in which
the Prince carries out such engagements. During the

tour his interest in the several departments grew until it was found that five hours had passed and the schedule of the visit had been completely upset. On the other hand, the present writer has known him to cut short a function which, in his judgment,was serving no particular purpose.

The same conscientiousness is applied to the Prince's speech-making. He is by no means a born public speaker in the sense that at any time he would rather be talking than listening. There have probably been many occasions when he would have preferred to be doing neither. But if he has consented to deliver a speech, let us say, in a provincial town, he takes great pains to make it allusive, constructive and to the point. His practice is to obtain recent issues of the local journals, to search them for trends of opinion and policy, to study the history of the town and its environment, and even to memorise passages relating perhaps to its past industries or to the nature of the inhabitants. If the visit is one of major importance, a draft of his speech is prepared, and is based on what he has studied and on the points he intends to make. When the time comes to deliver it, he adheres to the general form of the discourse, while allowing himself enough elbow-room for hints and comments arising out of the immediate circumstances. In so crowded a life as his it is not possible for him always to speak without manuscript. Moreover, in a routine matter, such as a reply to an address of welcome, the speech is frequently prepared by a secretary. It is a mistake to think of the Prince as an inexhaustible fountain of " sayings of the week." Of necessity, he must very often be a mouthpiece for impersonal and frigid politeness. To be set against these instances are others which have proved his ability as an impromptu speaker. For the most part these have occurred during recent years and have witnessed the successful result of a very real struggle with shyness. In this his accomplishment and that of his brother, the Duke of Kent, are similar. Both passed through a phase of diffidence. It was a question not so much of being at a loss for words (though neither has been afflicted with verbosity at any time), as of being disinclined to make a public speech if it could possibly be avoided. In the Prince's case that phase has long passed. His activities and interests were not such as to assist him in taking refuge behind that long-suffering formula, " unaccustomed as I am to public speaking." So accustomed has he become that he has sometimes surprised a gathering with a short speech when none was expected, as for example, on one occasion when he attended a Queen's Hall concert, which had been arranged on behalf of the Westminster Hospital, and used the interval as an opportunity to make an improvised plea for the hospital's funds. At such a time the workings of his mind can be clearly observed. That speech was brief, well-informed as to the statistics of the hospital's cases and expenses, had an air of racy good-humour and paid tribute to the musicians who had organised the evening, the sisters, May and Beatrice Harrison.

The more formal speeches of the Prince are perhaps less directly illuminating as to his mental processes, since they have been prepared in consultation with knowledgeable people and with great deliberation; none the less they repay close study in that they bear witness to the thoroughness of his application to the subject in hand. With this object, the author proposes to put before the reader an analysis of a typical example among the Prince's speeches, that which he delivered on November 22, 1934, in the London Guildhall at the centenary dinner of the Royal Institute of British Architects. He was addressing over two thousand distinguished architects (the fact is worth bringing to the notice of those who may have been unaware there were so many), and seized the chance of putting before them a plan for the mass production of houses to cure the slum evil. " I ask you," he said, " to carry the principle of mass production over to architecture and the building trades. I am convinced that in no other way will it be possible to raise the living conditions of the great majority of our people. They should have better conditions, and they can have them by these means. I am sure that the principles of mass production can be applied to housing, and I am equally sure that you can do it, and that you will be able to overcome any barriers of prejudice that may exist." So direct and simple a general enunciation made an admirable opening to the address.

When the Prince proceeded to develop his theme, simplicity of language and clarity of thought remained the prominent features. He went to the root of the matter in singling out the mean, narrow, twisting street as the chief cause of two evils, namely, traffic congestion and want of civic pride. Then, without elaboration, he made the sequential point that the evils could be removed by constructing higher buildings and allowing more space between them. He also put before them the possibility of making areas where only fire-engines and refuse trucks would be permitted to enter. This part of the development was brought to a culminating point in the following passage : " In other words, we should take a bigger and more generous outlook on the planning of our cities, following the trend of our times, which is to have less of the limited group of individuals and more of the national point of view."

In the next episode of his oration the Prince took for starting-point the contributions of science to the devices for domestic convenience and for improving exterior and interior architectures ; then suggested that to housing could be applied those principles of mass production whereby motor-car makers and multiple stores had brought new amenities within reach of the majority. At this stage he judged it tactful to recognise a difficulty —which is the method of every good advocate who wishes ultimately to bring home his point with increased conviction—the difficulty of reconciling æsthetic and utilitarian requirements. This recognition served to introduce a criticism, none the less acute for being wholly without harshness. "I think," the Prince said, "this difficulty lies in the fact that as artists you have been devoting your time to the consideration of the abstract ideal, which is good in itself when you are considering only the individual client. You must give consideration to another, a greater and more important ideal, designed and working for the great majority of our people, instead of studying the needs of the minority which is ever dwindling."

Next was introduced the note of personal appeal which the Prince knows so well how to sound, varying its pitch, quality and stress according to the composition of his audience. He reminded this company of architects of his great concern for the masses of British people and for the improvement of their conditions of living. He told them that his visits to the distressed areas and the slums of great cities had impressed on him the absolute and urgent necessity for drastic demolition and rebuilding. He blamed the architects and builders of the nineteenth century for giving so little consideration to the housing of the great industrial groups. Those of the present day were presented with an opportunity. As a further development of his theme the Prince suggested that the opportunity should be extended " to the schools and buildings in which the masses are reared when they are children and the hospitals in which they are treated when they are sick."

As a speaker, the Prince does not underestimate the value of peroration, although he avoids the luxuriant burst by which some orators bring themselves to a full close. The speech we are considering had a characteristic end: "To-day we are not the race of individualists which we were in Victorian and Edwardian times. We are now living—mostly because of the results of the World War—in a world which is more collective in principle than individualistic. Wealth is more evenly distributed throughout the country than it has ever been, and the interest of professional men, in common with the interest of commercial men, is being more directed to a consideration of the mass of the people and their requirements than it is to the individual client or the more selective group we commonly call Society."

The speech is a good example of the Prince's method of address on occasions of importance. It is a method which is sparing of words and which shows, moreover, a marked preference for the shorter words of the language. So is left an impression of common sense plainly and incisively expressed ; and this impression is deepened by a well-phrased delivery and a care not so much for intonation as for verbal emphasis. The choice of words, in itself, is often an interesting revelation. In spite of the Prince's affection for America and her people, there is no trace in his speeches of that pseudo-classical habit of mind which causes an American, who wants to book a seat, to " make a reservation." Nor is there any evidence of that true classical mindedness which informed the phrases of such an orator as the late Earl of Oxford. Where the Prince speaks thus : " I am sure that the principles of mass production can be applied to housing and I am equally sure that you can do it," the late Earl of Oxford would have spoken after this fashion : " Though rebuilding is not a light thing to be done precipitately, I am not without hope that the principles of mass production will eventually be found to be applicable to housing ; and I am inclined to express the further hope that, despite countervailing disadvantages to yourselves, you will sooner or later have the supreme satisfaction of discovering that these things, after all, can be accomplished." There can be no doubt that the Prince's pointed, urgent style is, in this particular case, the more appropriate both to its subject and its period.

Since this appeal to architects has been considered here in some detail, it will be appropriate to mark its immediate effect. Before it was delivered there had been among architects a movement towards the ends to which it called attention. The Prince had but to state his views to give impetus to the movement. Stating them, as he did, with emphasis and great earnestness, he made it possible to look for the achievement of practical results within a short period of time. Many of the accomplished architects of the younger school had already realised that their careers would be found, not in designing individual houses, but in answering the need for large blocks of dwellings, providing the essentials of a healthy and economically-run home. Providing, too, an element of dignity. For that is as essential as the rest.

To many people the very thought of " large blocks of dwellings " suggests the last dreary stage in the complete mechanisation of man. They believe that mass production can only end in mass thinking and mass living. They point to radio as an agency of mass-produced education and to the slow killing of all imagination which must ultimately result from that. They have good reason for their fears, especially with regard to radio's influence. But even in this connection, and certainly in connection with the housing question, the drilling of men's minds is not an essential part of the movement. That fatal effect can be avoided by a wise dispensation. In England the dispensation of radio, in some of the more important spheres of influence, has been anything but wise. The architect of to-day and of to-morrow must take heed and avoid the errors of the radio-builders. He must build in mass, yes ; but he must also build wisely. His large blocks of buildings must on no account lead to the mass production of block-heads. He must always allow room for imagination's play, even if he cannot always ensure that the room shall have a view.

In matters of utilitarian detail, mass production can be applied to housing more thoroughly than it has been hitherto, and without danger of stunting the occupants' mental development. Doors, windows and various other parts are already produced by machinery. The next step is to produce in the same way a complete kitchen unit, enabling sink, copper, cupboards and so forth to be fitted into a fixed design, as the parts of a mass-produced engine are put together. Soon after the Prince had given his address to the Royal Institute of British Architects a representative of that body gave his opinion as to what would be the first move towards the mass production of houses. It would be "to ask the British Standards Institution to establish standards for all building materials, and then to ask the Ministry of Health to use its influence to see that these standards are adopted throughout the country." This would mean an increased importance in the findings of that committee which was appointed by the Ministry of Health to consider the materials and methods of building flats for working people of small means.

The committee has heard the evidence of technical experts and is fully expecting to show that the Prince's appeal can be speedily realised. The dangers of so complete a standardisation cannot be overlooked, of course ; but in the first place, they are far less threatening in the purely utilitarian field than in the more arable field of culture ; in the second place, the dangers can be minimised by architects whose imaginations work in terms of human as well as æsthetic values ; and in any case the dangers of standardised building are as nothing compared to the insidiously evil influence which must always threaten the community so long as slums exist. There is no need to look upon this mass production of dwellings as being anything more than a temporary measure, a way of escape.

Before making that appeal to architects the Prince had already been giving active support to re-housing schemes in various parts of the country. One of these had been started by the Leeds Housing Trust, Limited, a public utility society which had undertaken to build sunshine

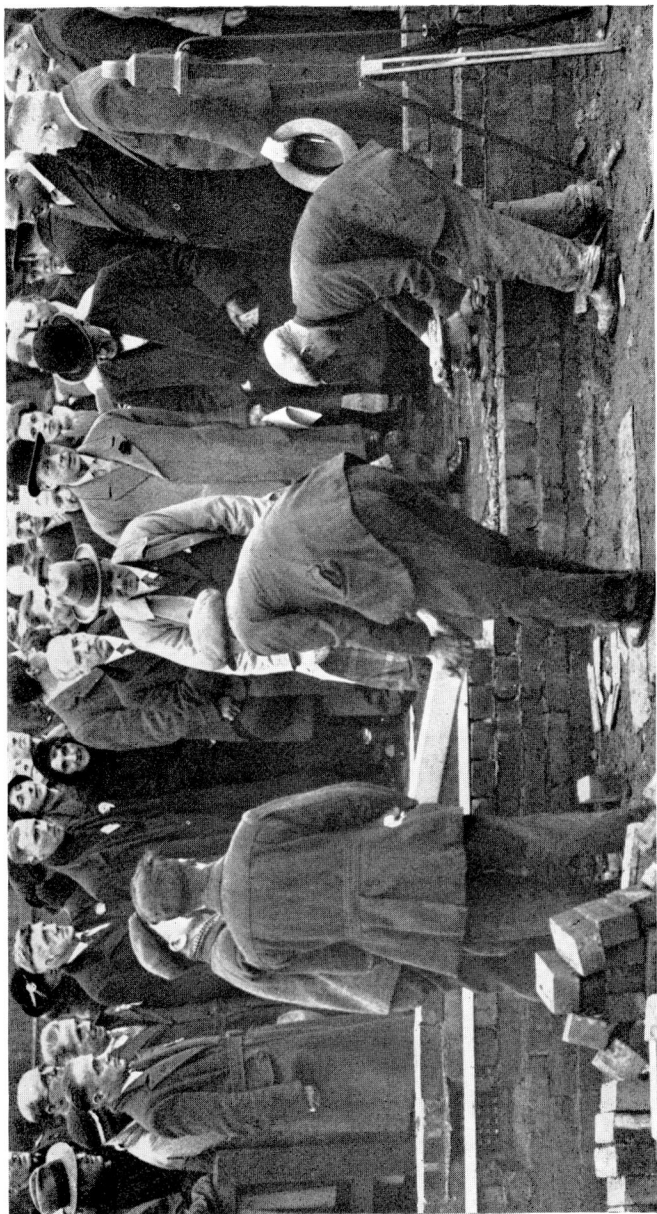

Photographic News Agency

With the Unemployed in Durham

flats to accommodate 280 people from East Street, on the edge of one of the city's slums. The scheme had the support of the Archbishop of York, the Roman Catholic Bishop of Leeds, Lord Moynihan and Lord Halifax. The society was greatly encouraged when a letter from the Prince arrived, congratulating them on the headway they had made, and on their success in building at a reasonable cost. (The contract for the first block of flats had been placed for a sum of just over £18,000, which represented something very like the finance committee's estimate.) In his letter the Prince emphasised how valuable the work of public utility societies could be, and how important it was to encourage all forms of voluntary enterprise which had for object the improvement of housing conditions.

At the time when the Prince sent that latter his ideas were being realised in the completion and opening of a block of flats called the " R. E. Sassoon House," in St. Mary's Road, Peckham. These had been erected, through the generosity of Mrs. Meyer Sassoon, at an exceptionally low cost, and were let at small rents with no assistance from the Exchequer or the rates. At the formal opening of these flats Sir Samuel Hoare gave some figures to indicate the progress of slum clearance and rebuilding. During the six months ending September 30, 1934, the number of slum tenants who were actually re-housed in new buildings was 50,000, which is about a quarter of the figure attained during the sixty previous years. In addition, private enterprise had been providing new houses at an unprecedented rate.

In this connection Sir Samuel Hoare observed : " There is here a great opportunity for people of good-will to show in a really concrete form evidence of their sympathy with the objects of the slum crusade. In these days of low rates of interest on investments in gilt-edged and similar securities, investors in shares and stock issued by public utility societies may look forward to a return on their money hardly less favourable than if they put their money into Government stock; but the dividend to which they will look forward with most satisfaction lies in the happiness radiating from the homes which they have provided."

So pretty a picture of the investor may well prove to be a little premature; to see so sudden a change in the psychology of investment is to be looking out upon an unnaturally rose-tinted world. Still, there are doubtless many investors who, if they could be sure of the yield from stock issued by public utility societies, would be quite ready to share in the general satisfaction of having done their part in the slum crusade. For there *is* satisfaction in the thought that a man, by doing himself a good turn, can automatically be benefiting others. It makes things so much easier.

Unhappily, things are, for the greater part of the time, difficult. There is another side to human nature, one that was shown in a unanimous resolution passed on the very day when " R. E. Sassoon House " was opened. This took place at a demonstration convened by the National Federation of Property Owners and Ratepayers. The audience comprised members of property owners' associations in all parts of England, Scotland and Wales. The occasion provided a typical example of the kind of difficulty which the Prince of Wales and his supporters are encountering in their anti-slum drive. Sir John Lorder, the Chairman of the Federation, began by stating that the meeting sympathised with the Government's determination to abolish property unfit for human habitation. But, or so the remainder of the speech appeared to suggest, the Government must pay for the privilege of adding that bright feather to its cap. The payment would be made under the heading of " equitable treatment." That was all the meeting wanted—equitable treatment.

Sir John confessed that he was a member of the Church of England, but that did not deter him from giving the Church this enlightening piece of his mind: " The

popular cry, ' Down with the slums,' has been taken
up by the Church and many religious bodies, by politicians, local bodies, busybodies, and any other crank
who thinks he can ' down ' something. The Archbishop
of Canterbury, the head of the Church of England, has
said, ' Do away with the slums,' but he does not add
that there should be equitable compensation when that
is being done. The Ecclesiastical Commissioners have
some of the worst slums in the country. As a churchman
I cannot conceive how the head of the Church can say,
' Clear out the slums ; hang everybody else.' That is
what it amounts to."

This zealous, if inelegant, pronouncement is handicapped by an erroneous statement. In the majority of
cases, the Ecclesiastical Commissioners do not possess
slum property ; they hold the sites by lease, but, at
the present time, are not in a position to deal with the
buildings on the sites.[1] Nor are the words which
the speaker has put into the Archbishop of Canterbury's
mouth any more convincing as a fair representation of
Dr. Lang's views than they are as an impersonation.
Indeed, the demonstration as a whole left an impression
of inaccuracy and lack of discipline, not to say of
sheer bad temper.

One speaker complained that no differentiation had
been made between the owner-occupier and the ruthless
extortioner, and it may be readily admitted that such a
distinction should always be made. The truth remains
that the owner of slum property *ipso facto* has put himself
in the position of being regarded as an extortioner.
Whereas the movement towards reformed housing
should have started from his camp, he has waited for
others to put it on foot. Thanks in large measure to the
Prince's whole-hearted support, the movement has
gathered great momentum in a comparatively short
period ; so much so that the slum owner, taking fright,

[1] In most of the cases where they own the actual slum property
they are carrying out rebuilding schemes.

falls back on a demand for "equitable treatment." Coming from him, the phrase can hardly be said to be persuasive. Slum-dwellers have not had equity from him.

In its narrow obstructive spirit, that convention of property owners brings to mind the early nineteenth-century debates in the House of Lords on the subject of child labour. In those dark days it wanted but one merciful word on behalf of those children to make sure of a stubborn opposition. If one noble lord went so far as to call attention to the practice of employing children to sweep chimneys with their bodies, and to men advertising "small boys for small flues," immediately he was opposed by others who urged the House to leave such reforms to the public's moral feelings, to avoid all such sentimental, un-English legislation. So with present-day slum landlords. Only in this instance the complaint is that the legislation is un-English in being harsh and, if anything, unsentimental. The opposition they bring to such reforms as the Prince of Wales is supporting is based on side-issues, the inculcation of cleanliness among tenants, for example, and the campaign against the bed-bug. Upon the main principles they can construct no contrary case, just as the House of Lords a century ago could construct no case in support of child labour. In both instances, apathy can be seen as the chief impediment to logical thinking. Had the slum landlords in general been less apathetic in the past, housing reform would not now have become so urgent a necessity.

Another repercussion of the Prince's appeal to the architects was heard on the night following its delivery. In the course of his Chadwick Public Lecture at the Royal Society of Arts, Sir Raymond Unwin remarked: "Society cannot afford to let its members remain below a certain standard of home life. The community must frankly accept the duty of providing dwellings up to the desirable standard for those sections who cannot provide them for themselves. This must be accepted as a public service." How far a lecture at the Royal Society of Arts can influence public opinion there is no way of measuring with any degree of accuracy. There is good reason to believe that some of these august institutions serve, not as platforms, but as mausoleums, for the quick no less than for the dead among our teachers. It is unlikely, however, that Sir Raymond's words will be fated vainly to reverberate or prematurely to be buried. As President of the Royal Institute of British Architects, he had listened to the Prince's forcible plea, and in this passage from his own lecture, his sympathy with the appeal is clearly revealed. Good neighbour the Prince has always been; and good advocate, too; but in all probability he has never done the ordinary worker a better turn than on that centenary occasion when he bearded the architects in their den.

CHAPTER 9

GOOD NEIGHBOUR (*continued*)

A word to the idly curious. The Prince's wardrobe. No aspiration to be "the best-dressed man." His sense of humour. Cracking Scots jokes. The Prince on books and newspapers. A tribute from the Archbishop of Canterbury. The Prince among the farmers. The Albert Hall speech, 27 January, 1932, and its three points: (1) A fresh response to national service. (2) Opportunity is at our own door. (3) "Away with depression and apathy: they are the Devil's own!" Effects of the speech: a check to the tendency of making the State's increasing power an excuse for individual indifference.

THE theme of the Prince's neighbourliness is open to a variety of treatments, for it is multiform in itself. To some, and their numbers are many, the theme is chiefly interesting in its more trivial aspects. They thirst for knowledge which, in terms of liquid refreshment, may be described as long and soft. They are curious as to details of the Prince's daily life, the time he gets up, the time he goes to bed, the books he reads, his hobbies, his friendships, whether he prefers the company of men or of women, his conversation, his clothes, his lucky day, his favourite cigarettes, his favourite colour, dish, wine, tailor, pleasure resort, theatre, motto, and so on and on, insatiably. They would like nothing so well as to submit the Prince to that kind of catechism which has become a regular feature of theatre programmes, nothing so well as to learn (even though they know the answer must be fabricated) when he feels at his worst and best, his pet aversion, his opinion of bridge and—ah! what strange satisfaction is here!—the Christian name he sets above all others. Not all these curiosities, it is true, are equally idle. And in that list prepared for stage artists there are other questions which, if not too lightly answered, might lead to uncommonly illuminating results in the Prince's case ; not least that ingenuous but devastating enquiry : what would you do if you were Prime Minister for a day ?

Now, some of these questions are to be considered in a later chapter. But there are others which fall naturally into place here and now. Those who, in days gone by, were nurtured on Graham Wallas's *Human Nature in Politics* (and also many who were not) will realise what importance a political candidate must attach to personal appearance when he presents himself to his constituency. He may decide to adopt an idiosyncrasy, such as a pipe, hat, monocle or long hair ; he may dress conspicuously well or conspicuously badly ; he may choose to appear in a strong man act, or again as being filled from top to toe with the milk of human kindness. Whatever choice he makes as to the character of his appearance, it must in any case be memorable.

In a modified form this same question arises in connection with the Prince's public appearances. Before a tour of one of the Dominions, or a visit to the provinces, or an official function in a foreign country, he has a careful consultation with his staff on the subject of appropriate dress. To the Prince this subject is as important as his choice is wide. It has been said that no man in the world possesses a larger wardrobe. Greatness, Malvolio was informed, sometimes occurs with birth, sometimes is achieved, sometimes is thrust upon a man. So with wardrobes. The Prince's can be said, for the most part, to have been thrust upon him. For his private tastes in dress are simple enough. He is at one with the trend of the times in requiring his clothes to be, above everything else, comfortable. For all that, if at any time he has been thought to be encouraging laxity in standards of dress, certainly he has been entirely mistaken. There have been times when a studied carelessness marked his appearance, as for example during some periods of his Australian tour. (Be sure that those grey flannel bags and the shapeless hat were not produced without a preliminary consultation, even if there is a possibility that the vote went against them.) With the rest of his generation he passed through the phase of reactionary extravagance which the gloomy and unbeautiful stiffness of the Victorians made inevitable. But since the field for sartorial invention is far more restricted for males than for females, the Prince was never obliged to set or conform to any excessively outrageous fashion.[1]

Although the Prince's styles of dress are followed by many men in England, on the Continent and in America, he has not shown the smallest desire to be a dictator of fashion. Sometimes a slight variation of his has been generally adopted, as, for instance, the omission to wear gloves at social functions, in which he was followed a few years ago. At other times, he has been content to be alone in his judgment of detail. At a reception some years back, for example, he appeared in the then unheard-of combination of dinner-jacket and white vest ; on another occasion, he attended a banquet with his father and brothers, and chose the way of singularity by wearing a flower in his button-hole ; at another period, he was bold enough to advocate the restoration of the unpopular " boater."

Those who describe him as the best dressed man are paying him less of a compliment than they intend. He has better taste than to aspire to any such distinction. Always he dresses with meticulous care, appropriately

[1] To realise to what lengths (rather, to what brevities) fashions in women's clothes do run, it is necessary to look no farther back than the year 1926. At that time Goodwood ordained that knee-caps should be exposed, that dresses should uniformly fall in one straight line from shoulder to hem, that they should have about as much shape and character as a sack, and that heads should be thrust into hats of the coal-scuttle type. Even the débutante went to Court in short, wide dresses, and dance frocks were decorated with conglomerations of silk grapes and were designed to display the leg in a flesh-pink silk stocking.

As the Duke of Rothesay

and with just the right emphasis upon individual style. He permits himself enough flexibility to avoid the reproduction of a fashion-plate. And, unlike some members of past Royal families, he does not leave the arrangement and the overhauling of his wardrobe entirely to his valets, but carries out his own inspection with great regularity. Nor does he invariably leave every detail of cut and style to his tailor. To those who make close observation, the general scheme of his clothes will frequently be seen to embody a suggestion of his own.

As for the routine of his life at York House, there is nothing extraordinary to reveal. The morning's work, which is, of course, largely conditioned by the letters he and his private secretary have received, begins at ten o'clock. To many of these letters he sends personal replies; to others Sir Godfrey Thomas attends, after discussing their contents with the Prince. Sir Godfrey and others of the staff have a suite of offices on the ground floor of York House. The Comptroller is also regularly in discussion with the Prince, who is both vigilant and orderly where his household expenses are concerned.

The type of enquirer suggested at the beginning of this chapter would perhaps be disappointed by the results of a conducted tour through York House, especially if he were looking for the ornately romantic environment which, once upon a time, was associated with rulers and princes. For, truth to tell, the utmost simplicity prevails in the Prince's house. To describe his rooms as being unmistakably those of a bachelor is to convey all the essentials of a true impression. A small bedroom, an adjoining den, the far from elaborate reception rooms, pipes, newspapers, books (sea yarns and detective stories prominent among them), a gramophone with an up-to-date collection of dance records, a wireless set, a Cairn (by name Cora)—here are sufficient items of the inventory to supply a working hypothesis as to the manner of the Prince's life at home.

Our importunate questioner will doubtless be desiring also to know something of the Prince in moods of relaxation, and particularly something relating to his sense of humour. It is only necessary to hear him delivering some of his public speeches to catch a reflection of that quality in him. He is quick to catch the mood of the company he is in. An instance worth recalling was his speech at the 1934 festival of the Royal Scottish Corporation. (Incidentally, the event also witnessed his nice perception in choosing a suitable dress. Since he was expected to eat haggis and drink whisky, he appeared in full Highland costume, with Royal Stuart tartan kilt, white lace jabot and skiandhu.) In the course of that speech he alluded to the origin of the rumours that Russian troops were passing through Great Britain during the War.

"I have been trying to learn Gaelic," he said, "just as I have been trying to learn the pipes. Gaelic is a great language. I am reminded of the rumour that got around during the War when a squadron of Lovat's Scouts were heard talking Gaelic in a train. At once the story spread that the Russians had arrived." That night he had many other stories to tell, and acted them all to the very life. A true-blue Scot who was there turned to his neighbour and commented upon the excellent Scots accent which the Prince assumed for these stories. Of one of these the hero was a novice golfer, an Englishman, who was playing at Gleneagles. "When he had done half a dozen very bad holes, he asked his caddie, 'How many strokes have I taken?' His caddie answered, 'I dinna ken, sir.' The Englishman became annoyed—even more annoyed than he was with his ball. He said, 'You call yourself a caddie, and you don't even know how many strokes I have taken for six holes.' And the caddie answered, 'Judging from your play, it's no' a caddie you need, but an accountant.'"

This address was an instance of the Prince's impromptu manner. "I was determined," he told those festive

Scotsmen, "not to read a speech to you to-night. I remember the words of the old parishioner who had listened to the new 'meenester's' first sermon. He was asked what he thought of it and he answered: 'In the first place, it was read; in the second, it wasna' well read; and in the third, it wasna' worth reading.'" The end of the speech shows the Prince alive to the fact that if you choose to laugh at the people of Scotland, or to laugh with them, you will do well also to let your respect for them be shown. This was his tribute: "Scotland still has its great record of pioneer work throughout the world. I have travelled a great deal, and there is not one part of the world where I have found the best industries, the most going concerns and the liveliest institutions not founded and run by Scotsmen."

A list of the Prince's engagements, even for a few weeks, when he is on duty in London, will give some idea of how comprehensive his neighbourliness must be. So numerous are the calls upon his time that the engagements he accepts can be taken as a very fair guide to his own greatest interests and sympathies. And those who insist upon the catechising method, cannot do better than peruse the Prince's own direct statements in order to form a clear impression of his inclinations, tastes and appraisements. For, although his set speeches are prepared in conference with advisers,[1] it would be a mistake to suppose that his is a minor part in those conferences, or that his own judgments are overruled. To an expert he will always give ear. But, without being in the least opinionated, his views are clear and wholly consistent with the development of his character.

The reader, therefore, could hardly have a better approach to his mind than by way of his public utterances. If, for example, he had a mind to know what the Prince has been thinking of the publishing glut (that

[1] Before delivering a speech on a given subject, the Prince sometimes favours the plan of inviting specialists to an informal dinner-party.

most revealing symptom of our times), he will be wise to turn to the address he gave on 16 November, 1934, as Master of the Worshipful Company of Stationers and Newspaper Makers. At that gathering, both the Prince and the Archbishop of Canterbury spoke with such a liveliness of spirit as to belie the official description of the event as a Livery dinner of the Guild.

The Archbishop indulged in the dream of exercising the great powers (with little responsibilities) which once belonged to his office. He saw himself with dictatorial might and burning all heretical and seditious books, burning the sermons and books of certain eminent divines whose names, since this was a dream, he did not think it advisable to disclose. He saw himself drawing up a list of all the best sellers among books of the past ten years, and burning them because of the offence of lowering the standard of literature ; then proceeding to the newspapers, drawing up another list and giving his orders to burn the lot. He further envisaged the delightful possibility of summoning to the Star Chamber all editors, sub-editors and reporters who omitted to report his speeches verbatim. " I would ordain," Dr. Lang said, " that henceforth the Archbishop of Canterbury should be included in the existing list of those who always enjoy verbatim reports, namely, the Prince of Wales, the Prime Minister, General Smuts and Sir James Barrie."

To a certain extent the Prince showed himself to be in sympathy with the underlying idea of the Archbishop's fantasy ; but he also reminded his audience of the importance of preserving freedom in the expression of opinion. Indeed, this address is especially interesting in throwing light upon his independence of thought and judgment. After some preliminary allusions, he began by reminding the guests from foreign countries that the Worshipful Company of which he was Master had been founded early in the fifteenth century for the protection of the manufacturers and vendors of books,

At Gower Street Hospital

and that, as a result of a recent amalgamation, they now concerned themselves with the protection of newspaper-makers as well.

"You may rightly ask," the Master remarked, " what is the nature and extent of protection demanded nowadays by publishers and Press ? I sometimes feel that the boot should be on the other foot, and that it is the public which needs protection against the flood of printed matter that is daily and hourly poured upon its defenceless head. One only has to pick up any newspaper at any hour of the day or night, or turn the pages of any publisher's list, to realise that of the making of many books there is still no end ; and the weekly output of printed matter from Fleet Street involves one in figures that, as regards weight and mileage, are astronomical in their proportions. Protection, indeed ! Has there ever been a freer trade ? I sometimes wonder what happens to all these thousands of books, what happens to these tons of newsprint. I have always been the first to en-courage a ' growing industry,' and even if some of the books remain unread, if some of the newspapers are returned unsold, at any rate binders, printers, and many others must have been employed in their production, which in these days is all to the good."

There, clearly, speaks a realist. Into that passage we are perhaps entitled to read a point of criticism—to see there a gentle nudge for the dreaming Archbishop. It was all very well for the Archbishop, even in fun, to emulate the peppery impatience of " dear old Fisher in the days of the War." For the bonfire which in imagina-tion Dr. Lang had started, could so easily get out of hand. There were so many other questions involved, and the Prince's reference to the skilled trades employed in book producing was a most timely hint that we should never spare too many pennies for the guy.

" Seriously speaking," the Prince continued, " we have little to complain of. With all this uncontrolled spate of printed matter one might be inclined to favour the idea of ' restriction of production,' an economic theory of which we hear a certain amount these days ; but restriction of any kind in regard to a genuine expression of opinion, however extreme, is, I am glad to say, entirely contrary to our belief and to our traditions. We should be thankful that in this country we enjoy freedom of opinion, freedom of discussion in our books as well as in our speech, and that we can point with pride to a free Press."

If we pause to underline those sentences, it is because they are worthy of a place with the most memorable of the Prince's declarations. It is not often that he takes sides in his public addresses, but here we find an unmistakable rebuke to those who, thoughtlessly falling in with the ideas of a few other countries, seek to override the quintessential nature of our national life, whether in relation to politics, religion, literature, professional sport, education, or any other sub-division. The passage becomes even more forcible if the date of the address and the events of that period are borne in mind. It is then set in a context which, by contrast, gives it a peculiar eloquence. For it was a period which appeared to mark the very culmination of national conflicts and hatreds. Short of war itself, it is difficult to imagine a time of more bigoted and intense bitterness. To numbers of English people that plea for freedom of opinion and discussion must have had the sound of a pleasing melody.

Before we leave this scene at Stationers' Hall and this picture of the Prince wearing the badge of Master of the Worshipful Company, we may appropriately give attention to the conclusion of the Archbishop of Canterbury's speech. It took the form of a most notable tribute to the Prince, " to his manifold public services for all that belongs to our common life, for the sick and not least for the unemployed, and for that embassy of Empire, which the Prince fulfils in every part of the world, and, I begin to think, in almost every language.

Have I not heard the Prince this evening conversing in Spanish with the Brazilian Ambassador? It is no exaggeration to say that future historians will look to the Prince's speeches to learn the best that can be said of the industrial, social and commercial life of his day and generation."

After thanking Dr. Lang for these references to himself the Prince remarked: " I think if the Archbishop of Canterbury had been brought up as a diplomat he would have told a white lie this evening, and instead of saying that he had overheard me talk Spanish to the Brazilian Ambassador he would have said that he had overheard me talk Portuguese."

It is a fact, nevertheless, that Spanish is one of the best of the Prince's linguistic accomplishments. His ability in this direction will be more fully discussed in the chapter which has been allotted to the subject. Meanwhile, it is of some interest to note that whereas he began to study Spanish in a mood which was but half serious and for a quite capricious reason, he was very soon applying himself to its mastery with the greatest diligence, having discovered and called in a first-rate teacher in Dr. Antonio Pastor.

When the Archbishop of Canterbury spoke of future historians referring to the Prince's speeches as a guide to the different aspects of the present age, it can be assumed that he was thinking no less of the variety than of the intensity of the Prince's interests. The view of him we are now taking—the view of him as good neighbour—must necessarily be incomplete; for besides the official manifestations of this quality there are many others of which not even the most practised journalistic eavesdropper ever hears. But the official occasions are often very reliable indications of the places where his strongest interests lie. When he pays a visit to the Smithfield Show, for example, it can be taken for granted that he is putting in as much a personal as an official appearance. Farmers welcome him there as one who can talk their own language. The ovation he received at the 1934 show witnessed his easy popularity among them. They saw in him the youngest representative of a line of Royal farmers from whom the ancient show has always derived support.

Major Hilgrove McCormick (the present secretary to the Duchy of Cornwall) accompanied him as he walked round inspecting the prize animals and talking with herdsmen and shepherds. Many were reminded of King Edward's visits to the show; he, too, had that manner of genial and keen curiosity where farming was concerned. But for all his affability King Edward did not object to the president and councillors wearing top-hats for the occasion. Could any dress be less appropriate at a cattle show than top-hat and frock-coat? We can only suppose that the councillors of that period preserved the custom as a decisive way of showing they were so much higher than the animals. The bowler hat marked the greater informality of the Prince's visit. Custom prevailed, however, in the manner of inspection, the prize cattle and sheep being drawn forward for the Prince to see as he walked from end to end of the Royal Agricultural Hall. The pigs in the Gilbey Hall proved less amenable, for the Prince arrived there during a general siesta.

Of this excellent show the Prince made a point of seeing all that was outstanding—among the pigs, the King's Berkshires and Lord Daresbury's exhibits; among the sheep, Mrs. Jervoise's black Welsh mountain sheep; and, of course, the King's cattle as well as his own. He showed great interest in a very fine lot of Devons—the breed he keeps on his Home Farm. Then there was the champion, Mr. Cridlan's Aberdeen-Angus heifer, Evergreen. She had been given pride of place in the middle of the hall. Round her pen was a crowd of admiring breeders and butchers who, in their minds' eyes, were already selling her by the pound. Evergreen was unmoved by the throng. Had she not around

Arriving at Hull
(*For a tour as Patron of the National Council of Social Service*)

her enough prize cards and rosettes to assure her of immortality?

The Prince spent some time admiring Evergreen, and offered Mr. Cridlan his congratulations. Mr. Cridlan had a tale to tell. He had bought Evergreen's sire, Speyside Pike, at three years old from the Prince at a Banbury sale. (That bull the Prince had bought in Perth as a yearling.) So, Mr. Cridlan wanted to say, some of Evergreen's unmistakable glory was due to the Prince. Alas for such transient splendour! The champion was sold for £90 to a Glasgow butcher.

Before the Prince left the show he found much to interest him in some of the side exhibits, for example the portable garden and farm buildings made in the British Legion village, Aylesford, Kent, and also the Ministry of Agriculture's demonstration of the grading of animals on a dead-weight basis.

No speech was delivered at the Smithfield Show. The Prince knows the English farmer well enough to appreciate his preference for deeds above words. In that, his and the farmer's tastes are alike. But at the risk of overstressing the orator in him, reference must be made here to one more speech, for it is, in truth, outstanding among all the Prince's appeals; outstanding, first because it is addressed to the youth of England; second, because of the period to which it related; third, because of its immediate effect. This was the address he gave in the Albert Hall on January 27, 1932. None who heard it could fail to recall the three clear divisions of the speech, the first being devoted to an earnest plea for a renewed response to national service; the next insisting upon the opportunity which was at each man's door; the last leading up to the exclamation, "Away with depression and apathy! They are the Devil's own."

No other of the Prince's speeches can be said to have been more necessary. It was spoken during a period when the State's power was increasing all the time, a tendency which led inevitably to a weakening of individual effort. Its effect was to make people aware of the dangers involved in a too great reliance upon the State. Not by any great command of eloquence did the Prince make his points in this address. At no time has he striven for that distinction. " To me," the Prince Consort once said to Queen Victoria, " a long, closely connected train of reasoning is like a beautiful strain of music. You can scarcely imagine my delight." Nothing could be in sharper contrast to the Prince of Wales's ideas and methods than that self-conscious avowal. He makes no pretence to be able to persuade by sheer force of reasoning, and certainly is never tempted to make a song about it. He relies wholly upon his own sincerity of spirit. By that alone he has persuaded the majority of his countrymen, as well as the thousands he has met in other countries, that, of their neighbours, he is one of the very best.

CHAPTER 10

MAN OF THE WIDE WORLD

Work for British Empire Exhibition. In the Western shires. "Time off" in Canada. Revisits his ranch in Alberta. Home again. Opens Wembley Exhibition. Visit to United States. Meets President Coolidge. To the ranch once more. Sails to South Africa in the *Repulse*. The tribes in motley dress. Studies agricultural peculiarities of Africa. Boers and English join to greet him. The Prince essays a speech in Afrikaans. Journey through the Free State and Rhodesia. Mr. Bonar Law's tribute. President Alvear persuades the Prince to visit South America. Expenditure of the Prince's tours criticised. An enquiry made. Stimulus to trade with the Argentine.

TO call the Prince a man of the world is to underestimate the extent of his experience. The phrase is too limited in meaning, is too overworked to carry a complete impression of all that he has harvested from a wide field of experience. When a man is described as being of the world, somehow—perhaps for no logical reason—one pictures a frock-coated figure with thumbs thrust into the arm-holes of his waistcoat and mouth open to deliver an endless succession of after-dinner speeches. The world, of which this figure is, becomes, in impression, a conglomeration of banqueting halls, the West End by night and the Stock Exchange by day. With that figure the Prince has never been identified. The world he knows and the experience he has garnered, entitle him to be relieved of so hackneyed a description.

In this narrative we have already followed him for many thousands of miles of travel. Many thousands remain still to be recorded. So extensive a travelling, indeed, that we cannot hope to follow every turn of it, if we are to make a book of reasonable length.

The prelude to further adventure was the British Empire Exhibition, of which the Prince was President. He accepted this office, not as a compliment to be passively received and shelved, but with the intention of following up the results of his Empire tours. There was example for it. The great Exhibition of 1851 had been planned by the Prince Consort and had been made a great success as the result of his skilful direction. The Prince of Wales threw his full weight into the organisation of this Empire Exhibition and wisely sought the alliance of his " very good friends," the Press. These he entertained at lunch in the Exhibition grounds at Wembley with the object of stirring up enthusiasm for " a project of the highest Imperial importance." He was not going to be content, he said, with an ordinary success. It was to be a brilliant one ; and home trade and that of each Overseas Dominion were to share in it. He had faced many set-backs while organising the Exhibition, but he was glad to assure them that it was now on a sound basis. He pointed out how bold a challenge to other nations this was—to be launching such an Exhibition so soon after the industrial chaos which the War had left. This, then, was to be a well-considered gesture. Its immediate object was to build upon the spirit of unity which had animated the Empire during the War-years. He expressed the earnest hope that his Press friends would give the venture their whole-hearted support.

After this exhortation, which ranks among the best of his speeches, the Prince thought a personally conducted tour of the Wembley show-grounds would be a good move. That lunch and tour went a long way towards ensuring the Empire Exhibition's success.

In an earlier chapter reference has been made to a holiday the Prince took at this time on the E.P. Ranch in Alberta. He was intent upon making this the more enjoyable by crowding the preceding period with official engagements. Then he could, indeed, believe that he was

As Indian Chief, " Morning Star "

taking time off. So he carried out an extensive tour of the West Country. Between Bath and Weymouth he learnt as much as possible about the country, and in the best way possible, namely by conversing with the men and women who worked there and belonged there. He did not leave Dorset without calling on Thomas Hardy. They had lunch together. Who will doubt that the Prince picked up more real and solid information about the West in that one hour than on any other occasion during the tour?

Then came the call of the North. Answering it, the Prince went to Newcastle, gave time to make contact with the ex-service men there, to visit the mining districts of Northumberland and Durham and to see what wonders Armstrong Whitworth's could show; and afterwards, always in earnest enquiry, devoted the same care to a visit to Nottingham. Not until 6 September of that year (1923) could the Prince be sure that he was safely on holiday. On that day there sailed from Porstmouth the Canadian Pacific liner *Empress of France*, with Lord Renfrew, Sir Godfrey Thomas, Sir Walter Peacock and Brigadier-General Trotter among the passengers. Everyone knew who Lord Renfrew was; but everyone, on the liner and in Canada, willingly pretended to know nothing whatsoever about him. A pleasant little game! It is called " travelling *incognito*."

Incognito this traveller remained as he passed through Quebec, Ottawa and Winnipeg. But when the Chiefs of an Indian tribe saw him, they knew well enough that this Lord of Renfrew was none other than their own Chief Morning Star, returning. And as such, they insisted on hailing him. Then followed those few weeks of free and not so easy life with his fellow-Albertans. When on 13 October, Lord Renfrew came aboard the *Empress of France* for the homeward voyage, his *incognito* was again dropped that he might receive the salute of officers and men.

No holiday in the Prince's career had been more

necessary than that interval on his ranch, and by none had he been so well and immediately restored. When he arrived home, he accepted without question a crowded list of engagements, including visits to North Wales, Edinburgh and Dundee. Then, after a flying visit to the French Riviera, he returned to London on 24 April, 1924, for the opening ceremony of the British Empire Exhibition. For all the triteness of the expression, we need not hesitate to call this a proud moment. Nor need we be deterred (by the memory of its ephemeral façade) from describing the Exhibition as a concrete representation of many of the Prince's ideals. Let his own words testify. They are taken from the broadcast speech he addressed to the King at the official opening of the Exhibition—an event which stands as a land-mark in the early stages of broadcasting in England.

" As President," he said, " I ask you graciously to declare open to your people the British Empire Exhi-bition. . . . I hope, sir, the result of this Exhibition will be to impress vividly upon all the peoples of your Empire the advice that you have given to them on more than one occasion, that they should be fully awake to their responsibilities as the heirs of so glorious a heritage ; that they should be in no wise slothful stewards, but that they should work unitedly and energetically to develop the resources of the Empire for the benefit of the British race, for the benefit of those other races which have accepted our guardianship over their destinies, and for the benefit of mankind generally."

More than ten years lie between now and then, and if we turn a backward look we see public opinion moving over them in a series of waves. Not long after that speech was made there was a period during which its sentiment was out of fashion. That phase was fol-lowed by another in which racial pride was once more a virtue fervently to be advocated. Note the order of those benefits to which the Prince referred ; benefits, first to the British race, then to those races which have accepted British rule or guardianship, lastly to mankind in general. Is it not true that the main division of opinion on all important Imperial questions is caused by disagreement as to the order in which those benefits should be placed. First Britain, then the Empire, then the world, say some. Others hold that the Empire unquestionably must have first consideration. Others are emphatic that if the human race in general is put first the rest of the benefits will be added to us. Shall we ever be unanimous on so fundamental a question?

In one respect, the Prince's Wembley speech has been reinforced by subsequent events. Aware of their vastness and richness, he spoke of developing the Empire's resources. But since that time a new vista of resources has been brought before our eyes. In a recent essay a Fellow of the Geological Society describes our insignificant mining activities as being no more than the scratching away of a little rust from the earth's surface. He refers to the limitless quantity of mineral wealth in the world and then makes the rather miraculous calculation that of this immeasurable quantity half is contained within the boundaries of the British Empire. Still, even if our minds cannot grasp what is meant by halving an immeasurable quantity we understand the gist of the matter; especially when this authority, estimating Africa's thickness to be twenty-three miles, declares that "even the top mile contains sufficient metallic ore to supply the world for many thousands of years." He cites the wealth of "blue asbestos" and chromium in British Africa, and points to Ontario and Quebec where there are the largest of all the known deposits of beryllium which can be worked on a commercial scale. So convenient are the qualities of beryllium that he calls it a wonder metal, and believes that it will prove of inestimable value in the construction of aircraft.

"The nation possessing its most abundant deposits," he writes, "may very easily find itself one day in virtual control of the world's aircraft." Beryllium, in fact, is a godsend on the one hand, and, on the other, is likely to be a confounder of politics. Oil in Northern Alberta, helium in Southern Alberta, Canada's nickel, Australia's cadmium, India's manganese ores, and molybdenum ores in Canada and Australia—these are quoted by this authority as being but a foretaste of the treasure concealed, and as yet fast-bound, within the lands of the British Empire. " That they should be in no wise slothful stewards." The Prince's words become more pointed if we think of them as an utterance of the present time. With the future, they are likely to become increasingly urgent. As for mankind in general benefiting from these vast resources, the only danger appears to be that the earth will prove too lavish with her gifts.

After he had seen the British Empire Exhibition launched and in good working order, the Prince made plans to renew his acquaintance with the United States as a result of an invitation from President Coolidge. Towards the end of August he sailed in the *Berengaria*, and after a fast crossing to New York, proceeded without delay to Washington and lunched at the White House with the President and Mrs. Coolidge. He was in Washington little more than two hours. Indeed, the whole of this visit to the States was something of a feat ; its speed and hustle left even the Americans a little surprised. A feature of the visit was the number of welcoming letters the Prince received from strangers. So far from being annoyed by his fan-mail, he made a point of thanking these well-wishers in a farewell message. In no other country more than in the United States has he been so continuously conscious—can we say without being misunderstood, so acutely conscious ? —of the right hand of good fellowship.

There was a reason for hustling. Time was short and the Prince's objective was Alberta. He knew that opportunities for living on his ranch would be rare and was jealous of every day which was lost in arriving there. On this occasion he made a point of studying labour questions and conditions in Canada and as a result of first-hand knowledge has often been able to give sensible advice to those who are inclined to see all the advantages of emigration and none of the disadvantages. Not that he wishes to discourage those who are considering that great adventure; but that he would like no man to embark upon it in ignorance or half-knowledge or without an unmistakable sense of vocation.

In retrospect this period of the Prince's career bears remarkable witness to his energy and concentration. There were those who at the time saw in his voyages and tours evidence only of an unchecked restlessness. If restlessness accounts for the record mileage of that period, it was not unchecked, and most certainly not undirected. Added to a young man's natural desire to see as much of the world as possible, was the thought of the task he had set himself to accomplish. So long as South Africa was left unvisited, that task was unful-filled. Next year he would go there, taking in West Africa on the way. He would bring his Grand Imperial Tour nearer completion. Above all, he would add a little more to the store of his knowledge of humanity.

The Prince's words and deeds have been in close harmony throughout the twenty years which this narra-tive covers. To his speeches he admits no high-sounding, flowery phrase. Always they are well-considered, eminently reasonable pronouncements, whether gratitude or pleading is the burden. Whatever he pronounces, that, in spirit and in fact, he performs, so that both words and deeds reflect the clear sincerity of his motive. His Empire tours are but the natural counterpart of such a speech as that which he delivered at the opening of the Wembley Exhibition.

In the spring of 1925 began the African tour, the Prince sailing in H.M.S. *Repulse*. Humanity did indeed show a new face when he landed at Bathurst. For an occasion of this kind the natives made it quite clear that they were dressing. Rarely though this was asked of them, they had no great difficulty in finding the solution. Some fitted themselves into strange, fancy dress uniforms, suggesting that Mr. Willie Clarkson might have passed that way at some time. Others deemed a top hat and a change of loin cloth to be the correct wear. The point here, surely, is, not the quaintness of their devisings, but rather the friendliness which could persuade them to go to such lengths. Out-of-the-way, too, were some of the gifts the Prince received from the chiefs as he journeyed along the West Coast. Plague threatened to stop the proposed visit to Nigeria, but the danger was circumvented by the Prince making for Iddo Island on a tender while the *Repulse* stood by. That is the kind of incident which is continually lighting up the Prince's tours as we follow them. Every stopping-place on the route was worth the trouble of some specially thought-out sign of recognition. To explain these incidents as mere showmanship fails to account for their spontaneity. The response to this particular gesture in Nigeria was no less spontaneous, for a great shout went up from the natives and was sustained for half an hour.

The Prince then journeyed to West Sudan and at Kano took part in a Durbar to which came a band of twenty thousand horsemen under Moslem chieftains. To their greetings and shoutings he replied by raising a clenched fist after their own manner.

Meanwhile Capetown was preparing a welcome which should at least equal any that the Prince had previously enjoyed. When the time came, it seemed to surpass them all, so high-spirited was it and so variously expressed. It was as if the people were striving by their welcoming breath to lift the fog which had settled on the town and marred the Prince's first sight of it ; and if the reader thinks that too fanciful a notion he must know that in any case, the fog took sudden leave soon after the Prince's arrival, and all the beauty of the place was spread before him. The Earl of Athlone received him.

Prominent among those who had assembled to greet him was General Smuts, that enlightened man by whose wise counsellings we have never failed to profit. For his address to the great throng of English and Dutch which had gathered on Grand Parade, the Prince was compelled to speak through a microphone. The fact is mentioned because that little object was not then the ubiquitous instrument it has since become, and also because the Prince, at that time, preferred to speak without it if possible. In that, his taste and judgment are much to be commended.

Outwardly, this Capetown festival presents little to the recorder to distinguish it from the acclamations of other capitals which the Prince has visited. There was a State Ball, of course; and to add that it was " magnificent " seems to be excessively redundant. There was, of course, an honorary degree, and in addition the Prince was installed as Chancellor of the University. There were the usual banquets, inspections and foundation-stones. A visit to the naval station at Simon's Town was included in the programme; and there were various expeditions to the outlying country which were outside the official programme.

A catalogue of these items would fail to convey any essential difference between this and the punctuating marks of the earlier tours. A difference, however, there unmistakably was. Not one of degree in the warmth of the welcome, but rather one of kind in its spirit. There were problems to be faced, racial problems and political. If the problem of race was a less prickly obstacle than in India, it still necessitated a careful approach, and as for republican feeling, it could hardly be expected to vanish as a result of a Royal visit. The danger was that it might run more strongly for that, if not menacingly. In this matter, the Prince rose to the occasion as successfully as he had done in Canada and Australia. He had little difficulty in making the meaning of his visit clear. His own democratic nature was at once apparent. And as a man, the South Africans liked him. That was the important thing. It is a simple statement to make, but since the fact itself is also simple (even if the implications are deeper), it needs no elaboration. On one of the banqueting occasions, the Prince during his speech essayed a few sentences in Afrikaans. That may seem a naïve incident to bring forward as evidence of his tact. But the effect was far greater than its artlessness would seem to warrant. It was taken to be, as indeed it was, a sign of the desire to break down the barrier of language—a desire to approach the natives more nearly and to know their thoughts.

The Prince now turned to the less populated parts of South Africa, passing through the settlements of Dutch-speaking Nationalists, and being welcomed by mayor after mayor, each of whom was eager to impress upon him the superlative attractions of his town, each of the mayors, especially he of Uitenhage, hoping that the Prince would commit himself. But the Prince would not be drawn. Good-humouredly he reminded them that he was a traveller and one whose words were widely published. He asked them to consider the point: if he declared for Uitenhage, what would Riversdale have to say about it, and Oudtshoorn, and Addo and Grahamstown?

Civic pride is a fine but sometimes awkward thing. In these outlying parts the Prince often found it difficult to handle. The more remote the township, the more importunate were its claims. It was necessary to bring the technique of conciliation into play. The mayors, for their part, were not niggardly in their tributes. They spoke of the sinking of class, race, creed and colour differences, and of the common feeling of joy which the visit of King George's ambassador had brought; they spoke of the British Throne as being the centre of all their national aims and ideas; they spoke of their conviction that the Prince's visit would do much to

Central Press Photo

In the Bathurst Colony, listening to Native Music

further in the South Africans a more powerful sentiment of attachment to the Crown. The words, in fact, were frequently conventional and formal. In print they bear a disconcerting likeness to vain repetitions. But they were not vain; and in those districts opportunities for repeating them were only too rare. These carefully worded addresses were comparable to the top hats with which some of the natives crowned themselves, and the bishop's hat and coloured gaiters in which one of the chieftains exhibited his loyalty. Apt in expression they may not have been; but the momentary ardour they conveyed was unquestionable.

Strain and climatic variations began to overtax the Prince's strength during this crowded period. He could not catch up with his minimum requirement of sleep, and in one instance, postponed his arrival in an attempt to do so. The exacting tour was full of surprises. In some places he was greeted by choirs of children. In others, Zulus danced before him. Once he was "kidnapped" and carried to Rhodes University. Soon after he was advised to take a rest, if indeed it was not enforced by utter fatigue. He took refuge in some long protracted games of golf.

A few more towns were visited before the Prince journeyed to the Free State. In all his life he has probably faced no more cosmopolitan crowd than that which met him at Jagersfontein. Boers and English joined to make his entry into Bloemfontein a memorable one. He was met on the way by more than a thousand Boers whose wish it was that he should lead them back in procession into the city. Kroonstad, Bethlehem and Harrismith were included in the tour, but the Prince's stay in the Free State was not long. He was there long enough, however, to feel how genuine was the welcome from these people. "So spontaneous and so unaffected" was his own description of them.

He did not pass by the colony of four hundred lepers near Maseru. He spent an hour there. There is no way for the present writer to describe the experience. How could it be communicated? The thought of that horror ties a man's tongue.

It was at Maseru that the Prince was embarrassed by being credited with supernatural powers. He had done nothing to deserve it, or rather nothing that he was aware of. It was true that, when he arrived there, it started to rain, and that the weather then became so bad that the grand Durbar which he was to attend was cancelled. But to arrive at a place, especially if it be for diversion, and to find that it has just begun to rain, is not to be fairly accounted a phenomenon. These natives, however, followed other lines of thought. To them the coincidence was so much a phenomenon as to be a miracle. The White Prince's arrival had broken the long-drawn-out drought. No doubt he had come for that purpose. The ruined Durbar was a detail.

The Durbar did, in fact, take place next day, for, by an almost equal miracle, the weather began to improve. The next stage of the tour was as exacting as it was interesting. Durban had prepared almost too lavish a programme. Thousands of children greeted him there, thousands of ex-service men assembled to do him honour, thousands of Natal Indians were drawn up for inspection. Another banquet, another parade of Zulus, another miscellany of celebration. The new Graving Dock was ready, too, for him to open. It was called after his name. A tour of the battlefields was, of course, arranged. Let us not presume to interpret the Prince's thoughts as he passed through these. But we ourselves can stop to ask why these were ever allowed to become fields of battle in a land which was now in such an effervescence of goodwill towards England—and mankind in general. The evidence of goodwill which the Prince received in Pietermaritzburg, Vryheid, Newcastle, Dundee and Johannesburg was so convincing that it was difficult to believe there had been conflict a quarter of a century before, or to believe that the conflict had been inevitable.

If of all these civic welcomes that of Johannesburg stands out, it is because the Prince's arrival there coincided with his birthday. In the Transvaal he made many long expeditions to far-away districts and showed a continuous interest in the particularities of farming there. Formidable, too, were some of the distances which the natives covered to meet him. To enumerate all the official functions and occasions which were crowded into the final stages of this African journey would, perhaps, explain the exhaustion that intermittently threatened the Prince, but would do little to convey the richness of his experience and impressions. We can record that he visited Rhodes's tomb, was acclaimed in Rhodesia, opened more new-born universities, received more degrees, carried out so many more reviews and inspections, returned to the Cape, descended a mine at Kimberley and so forth. But these things, important though they were as duties, form only the scaffolding of the structure which the Prince was attempting to build up.

He regarded this and his other tours as the full-time job he had been fortunate enough to find. For a young man, still experimenting, still gathering in experience, it was a big, rather frightening job. If keenness was all that was wanted, he could have been completely confident. Unfortunately, to be over-keen was in some circumstances a disadvantage, and led to wrong judgments. He was always conscious that the British Government regarded his missions as an experiment, that public opinion in England would be judging his success or failure by cold results, and not by the glamour of his receptions in all parts of the world. His desire to make a success of his tours made him earnest and serious beyond his years, almost as earnest and serious as the generation of twenty-year-olds who have since arrived. Among the various speeches of approval or criticism on the subject of his work, one has claim to be quoted here, both because of its sensible expression and because of the encouragement it gave. The tribute came from Mr. Bonar Law.

" There is one young man," he said, " who has set a peculiarly good example, and whose intercourse, not only with leaders of Governments and public men, but also with the masses of people with whom he has been in contact, has been of immense value in bringing about a closer understanding and creating underlying conditions of co-operation. I mean, of course, the Prince of Wales. Not only have the Prince's Empire missions been followed with great interest by the whole of His Majesty's subjects, but also the whole civilised world has intelligently observed the experiment of the British Government in sending out this young member of the House of Windsor to gain trade for themselves and their Dominions. Napoleon once sneered at England for being a nation of shopkeepers, and, in truth, even fifty years ago prosaic trade seemed to be a poor thing compared with the romance of Courts. Despite the many-sided excellences of the late King Edward, he was not what you would call a commercial man. King George is more of a business man, but for sheer commercial brilliance the Prince easily overshadows even His Majesty."

When the Prince was in the Transvaal some of the natives who had journeyed so far to see him, and perhaps had expected to see a kind of god, could not believe that this undemonstrative young man was he, when they were brought to meet him. To reassure them, the Prince spoke a few words to them in their own tongue. " I'm your man," he said. To the British Government he had, in effect, said the same thing. And here was Mr. Bonar Law asserting that this was their man without a doubt. To those for whom the " romance of Courts " was an all-important ingredient of life, that gradation which the speaker introduced by beginning with King Edward's deficiency of business sense and ending with the Prince's abundance, will, no doubt, seem to be the sorriest of come-downs. The only way to answer such people is to repeat, as blithely as possible, the eternal platitude that times have changed. We have lived to see a Prince of Wales who gets busy and gets business. That it should come to this!

On the way back from South Africa the Prince landed at St. Helena, and there received yet another ovation. One incident on that island can be aptly set down here; near the tomb of Napoleon the Prince planted an olive-tree. We may, if we like, regard that act as helping to soften Mr. Bonar Law's rhetorical reference to Napoleon, as well as Napoleon's reference to ourselves. We may do that, if we like. It all depends upon how far imagination will carry us.

The Prince was soon on his way again to get more business. Before returning to England he set out for a new objective, South America. The 14 August of the same year found him arriving at Montevideo. He had received an invitation from President Alvear to be his guest in the Argentine, and had accepted without a moment's hesitation. Here was a unique opportunity of getting on with his job. In answer to those who were inclined to criticise his frequent leaves of absence, he would make this a trade tour of outstanding importance. (His position was once again not unlike that of the Prince Consort when, after planning the Great Exhibition of 1851 for the promotion of international trade, he found himself strongly opposed by some sections of the English population.) His immediate object was to open up channels of commerce between England and the South American republics, channels which hitherto had been insufficiently appreciated. And the Argentine Government also expected profitable returns from the visit. How much, can be gauged from the fact that a sum representing more than £30,000 had been voted towards the festivities.

Almost we are persuaded to use that disreputable epithet "colourful" in description of this tour. More disreputable still, and yet a literal statement, would be to speak of a riot of colour. For at every stopping-place the streets and the crowds went bewilderingly gay. The

Prince played up. When the President of Uruguay came aboard H.M.S. *Curlew* to welcome him, the Prince wore the bearskin and scarlet uniform of the Guards, which had proved the most popular of all the uniforms he wore in Africa. (This question of dress looms large on all the Prince's official tours, and he and his staff must give it most careful consideration. The South American tour was the ultimate test of showmanship.) Mounted police guarded the procession to Government House, outside which the people of the Republic had assembled to shout welcome to the Prince. He appeared on the balcony to salute them and then reviewed a military march past. (What an asset, incidentally, has the balcony been to Royal pageantry as well as to romantic drama! How many are the conflicts which have been resolved by a well-timed appearance on that narrow stage!)

Buenos Aires was the next port of call. Now began to rise a tide of enthusiasm greater even than that which President Alvear had, in his dreams of this visit, projected. As the Prince sailed up the estuary of the Plate, a salute of twenty-one guns was fired. When he landed, the crowd gave vent to its excitement with a vocal hardiness and quality which few other crowds in the world could approach. The tour was a succession of " scenes." Journalists plunged into an orgy of description. Reading their words now, we see that some were overwhelmed and lost their senses. So much colour, so much shouting did but throw their words into confusion. Such riches did more than embarrass. They bowled the journalists completely over. Here, at a distance, we enjoy advantage.

We can set down a few of the incidents in more sober vein. We can tell how the Prince was driven through the streets in a carriage drawn by four black horses; how the people threw flowers into the carriage; how the night was given to a banquet, to fireworks and a torch-light procession; how Señor Basualdo lent the Prince his house in Buenos Aires; how the Prince and the President sailed in a yacht to Avallaneda; how almost every path the Prince took was strewn with flowers; how almost every occasion was accompanied by the songs of children; how a choir of fifty thousand boys and girls had been coached to sing "God Bless the Prince of Wales" in English. We can relate all this and then, perhaps, will be in a mind to ask if these could possibly be the preliminary flourishes to a business deal. The question is reasonable. The answer is that each race has its own peculiar way of doing business. This was the Argentine's way. The more realistic aspects of the tour included many an inspection of the processes involved in the chilled-meat industry, from the farming of the cattle to the slaughtering (aided by blessed science) and the meat-dressing.

Everywhere the mingling of business and pleasure was made a fine art. During his visit to Liebig's Stud Farm, the Prince was entertained by cowboys to an open-air lunch of freshly killed mutton and fresh fruit, which was accompanied by music from a guitar band. Whatever the Prince's views on "music at meals" may ordinarily be, he was delighted by this particular band, and at the end shook hands with each of its members. That was a day in the saddle. He rode round the great farm, saw a performance in which a stampede and a round-up were staged, and as finale, watched the gladiatorial display of a rodeo.

The Argentine mission was watched by some sections of the British Press in a fault-finding mood. Every significant incident was closely reported, not to mention many insignificant ones. Gradually the fact emerged that the Prince was making a thoroughly good job of it. Adverse critics might still adhere to their general principles, but found their case considerably weakened on this particular point. Meanwhile, the Prince was encouraged by the messages which his father was sending by cable.

Another State (and balcony) occasion was the Prince's reception at Government House where the ovation was spirited to the point of riotousness. A choir of girls

sang "God Save the King" in well-drilled English;
then innumerable pigeons were let loose, regardless;
then came a moment when, their excitement reaching
boiling-point, a group of young men were moved to try
their strength with the police in an attempt to get a
closer view of the Prince. That evening the Prince went
to the renowned Teatro Colon and saw a play which,
whatever its merits, could hardly have been judged
brilliant in comparison with an audience representing the
wealth and beauty of Argentine Society. Of that evening
the remaining impression was that a masterpiece had
been seen, in the auditorium if not on the stage.

An extension of the journey to Chile led the Prince
into rough weather. The train was delayed and the
official functions were enacted in cold winds and rain.
But there were crowds for the Prince's arrival. A review
of thousands of boy scouts was one of the chief items of
this programme in Chile, to which an impromptu coda
was added, when the snows came to prevent a departure.

This South American tour is among the most interesting of all the Prince's travel achievements. For one
thing, it improved trade relations with a foreign country.
For another, it was undertaken in a challenging spirit
which made it necessary to secure so much the more
tangible results. To answer those who considered that
the expenditure involved in these tours was too heavy,
an enquiry was made and the auditors appeared. The
findings showed the Prince's expenses to be, if anything, lower than what could reasonably be allowed.
After all, when a country chooses to spend £30,000 for
the entertainment of a guest, it is to be assumed that the
guest's own outlay will be reduced, for the time being,
to a minimum. And when the said country happens to
be a Republic and the said guest happens to be a Prince,
can we not also assume, without implying the least
ingratitude, that the sum was voted for the promotion,
not merely of idle amusement, but primarily of sound
business?

CHAPTER 11

MAN OF THE WIDE WORLD (*continued*)

Activities from 1926 to 1928. With Duke of Gloucester to East Africa. Odd games of golf. Port Sudan in the heat. A strange welcome in Kenya. Stalking 200 lbs. of ivory. A close shave. Enter lion. Bad news. Non-stop return.

THE time had come for the Prince to take account of his bill of health. Up till now he had rarely been able to withdraw from the stare of the public eye. The play in which he was taking part had been so constructed that he could leave the stage only for comparatively brief intervals and, even then, he must wait in the wings listening for his next cue. He now began to consider the possibility of taking a holiday which would involve as little publicity as possible. He began to consider this ; but before it could be realised, there were innumerable engagements to be carried out in England. He had no sooner embarked upon this heavy programme than it was interrupted, first by the death of his grandmother, Queen Alexandra, then by that hunting accident which resulted in a broken collar-bone, and to which reference has already been made. Soon after, the provincial programme was resumed. Birmingham saw him a month or so after the accident. As the Earl of Chester, he travelled to Biarritz for a brief holiday. Then came news of the General Strike, and he immediately returned to London, flying for the last stage of the journey.

The list of towns he visited during 1926 suggests that he was attempting to complete two years' work in one. The period marks an activity which can only be called feverish. It also marks a clearer understanding

and fuller appreciation of his spirit among his own
countrymen. They began to see him as a man of his
time. They saw that in some ways his position made
things difficult for him, and hindered him in his progress
towards certain reforms. They saw him, too, as a realist.
In few of his speeches did he omit to sound the unsentimental note.

At the opening of the North-East Coast Exhibition,
for instance, he impressed upon his audience that it was
hopeless to think of maintaining the supremacy this
country enjoyed during the nineteenth century, and
warned them against losing valuable time by looking
back regretfully to that too-good-to-last era. Those
spacious days would never return. We had fallen behind,
and there was no need to think that it was pessimistic
to admit the fact. The admission rather was the first
condition of success in the future. Our economic
prestige could only be restored through courage and
imagination. How could we show courage? By
ruthlessly scrapping all methods and machinery that did
not satisfy the most modern standards. And imagination, how could that be shown? By exploring every
commercial avenue overseas.

So did the Prince speak on that occasion. A new force
can be felt in his utterances of this period. His experience, we feel, has been well invested. It gives him leave
to speak his mind more freely. Sometimes we detect an
undertone of impatience in his sentences. Having seen
so much of the wide world, he is far from satisfied with
some of the conditions and standards of life and business
in England. But there were reactionary forces to be
overcome. His call to scrap all out-of-date methods and
machines—to scrap them ruthlessly—was not favourably
received in every quarter. Vested interests offered
formidable opposition. The Prince could but sound the
call. He could not expect Jericho's walls to collapse
miraculously.

That which was within his power he performed with

increasing good judgment and ability. His activities at this period have the appearance of a big drive, a crusade. Surveys of motor works, printing works, newspaper offices, mines; support for all manner of municipal enterprise throughout the country; attendance at agricultural shows, meetings for hospital funds, meetings of the Slum Improvement Society, the Mental After-care Association, and a miscellany of other social and commercial organisations; attendance at the British Legion Conference; special journeys to welcome distinguished foreign visitors to England; yet another trip to his Canadian ranch—the enumeration of even these few items of his work from 1926 to 1928 will, perhaps, convey an impression of the kind of task he had set himself to carry out. The mere look of this programme is enough to suggest the Prince's width of outlook and active sympathy. It is not a list of hobbies. Nor does it represent the kind of spare-time social work which is customarily adopted by those who lead an otherwise (and even in this respect) strictly useless life. Crusade we have called it. The word is used advisedly. If we take it in its simplest meaning—an expedition against infidels—it expresses very fairly the recurring motive of the last twenty years of the Prince's career.

During the past eight or nine years, the motive has been given greater emphasis, has been more intensely developed, has emerged more variously. The infidels can be said to be all those reactionary forces which hinder progress towards a more harmonious national life. In broad terms, that is the explanation of this crusade. (And to those who object that the terms are altogether too broad, the writer would suggest that it is by narrowing the component issues too persistently and with little or no awareness of the question in its entirety that the air is made as hideous with discord as it is at the present time.) The Prince, of course, is not alone in this crusade, or in leading it. But of all the leaders in this country, he has personality's advantage in the highest degree.

It was not until September, 1928, that the Prince was able to claim an interval of complete rest from official undertakings. The project was an East African tour, in the company of his brother, the Duke of Gloucester. The party also included Brigadier-General G. F. Trotter, Lieutenant-Colonel the Hon. Piers W. Legh, Mr. Edward Brook and Mr. A. F. Lascelles. The autumn of that year was, in England, so beautiful as to make some of them a little regretful that they were leaving. They went by Marseilles and Alexandria. For the first part of the voyage the Prince lay low until the effects of vaccination and a para-typhoid injection passed off.

At Alexandria the Prince and the Duke were entertained by the High Commissioner at the Residency, part of the entertainment being provided by a galli-galli man who galli-gallied them into believing that he was hatching out a brood of chickens from the nose and ears of one of the audience. Next day the Prince visited King Fuad at the Ras et-Tin Palace, and there had a meal which in substance and in its manner of serving suggested that the King was a follower of French fashions. The King also placed his yacht at the Prince's disposal for his stay in Cairo. There was, of course, Tutan Khamen. He could hardly be passed by, with any pretence to politeness. So, pretending to be polite and fearing not a little boredom, the party went to the Museum. But so well contrived was the Curator's story of the discoveries, and so well delivered, that they were glad they had gone.

The golf that the Prince has played in Africa at one time or another would fill a chapter or two if we allowed it. It is enough to say that it was of an entirely unorthodox nature. Not meaning that the player was below form, but that the capricious nature of the courses was often at variance with the ordinary dignified tenour of the game. Thus, the greens were sometimes laid in red and blue sand, and it was no uncommon thing for the putter to find his green lifted and converted into a little sandstorm. They also tell you, even nowadays, of the impediment caused by the spoor of hippo, and of fairways which prove to be one long bunker. The Prince knows all about golf in Africa, its indigenous problems and diversions. The caddies, too, brought diversions after their idiom. One little dark face at the Gezira Club had christened himself Andrew Kircaldy. Another incident of the Prince's golf history is connected with the Great Pyramid of Cheops. When his party had paid this duty-call and had clambered to the top, there came to each of them an impulse to use the vantage-point in the hope of adding a few inches to his drive. Or perhaps it was not by impulse, but by long-considered plan, since they had troubled to carry clubs and balls to the summit. From the Egyptologist's to the purist golfer's, the shades of opinion on this prank will be many and fine. But the average man can hardly exclaim any other than " What a good idea ! "

The *Malda* took these holiday-makers on to Suez. Eleven days after leaving England they arrived at a place so overpoweringly hot that they did not wish to see it or remember its name. But later, when the glare had been softened, they went ashore and, as a result of accounts given by the young men who were stationed there, thought better of Port Sudan. The Prince, in fact, was almost tempted to spend some time there when he was told of the big-game fish which could be caught outside the harbour. But he contented himself with some tennis and squash and a dinner at the headquarters of the big-game anglers, where he heard stories that were certainly tall, but, for all that, may also have been true.

For the next few days and nights, the Prince experienced a Red Sea which lived up to reputation, even though the monsoon had done something to alleviate the sultry heat. In such conditions the last thought in the world was a game of football. Yet at Aden the Prince was asked by Major Birkett of the South Wales Borderers if he would watch an inter-company match and present a cup. The Prince consented. It was difficult to make this a wholly unofficial tour. On the way to Kilindini the heat intensified the problem of killing time. The Prince varied his daily routine by introducing a form of exercise which could be described as putting the sandbag, and another, equally hot-making form namely, learning the elements of Swahili. The rude ceremony of Crossing the Line came as a welcome opportunity for relieving feelings. The Prince relieved his by showing them, with whitewash and a large brush, how it was done.

Something of the gaiety with which Mombasa welcomed the Prince and the Duke is carried by the Arab's word *fantasia* and the Swahili word *ngoma*. The whole visit, in fact, was one long *ngoma*, except when it was *fantasia*. By the latter term the Arab means official engagements, such as, on this occasion, an inspection of the Old Fort which was built in the late-sixteenth century by Portuguese, and of the native quarter where Arabs, Africans and Hindus live with Japanese, Chinese *and* the Turks. In rough English *ngoma* is " making a night of it." Literally it is " drum," and from that is derived the feastings and merry-makings which depend upon an incessant accompaniment of drum-beats. The Governor of Kenya, Sir Edward Grigg, told the Prince that the origin of all jazz was to be found in *ngoma*. The Prince said he had no difficulty at all in believing it.

A Sunday evening service in the Cathedral and a sermon from the Bishop of Mombasa supplied a restorative after the fatigue of being so relentlessly entertained. Then arrived an experience which the Prince will always remember. After the service, the Governor brought an old, old man to present to him. " This is Wellington," the Governor said. Wellington? Yes, that was Chumah's nickname, or rather, his title. Chumah was a native who had been rescued from slavery by Dr. Livingstone and was one of the two faithful servants who, after Livingstone had died, embalmed his body and carried it on a journey of nine months and of seven hundred miles, to the coast. And here Chumah was, dazed, blinking and wondering what was happening to him. The Prince took him by the hand.

There was no way of travelling light in Africa. Picturesque and pleasing though the African customs of present-giving are, they sometimes cause an inordinate increase of luggage. A notable instance occurred at Mombasa during this tour. The Prince was about to leave by train for Nairobi, Kenya's capital, and distant from Mombasa about three hundred miles. He was at the station and, after inspecting the ex-service men and women, was ready to start. Loud calls were then heard. They came from two tall natives who were shouting that the crowd should make way for the Liwali. Then the Liwali appeared. He had brought a parting present. Would the Prince accept a carved elephant's tusk? There it was, being carried by three of his servants.

Now, it were best here to make plain to the reader what was the precise object of this expedition. The Prince had not come primarily to collect heads. Later on, as we shall see, he began to covet a trophy or two, but his chief wish at the outset was to observe, to photograph and film big game. So to shoot a wild beast, alive and in action, is far more difficult than to shoot him dead. The rifles this party carried were to be for defence. Incidentally, each man's kit included three pairs of strong, light boots, one pair of mosquito boots, one double Terai hat, three pairs of khaki shorts with cartridge-holders, three pairs of khaki trousers, three shirts, four changes of underclothing, six pairs of stockings, twelve pairs of thick socks, two khaki drill coats, one overcoat and one waterproof hurricane smock.

The arrival at Nairobi was *fantasia* indeed. An eye-witness described the station-yard as a combination of circus and flower-show. The assortment of races and colours in the crowd which lined the way from station to Government House, was almost as odd as the assortment of costumes. Even here the King's sons could not escape formal addresses of welcome and replies, and Guards of Honour drawn up for inspection. They were also expected to attend a *baraza*. This was an assembly of about two thousand chiefs, together with native councillors from all over the Colony and Protectorate. In this the Prince saw a signal example of an experiment in local government, one that had been tried there for four years. Among those presented to the Prince that day was the aged ruler of North Kavirondo, by whose willing aid the way to Uganda was opened up some forty years earlier. Mumia was his name.

Two other incidents at Nairobi find their way into this record. The first was the bringing of a cheque for nearly £400 to the Prince. It was a gift from the Freemasons of Kenya to the masonic charities in England. The other was the Prince's appearance on the race-course where he rode three races, in one of which he was second.

After a little time at Nairobi the Duke of Gloucester, accompanied by Mr. Edward Brook, started on an expedition towards Moshi. The Prince and his two remaining companions went back to see a cricket match. Then the Prince went to stay at Lord and Lady Delamere's magnificent farm at Soysambu. Soon after this the expedition to Uganda, which had been planned at the beginning of the tour, was on foot. Or rather, not yet on foot. By train to Kibos, by cars to Lake Victoria, by steamer to Entebbe, those were the preliminary stages. (Incidentally, the steamer—the *Clement Hill* of 1,000 tons —deserves to be named here, for she had won some fame through her stalwart service during the War, in the fighting near Kisumu.)

There is at Entebbe a convent which is the whole world to the nuns living there; never do they go beyond its walls and no newspaper or secular book ever reaches them. They speak French, but are of all nationalities. No man must ever see them. One of royal blood, however, can claim exception to this rule, for some curious reason. The Prince, hearing of this, decided to claim his rights. He was admitted, and stayed to tea.

There were still a number of official affairs to attend before safari could be said to be begun. Meanwhile incentive had arrived in the shape of a message from the Duke bringing news that he had shot an oryx. The Prince's party moved on. Presently they were joined by Pete Pearson, experienced elephant hunter, Captain R. Salmon, Game Ranger of Uganda and Dr. Peacock. The arrival of the last was timely, for not long after Brigadier-General Trotter collapsed with a heart attack as a result of the heat. He was carried unconscious from the *Samuel Baker* to the Nile steamer *Lugard*. It was an anxious time. The Prince gave up his cabin to the sick man and Dr. Peacock was in continuous attendance until they reached Murchison Falls. By that time the immediate danger had passed.

The Prince landed and went to look at a pool where there were crocodiles. He shot one stone dead and was much gratified. Hereabouts were herds of amiable elephants, buffalo, many kinds of antelope and gazelle. Hippo were rarely out of sight. Clumsy as these brutes can be —as, for instance, when one, ponderously satisfying curiosity, upsets a steamer at night—they are, in hunters' eyes, almost benevolent in comparison with the guileful crocodiles.

Malisa was the scene of the first big adventure. Captain Salmon had sighted three elephants and had estimated the ivory of one of them to weigh about 200 lbs. The Prince was tempted by the idea of the trophy and, in spite of the noon-tide heat, set out with Salmon and Pearson. Through thorn and elephant grass they covered fifteen miles in something like five hours. But never another glimpse of that ivory did they catch. The Prince, however, did not return empty-handed. Instead of 200 lbs. he brought back 135 lbs. of ivory as a result of one of his own shots—(he could not have missed, they said; it was a gift)—and photographed the prize. But the picture was taken not so much out of pride as out of relief; for at first the Prince thought he had merely wounded the beast and was depressed at the idea of a slow death. The elephant was found next day and, it was calculated, had died very soon after he had been hit. In any case the Prince expressed his disappointment in elephant-shooting. He was not carried away by the fact that this was his first. His points were that the sport was not a one-man show, that it was comparatively easy and unexciting and that there was more fun in filming an elephant than in killing one; that the risk in filming was almost equal while the intentions were more humane; that the elephant (looking so casual, sage and mild) did not incite the hunter's warring instinct.

For all that, another expedition was begun. The talk in camp was all of elephants, 100-pounders, 200-pounders (meaning a single tusk, of course), the disparity of tusk-weight between bull and cow, the damage they do, and, of course, their habits. It was on the question of damage that justification for another hunt was founded. On the road to Kigoya the natives are smallholders who have good reason to complain when elephants are too numerous. It was Salmon's job, and Pearson's, to regulate their numbers by means of the rifle. The Prince could accompany them on their round if he liked. He decided to go and Sir William Gowers and Mr. Lascelles went with them. Later on Sir William took a photograph which shows the grand finale of that particular show. A dead elephant with one tusk supplies nearly the whole background of the picture. Upon its prone form Lascelles is seated in triumph, although, to be fair, the victory owed nothing to him. Behind are natives with the guns. Salmon and Pearson are leaning familiarly against the hide of the beast; between them stands the Prince not yet quite free from the surprise he had been given.

This is what happened. They were following four poaching elephants. After a mile they spotted one and got within fifty yards of him. The elephant stood still, benign and unsuspecting. Here was a chance. The Prince and Lascelles began a whispered argument as to who should shoot the beast. Having accounted for one elephant, the Prince was not over-anxious to claim another. Besides, it had been agreed that Lascelles should have the next chance. Lascelles denied that any such agreement had been made, and fell to admiring the elephant, its magnificence, its balance, and, in general, its near-perfection as a work of art. All this to egg on the Prince to shoot. "Besides," Lascelles added, " single tuskers are rare." " So is a man with one eye," said the Prince. In fact the elephant's deformity was, in the Prince's opinion, a reason against shooting him. At length, the elephant settled the point by vanishing. Not into the thin air but the thick bush he had vanished. The party moved on. Salmon and Pearson expected to see no more of him. They saw and heard him soon enough. Ten yards away, on the right, he was trumpeting like a frenzied jazz-blower and plunging towards them. The Prince was in front with Salmon and Pearson ; he was chiefly aware of the trunk swinging up into the air and the single tusk. He changed his opinion about the tusk. It was an all-too-superb tusk, big enough for two pairs of tusks. Then, a scene of swift, instinctive action. Pearson, with his whole strength, pushed the Prince into a thorn bush. Pearson and Salmon, at point-blank range, put three bullets into the elephant's head. Their bull's-eye was the brain and they had missed. But the elephant turned away, and in turning, gave Pearson another shot. With that he killed.

The Prince picked himself up and Sir William Gowers came to commiserate with him. "But Pearson and Salmon !" Sir William exclaimed. " Why, they might have been shooting rabbits." But Pearson and Salmon were not taking any bows. The Prince fetched the basket and made tea. He handed a cup to Pearson and, as unexcitedly as he could, asked if that kind of experience was an everyday affair. "No, sir," said Pearson. "We don't usually go assing about arguing who is going to shoot the elephant."

Another encounter with an elephant was more circus-like, but even so, dangerous. The Prince had done some sightseeing, had attended some official functions, had played golf, had been lost with Salmon all night in the rain. The time had come for another safari. At eight o'clock in the morning on November 15, a strange procession set forth upon adventure—a Hudson, a Buick (which the Prince drove), two Willys-Knights and four lorries. Without doubt, this would have been a shocking sight to those single-minded sportsmen who rigidly believe in doing-the-thing-*properly*-or-not-at-all. But the Prince's time was not unlimited, and he was anxious to cover as much ground as possible. As for learning Africa's secrets—"My boy, she doesn't wear her heart upon her sleeve, you know"—as for listening to her heart-beats—well, perhaps another time.

The Prince, intent upon bringing home something alive, had borrowed a cine-camera from the Governor of Kenya. Two elephants were sighted. One posed like a very model for his picture. The other seemed to be doing so, but after a minute or so, began to enquire what it was all about. The Prince and three others were busy turning handles at a range of about twenty-five yards. They saw their model grow restive, stopped the picture and, with an occasional and ever so casual backward look, walked quietly away. The elephant, we suppose, had never seen a cine-camera before. He followed them. Craftily and imperceptibly, they increased their pace. Then came again that sudden jazz-band blare. They looked and saw him charging. No longer imperceptible was their retreat. They ran very fast, each choosing his own direction. Lascelles, it seemed, held the most attraction. The beast made for him. Lascelles sprinted and sprinted again, but could not hope to equal the elephant's forty miles an hour (which enragement might at any moment increase to fifty). One of the others, out of danger for the moment, fired an almost random shot. The elephant changed his mind and made off in another direction. The men stopped running. They could afford now to make light of the scene. But, remembering the surprising re-appearance of that other elephant, they judged it best, on the whole, to get back to the cars.

When the Prince went into Tanganyika, District Commissioner Orde-Brown was appointed as his personal conductor. Another notable addition to the party was Baron von Blixen who came as an extra-hand hunter. Von Blixen's fixed purpose was to provide the Prince with a lion. Lion-shooting, he was careful to explain, is a ritual. You must make an appointment with the beast. You do that by putting down " kills." That is to say, you shoot some of the more common fry, zebra in preference, disembowel them, and scatter the bait at various places within reach of your camp. You had better cover the bait with thorn-bushes, otherwise you will be keeping the appointment with vultures, and perhaps jackals and hyenas.

Von Blixen went to Kwakuchinga to prepare the bait. When the Prince arrived there, von Blixen sadly informed him that all the " kills " had been well feasted upon, but the lions had clean disappeared. Of course, there were always rhinoceros and buffalo. But having once mentioned lions, von Blixen could not now suggest anything which would avoid anti-climax. Meanwhile the Prince had the satisfaction of shooting a kudu, an African antelope, which, although not uncommon, is admired for its horns. This proved to be a mere " getting his eye in " for a larger adventure. Von Blixen had been at work again with his offerings of dead zebra to any lions that happened to be in the neighbourhood.

On November 21 he was a bringer of good news. He had seen lions. Eagerly he led out the Prince's party to bear witness. They wandered round for three hours. but no lion appeared. They came to some high grass, The Prince and one other were posted in the line of retreat which a lion might possibly take. Von Blixen, Legh and Lascelles went forth as beaters. They met with what must be called (in view of their occupation) success. A lioness and a black-maned lion were disturbed, but did not take the arranged path of retreat. Von Blixen now decided to depose Legh and Lascelles, and to beat alone. Legh and Lascelles were not inclined to regard their dismissal as being any kind of disgrace —neither then nor a few minutes later when von Blixen disturbed another lion. This, like the other pair, turned away from the expected line and into the bush. But von Blixen knew what noises to make and, although they seemed incongruous (being such as you might use to rebuke a kitten) none the less they were effective. The lion came out again. The Prince took aim (with a ·350 double-barrel Express), fired and missed. About 140 yards were now between him and the lion. He allowed himself time, took more deliberate aim. His shot knocked the lion over. He re-loaded and ran towards the spot where the beast fell. The lion got up and ran a little distance, then turned to attack. The Prince, now at close quarters, fired both barrels and the lion dropped in the long grass.

In its sequel the adventure tailed off into comedy. First they were careful to make quite sure that the lion was dead. Then the native boys began their expert work of skinning. It proved to be an old lion, measuring just over 100 inches. While the natives were at work, the party had lunch. If anyone there was more delighted than the Prince, it was von Blixen. He had promised so much, had been so sanguine that it had become imperative that he should produce a lion, if only to save his face. The reader can picture him despairing and driven almost to playing lion himself, at least in vocal representation, so that the guns might cock their ears and,

menacingly, mutter, " Let him roar again ! " Happily
the ruse had been unnecessary. No actor had been
required. Lion himself had entered, played his noble
part—and now was being skinned. Half an hour was
enough for that job. The natives' skill was a thing to
marvel at. One little false move can mar the prize.
The first cut is down the centre of the stomach ; then
down each of the legs. That is made to appear comparatively easy. But in skinning out the toes and opening out
the pads, the native becomes an artist. Then again to make
a clean business of skinning the skull, the art must be
the finest imaginable. When the skin is off, it is hung
in a shady, dry place, and dressed with wood-ash, alum
and arsenical soap. Perhaps, if the weather is favourable, two days are enough to finish the drying.[1] It can
then be packed and posted to the relative who for long
had been hopefully reserving a space on the drawing-
room floor.

For all the natives' deftness, the Prince nearly lost his
trophy. He went to bed early and before daybreak woke
to hear an animal prowling outside his tent. His boots
were near at hand ; he threw one of them through the
opening of the tent into the moonlight, by way of
enquiry. To this there was no reply; so he went to
sleep again. They found in the morning that the invader
had been a hyena which had been drawn by the lion
skin and had attempted to eat it. The boot had sailed
through the air just in time to prevent any serious
damage.

It was at Dodoma, half-way between Tabora and
Dar-es-Salaam, that the Prince first heard of the King's
indisposition. But there was no urgent note in the
message, and the tour was continued. Von Blixen was
now preparing to produce a buffalo, in the same manner
as with the lion, that is to say, partly as a stage-manager,

[1] For this information the author is indebted to Mr. Patrick
Chalmers who has compiled the book called *Sport and Travel in
East Africa*. (Philip Allan.)

partly as a sort of magician. The safari was in touch with Reuters and a cable arrived bringing reassuring news of the King. The Prince sent one back asking for more information, and then went off in search of von Blixen's buffalo. On November 27 they called at Kondoa where a code message was waiting for the Prince. But no one could translate the code. The Prince was anxious and hurried back to Dodoma. There he found cables from the Prime Minister, Sir Godfrey Thomas and Admiral Halsey. The news was bad. On November 28 at four o'clock in the morning, the Prince left by train for Dar-es-Salaam. There he was held up. The *Enterprise* was on her way to Dar at full speed, but could not be there for three days. Cables, a children's party, a trip to Zanzibar, dinner with the Sultan—these were some of the things that helped to kill time. At ten o'clock on Sunday morning, December 2, the *Enterprise* arrived. The Prince sailed without delay. Aden was reached three days later, Suez, two days after that, Port Said, after another two days. The ship started for Brindisi in rough weather and arrived on December 10 at noon. Sir Godfrey Thomas met him there with later news and changes of clothes. By the courtesy of the Italian Government a special train ran through to Boulogne where they arrived on the evening of December 11. At half-past ten that night—nine and a half days after leaving Dar—the Prince was at Victoria Station. Better news awaited him. He went straight to Buckingham Palace and, not long after his arrival, his father was asking to hear all about the elephants.

CHAPTER 12

MAN OF THE WIDE WORLD (*continued*)

To East Africa again. A 70-mile trek after a wild elephant. Two
film stars. Flying with Campbell Black round Kilimanjaro.
The Masai arena. A touch of malaria. The natives dance
for the Prince. Safari into the Sudan. Flying home with the
R.A.F.

SEVERAL months later, when the King had
recovered, the Prince called to mind the various
appointments that von Blixen had planned for
him and began to consider how he might keep them.
In addition there was an invitation from the King of the
Belgians to visit the Belgian Congo. So a new tour was
mapped out—first to the Cape on a visit to the Prince's
uncle, Lord Athlone; then to Rhodesia; then to Beira;
then to Dar-es-Salaam, Zanzibar and Mombasa. After
that, the safari could be resumed.

The Prince started from London on 3 January, 1930,
and sailed from Southampton on the *Kenilworth*. Normal
variations helped to keep the Prince on this side of boredom during the long voyage—a rough passage through
the Bay of Biscay, Madeira's gardens, inoculations, songs
and duets from Clara Butt and Kennerley Rumford, the
Equatorial horse-play once again, a whale, more songs
and duets, an albatross and the slow *tempo* marked
throughout by regular and rigorous exercise. The ship
reached Table Bay on January 20. This was an unofficial
visit to Capetown, but it was none the less exhausting for
that. The celebrations the Prince attended were only
equalled in number by the rounds of golf he played.
Indeed, it was only by the strict alternation of pleasure
and exercise that he was able to keep up with the calendar.
The outstanding occasions perhaps were Lady May

Cambridge's birthday party and the Navy's evening when Admiral Burmester gave a banquet at Simonstown and afterwards entertained the Prince on board H.M.S. *Calcutta*.

To Rhodesia the Prince travelled in the private coach of Prime Minister Hertzog, and from that easeful vantage-point watched the changing face of the country between Capetown and the high veld, from the friendliness of valleys with woods and vineyards and orchards to the dramatic ravines and mountain spurs. After the first night of this journey the Prince found that the high veld and a cold in the head had arrived together. At Belmont he was met and taken over the Boer War battle-fields. He was far from pleased at the sight of the memorials to fallen soldiers, so sadly neglected were they. The result of his visit was that provision was made for more regular and decent attention to these monuments.

Johannesburg from the train is not the most cheerful of prospects for a man with a heavy cold. The pleasure of descending Shaft No. 14 of the Crown Mine—that had been the first intention—was postponed, for the Prince recalled the time, five years earlier, when he had descended the Village Deep Mine, and the terrific and increasing heat as he travelled down. When the journey was resumed, the heat of the train seemed to be not much less than at the bottom of that mine. The Prince was ill and depressed. But Bulawayo's delightful aspect began to charm away his cold and to enliven his spirits. He went on to Beira and, by the S.S. *Modassa*, to Dar-es-Salaam.

At Zanzibar the Prince called once again on the Sultan. It was here that he decided to carry out an experiment which he had conceived in London before starting for Africa, a most delicate experiment, one that could only be attempted in a mood of utter dauntlessness. Is there anything more immutable than that tradition we call English Cricket? Nothing unless it be that we call

English Golf. Let us agree that these two Immutabilities are equal; for to propose a new kind of club is hardly less an effrontery than to suggest a wider bat or that the bails in future should be nailed to the stumps. The Prince had not actually proposed a new kind of club, but he had brought one from England and no doubt was hoping that, after trying it out " on tour," he would be emboldened to use it at home. This club was a patent, unbreakable driver made of steel. If any there had been disposed to heed the omens, the experiment could never have been carried out. When the Prince appeared on the links, there was a free and very determined fight among the native caddy-boys for his golf bag. Nor did the intervention of the fat caddy-master settle the point but rather delayed decision. We, knowing what followed, may suppose that the noisy conflict had robbed the Prince of the confidence which was necessary for so momentous a test. Whatever we may suppose cannot alter the fact that that unbreakable driver, made of steel, broke into two clean pieces at the very first tee.

After this experience the Prince considered it about time that he turned to safari; and when von Blixen and Finch-Hatton met him at Mombassa, they began at once to make plans. The result was the most arduous trek the Prince had known till then. Some natives brought news of a solitary bull elephant, the biggest they had ever seen. The spoor was discovered and off they went in pursuit. The country was a scorched plain. They covered ten miles in two hours and a half; then, as if they had merely come out for a picnic, they had a leisurely lunch. They went on till dark without a glimpse of the beast. The Prince then had his first experience of camping on an open plain. Just before he went to sleep (if he slept at all) he heard a lion roar. Distant it was, but in the stillness it seemed all-too-near, especially when, following it, the antelope's alarm cry was raised. Through another burning day they tramped, following spoor that at one moment looked fresh, at the next, not so fresh. Light of head and very sore of foot they were at the end of that day. And after the next day, hunger began to discomfort them, for rations had been cut down.

Before the fourth day could be begun, boots had to be put on, and that was now an exceedingly painful business. They had food and water for another twelve hours. It was at least thirty miles to the railway, but no one knew the way; and as against an indefinitely placed railroad there was the mammoth elephant's track, tantalisingly plain to see. Lamely, they followed the spoor. They did not dare to stop for a midday meal lest the habit of trudging on should be irreparably broken. At the beginning of the afternoon they came to a thickly wooded hill-land. Here they took separate paths, keeping within hailing distance of each other. But none had anything to call out about except the increasing roughness of the going. They were beginning to think they had been gammoned. Then, in a moment, the whole scene was transfigured in their eyes. The Revelation came first to Finch-Hatton. On his right he heard a movement, carefully stalked, and there it was, moving like a cloud's shadow along the hill-side. He signed to the Prince to come and take the shot. The great shadow sailed on. As the Prince was coming across through the thick bush, the elephant stopped dead. Then, having gathered from the air all the information he required, he barged through the bushes and vanished. The Revelation was over. The three men sat down and gazed sympathetically at their feet. Was the game, nearly uneventful and cruelly protracted, worth the candle? You who have not the hunter's spirit, will hastily answer, "No." You have no way of understanding the nature of that Revelation, no way even of believing that it was one. To have gone on blistered feet for seventy roasting miles and to have been rewarded at last with the awe-inspiring sight of a 125-pounder—ah! how can the ecstasy be communicated!

You, the non-hunter, will only sniff and say : " Better by far not to have seen those giant tusks than to be teased by the thought of having lost them." But the hunter thinks otherwise. The idea that he *might* have brought that ivory in triumph home but for that too-generous lunch on the first day or those blistering feet, but for the beast's prodigious ambling pace or the accident of stalking him down wind, but for this or that —the idea in itself fills the hunter, in his every sense, with sweet content, is in itself so rich an experience as almost to equal the very accomplishment.

How hard it was to remain pure naturalist can be illustrated by the Prince's encounter with a rhinoceros at this time. He had been enjoying an interval of golf and gaiety at Nairobi. Also he had done some trips over the Great Rift Valley in Campbell Black's Moth. At the end of one of those flights the party settled down to watch a rhino-movie which Legh had taken. A charging rhinoceros ! The film was a good one and at the end their blood was roused. When the Prince started on a trek to the Masai Reserve he promised himself a film of a rhino whatever else might result. On 25 February the expedition went forth. This was a filming, not a shooting party. Cars and lorries were in attendance and the Game Warden acted as watchman and swift messenger. " I have a big elephant in there. I shall have some lions for you this afternoon. I have a mother rhinoceros and her calf at Mashuru." The Warden was as obliging as a salesman behind a counter, and as embarrassing with the multitude of things he offered. A decision was made. The Prince would take the Mashuru Mother and Calf.

It started to rain. This was another kind of experience —to meet with the sort of rain which stormed your track into mud and, after twenty minutes, into nothing. But the guide knew where the track ought to be running, and the cars ploughed and lumbered on. They camped in something like a lake, but during the night the rain ceased. The next day dawned upon a translucent world. It seemed wholly composed of light, water and the greeny golden gleam of lizards. They walked four miles from camp. In the middle of a shallow river they found a great elephant, just standing there and musing. You would have said he knew the camera-men were coming. To help them in their work he began quietly to rock himself. If he could have smiled for the gentlemen, no doubt he would have done so, for clearly he was vastly pleased with himself and the sight of that watery world. They left him standing there.

They had not gone far before they almost stumbled over a rhino, asleep in the sun. This was not that mother rhino which the Warden had in store at Mashuru. The party decided that the Prince must make his own personal copyright film of this beast. But where a sleeping rhinoceros is concerned, a cine-camera had no advantage over an ordinary one. Movement was wanted. Would the Warden see to that? If they were really sure they wanted movement, he would see to it. So the Prince took up his position and got ready to film. The Warden informed the rhino that he was wanted on the floor, yelled at him. The beast, perhaps before he was awake, pulled himself up on to his legs, then blinked while his brain slowly put right the disorders of time. The swinging of that grotesque and formidable head meant that his senses were returning, especially his sharpest sense of danger. He turned and saw the camera-man and in an instant decided to charge. The camera-man, trusting in a last-minute change of mind continued to turn the handle. Finch-Hatton and the Warden (Captain Ritchie) prepared for trouble, and just as the rhino was putting on his intensest close-up expression, they both fired. The rhino turned to the left, the Prince jumped to the right. Then Ritchie fired again and the " gallant old chap " fell.

That tribute to the rhino's gallantry came from the camera-man himself. He thought it real bad luck that they had been forced to kill. Especially as the film was not a complete success. Somehow it had been difficult to concentrate on that close-up.

Still to come was the witnessing of a lion hunt in Masai, boldest of all the East African tribes. While plans for this were being made, Campbell Black took the Prince on a flight round Mount Kilimanjaro. They looked down on Lake Amboseli, on Tsavo River, on great stretches of bush and swamp ; they went on over the glaciers and among the mountain peaks ; they rose still higher and looked down on the white summit of the great mountain itself. When they were back in camp the Prince was informed that, unwittingly, he had brought four lions into the scene. The hungry quartet had been drawn by the dead hero of his film. The Masai fighters were already closing in.

They all hurried out. Two of the lions were still gorging when they took their places above the arena. It was like that—they might have been arriving at the Albert Hall to watch a heavy-weight contest. A definite and neat plan of attack had been arranged ; but it had been arranged by a white man, and a non-combatant,[1] and the natives soon made clear that they preferred going about it in their own way. Instinct and intrepidity formed the broad basis of their strategy, which indeed included little else save spears, swords, shields and war-paint.

A centre group of natives marched straight towards the two lions. The beasts slipped away into the tangled bush. Two other groups of natives joined this one in a cacophonous chorus and all went beating about the bush. The Prince complained that the natives were having the best of the fun. He and his companions were seeing very little, for all that their seats had been booked. An occasional glimpse of a lion flashing across an open space, that was the most they ever saw. The Prince said he would rather be in the arena itself. If he could

[1] Lord Delamere.

do nothing else, he could help in the bush-beating. So he, Finch-Hatton, Ritchie and von Blixen left their positions, followed the natives and, a little aimlessly, thwacked the thickets. They heard the chorus suddenly become more tense and strident. Over there to the side was a great confusion, and the four followers ran to see. The contest was over when they arrived. They saw only a dead lion with spears in its flesh. Then, immediately, that shrill chorus again, from another place. The spearmen ran towards the new arena, and the spectators struggled after them. They were in time to watch the next encounter. A lion came out into the open and, making for cover further on, was challenged by a tall native. The man was felled, but before the lion could kill him, the spears were flying again.

And now came the inevitable " touch " of malaria. It is one of the smaller mysteries of life that malaria should always be said to arrive in the manner or degree which is described as a touch. Whether this is due to any peculiarity of the fever itself, or to a sort of masonic understanding among White Men that the existence of the Thing must be as far as possible strenuously denied, that is hard to decide. What is certain is that no White Man, if he is truly White, is ever heard to boast that he once had a real big dose of malaria and no mistake. For the boast would be as good as a confession, a let-down. So we must be content to record that von Blixen had a touch of malaria, the merest flick we might call it. The Prince was next, and he was ill enough to make a return to Nairobi advisable. But perhaps his was but a touch after all, for a week later he was up and watching the races.

From now until his departure from Africa, the Prince became more and more active with the cine-camera. He was especially pleased with his success in stalking a sleeping crocodile on a slippery bank of the Aswar. But, of course, as in the case of the slumbering rhino, he wanted an action-picture. So he found a good view, shouted and then filmed the beast as it was plunging unenquiringly into the river. Later, there was an Aswar (that is as much as to say, an outsize) elephant which obliged him by waiting until he had put a new reel into his camera. Then there was a second obstreperous rhino, another charge at the camera, and once again Finch-Hatton was to the rescue. Finally, when they were on the way to the Belgian Congo, keen-eyed Finch-Hatton gave the Prince his opportunity of filming white rhinoceroses. He had spied a herd of twenty and out came the camera again. For once there was no danger. The Prince walked right up to the beasts. For all the heed they took, he might have been filming sheep. There seemed no reason why he should not attempt a close-up, they were so solid and untemperamental. But that was not so easy, after all. They were friendly, but shy. If the camera-man did not keep his distance, they kept theirs. They ran away, but only a few yards, then turned again in unruffled curiosity.

" White " is a far from accurate description of this beast. Rather should he be called the major rhinoceros. Only the elephant surpasses him for size. If you were hoping to pick him out by his colour, you would perhaps fail to see very much difference between him and the black rhino. He is, however, at least a foot taller.[1] His preference for company perhaps indicates a lack of self-confidence ; or perhaps instinct tells him he is becoming scarce and bids him fall back on the family group ; or perhaps he still remembers the blundering raids made by President Theodore Roosevelt and his party a quarter of a century ago. In any case, he rarely wanders from the herd. And now—although it is unlikely that the information has yet percolated through to him—man has come to his aid with a law for his protection.

In the Belgian Congo the Prince photographed a herd of red buffalo. The photography was a smaller feat than

[1] Here again the author is indebted to Mr. Patrick Chalmers.

the stalking, for this is a more dangerous animal than his black relations and must on no account be made suspicious. The problem was increased by the leeches—of land and of water—and since the Prince was wearing shorts, he became fully acquainted with their ways and means of attack. Indeed, this part of Africa is probably remembered by him as much for its little leeches as for its little people. The naturalist in him was discouraged for a time, and no pictures of leeches were taken. The pygmies, on the other hand, provided subjects for many admirable camera-studies, as the writer can testify. One that he saw has left a particularly clear impression. It shows two of these little people, both above the average age of their tribe, one wearing a loin-cloth, the other wearing a kind of bowler hat, a shirt and a kilt. He of the bowler is smoking through a stick which is twice his own height, while the nearly naked one is holding up the other end of the pipe. They have the air of being about to carry out a music-hall turn. Chopped grass is their tobacco and the more pungent it is, the better they are pleased. In fact, smoking is intended to be a direct assault upon the smoker's own throat and eyes. Tobacco is judged by the amount of coughing it can bring on.

The music-hall was suggested more than once to these Englishmen travelling through the Belgian Congo. The pygmies' *ngoma* was such an occasion, as the Prince's film of the ceremony faithfully shows. The *ngoma* at Okodengwe, too, was an entertaining event and resulted in one of the finest of the Prince's African films. Okodengwe is the name of the tribe's chief and after him the village where they live is called. The chief is a broad-shouldered, big-chested, serious-looking fellow who is obviously out to be admired and not at all to be laughed at. But the Prince had some difficulty in finding the native point of view. He did his best, more especially as the *ngoma* was held to honour him, to discover what precisely the dancers were at ; yet it was well-nigh impossible to connect their drilled but frenzied movements with anything but low comedy. Age counted for nothing in these performances. The whole tribe took part and, if anything, the village's oldest inhabitant was a little more remarkable than the rest for the extreme fantasy of his choreography.

Thus were homage and high-jinks mingled. As it happened Okodengwe provided the last high-light of the tour. Thereafter the journey was comparatively uneventful. The Prince was due in England on April 25, and on the first of the month he set out for the Sudan. For a hundred and fifty miles nothing more interesting than a stray elephant was spied. The Prince photographed the elephant. It was best to make sure. For all he knew, that might be the last he was to see in Africa. Then the party ran into the " long rains " which had arrived before their time. By air they reached Mongalla where the *Omdurman* was waiting. On the way to Bor the ship provided matter for the diary by running beautifully on to a mud-bank. This was not only an incident in itself but also introduced the incidental and nocturnal music of Mosquito. Next day the ship went leisurely on down the stream of the Bahr-el-Jebel, so leisurely indeed that the Prince was able to take exercise by walking the last ten miles to Bor. Nothing in the way of game rewarded him for his pains, but on the following morning they landed and after two miles came upon a congress of about two hundred elephants. Now, here is an instance of the Prince's aversion to killing game for the sake merely of killing. From the beginning he had made plain his intention of being naturalist first and slayer last. Only in the case of a genuine trophy would he be tempted to pit his life against the beast's. And, with a few exceptions and accidents and emergencies, that intention was carried out to the end. Among these two hundred elephants, for example, the Prince saw no tusks big enough to justify a kill, none big enough to persuade him to throw away a fine picture. He photographed the scene while sunshine and the trees assisted in the play of light and shadow.

In the Sudd country even the keenest observer may find time hanging heavily on his hands. Many rare birds are to be seen, it is true. (These travellers happened to see the giant shoebill on two occasions, a sight as rare as it is weird.) But the unchanging desolation of the country pulls a man's spirit down until he can only shut his eyes and wait for it to pass. If, after a slothfully moving hour or two he opens his eyes again to remark any slightest change in the prospect, and sees a single tree emerging from the surrounding papyrus sea, he can be accounted fortunate. So it was thought to be an almost exciting event when the party on the *Omdurman* saw a group of naked hunters. Hippopotamus was the prize these natives were seeking. What success they had already had, was hanging in chunks outside their tents. The Englishmen scrutinised the natives through their glasses, remarked them to be tall, fond of beads and ivory bracelets, fighters with the spear and artists in hair-dressing.

Farther north, the skyline was occasionally broken by a herd of elephants on the bank, and one of the Prince's photographs show them to be quite untroubled by the passing of the ship. But here again æons of experience have filtered through to form a solid instinct. These elephants of the Sudd know they are safe. The Prince's photograph reveals ten or eleven elephants half-hidden by papyrus and a few yards from the bank. It also includes a stretch of mud between the camera and the bank's edge. The stretch ensures the elephants' immunity from any attack from the river. It is swamp of the most treacherous kind.

The Prince and his companions were not sorry to leave the Sudd country behind. The solitariness it induced had been intensified by the great heat. Having come into the desert lands, they could now look back and cheerfully remark that they were glad to have seen the Sudd, could remark it so cheerfully in fact, that it was only too plain that they would be even more elated by the idea of never seeing it again.

They arrived at Malakal, the headquarters of the Upper Nile Province, twelve days after the safari into the Sudan had started. Punctually, eleven R.A.F. fighting planes appeared in the sky. They had come to fly the party to Cairo by way of Khartoum. Before going on, the Prince seized the chance of some exercise, first in a squash court, afterwards on a polo ground. They started next morning at eight o'clock and were in Khartoum soon after midday. During a dinner-party given by Sir John Maffey, Governor-General of the Sudan, the Prince's fever returned and he was ordered to bed. In the morning he was normal again, went sight-seeing in Khartoum and in the afternoon visited the none-too-green and almost impromptu polo grounds of Omdurman. The party stayed just long enough in Khartoum to experience the beginning of the hot weather season, and on a scorching day went to see the heights of Jebel Surgam, the scene of Kitchener's triumph. We have seen that in many of the countries to which the Prince has travelled, he has passed through the experience of some indigenous perturbation of nature. The Sudan failed him, in that the country was unable to produce for him one of the black and burning dust storms which are part of its reputation.

When they flew from Khartoum, they travelled over a hundred miles an hour for about seven hours. They were now at Aswan. Another four hours in the air brought them to Cairo, where the Prince started immediately on a round of engagements, including a visit to King Fuad; inspections of the Welsh Guards and, in gratitude for his journey from Malakal, the R.A.F. Squadron; and a service on Easter Day in the Cathedral. They sailed from Port Said on the *Rawalpindi* and reached Marseilles in the early morning of April 25. Within an hour of his arrival there, the Prince was flying again and by midday he was being greeted by Lord Tyrrell at Le Bourget. After lunching with the 34th Air Regiment of France he left Le Bourget with a squadron of French planes as escort. This squadron flew as far as the Channel, dipped in salute and went back. At Dover an English squadron met him and escorted him home.

We have recorded this homeward journey from the Sudan in some detail, not because it included events of great importance, or even of more than average interest, but to exemplify the Prince's thoroughness in carrying out a set programme, and his essentially adaptable nature. He was the first—it goes without saying—to pay tribute to the efficiency of the R.A.F., and he paid it in the kind of plain phrase which he is accustomed to use. The R.A.F., he said, had put up a remarkably fine show. We have seen how well deserved was the compliment. From the moment when the *Omdurman* reached Malakal to the arrival at Cairo, and again from Marseilles to the landing at Smith's Lawn, mile after mile was left behind according to schedule. But these programmes could not have been so well ordered without the Prince's co-operation. The R.A.F. was working with a man who, as traveller, was chiefly interested in saving time, a man, therefore, after its own heart.[1] The Prince's life in East Africa, after all, had been on a day-to-day basis. There was always to-morrow, and in the East African sun, to-morrow's insidious lure is only too apt to defeat to-day's purpose. From that sphere of enervating influence, which, however, he resisted by means of curiosity and a natural urge to be doing things, he had quickly passed to one in which each hour was allocated with nicety; from the sphere of safari to that of the

[1] The Prince's promotion (announced on New Year's Day, 1935) from Air Marshal to Air Chief Marshal in the Royal Air Force was a happy recognition of his association with that Service. At the same time he was promoted from Lieutenant-General to General in the Army and from Vice-Admiral to Admiral in the Navy.

State. The self-adjustment which has marked all the activities of his manhood was notably in evidence in this instance.

He was quickly in harness again, and, as was the case at the end of the African tour of 1928, embarked upon a programme of exceptional activity and variety. The dividing line between the official and unofficial aspects of the Prince's life is so fine as sometimes to be indistinguishable, a fact which necessitates a continual mental regulation, that leisure should yield a maximum benefit. Not everyone would wish to devote a holiday to trekking twenty miles a day through African bush and forest. To the Prince both the East African tours were real holidays, to be ranked with the visits to his Canadian ranch as being among the interludes of happiest freedom.

CHAPTER 13

MAN OF THE WIDE WORLD (*continued*)
(And some views on Empire Citizenship)

The Prince's second visit to the Argentine. Opening of British Exhibition in Buenos Aires. The Prince and Empire citizenship. The King and the family spirit. His Christmas Day (1934) address as a fitting prelude to his Jubilee. The Prince's contribution to the achievement of his father's reign.

SO many catch-phrases have been attached to the Prince's career in the past that it is far from easy for the average observer to gather from these a clear idea of the direction of his development. A single affix—" Conqueror," " Cœur de Lion" or " Peacemaker "—helps to convey some notion of the direction, if not of the actual destination of the subject's public life. But too many labels attached to one career lead to confusion. To convey a reasonably clear view of the Prince's manhood, it is necessary to discard many of the labels which have been hastily and unthinkingly stuck on to it from time to time. Also it is necessary to recognise that the Prince's abilities have pointed to a possible development in more than one direction. His peculiar problem has been to direct and develop his several talents that their maximum force might be realised. It is more than likely—the point is worth repeating—that with less of his time taken up by official functions, his sense of business would have carried him to uncommon achievements. Even as it is, not altogether without reason has he been described as " the Empire's best commercial traveller " and as a " big business leader."

Those who believe that the Prince's embassies of trade

represent nothing more than an exploitation of his personality in support of this or that project, overlook the fact that such an exploitation would hardly be possible, were there no signs of business acumen in that personality. They also overlook the sagacity which is required to choose among projects. There is no doubt that the Prince's trade embassies to the Argentine in 1925 and 1931 were among the wisest of his undertakings. The earlier visit was planned to include an historical significance, for that year was the hundredth anniversary of the first Treaty of Amity and Commerce between Britain and the Argentine. And during that tour we have noted that the Prince had more than a little difficulty in balancing those two elements of amity and commerce.

The Argentines were irrepressible. A profusion of flowers, lavish entertainments, the beauty of their people, the songs of their children—these in array served to express some of their warm-heartedness. Police cordons were ineffective in the face of such ebullience. Embarrassing incidents were a daily occurrence. (The embarrassment was felt not so much by the Prince as by his hosts.) There was the middle-aged woman, for instance, who, outwitting or outfighting the police, found her way to the Prince to tell him that they all loved him so; and there was the young and beautiful girl who conquered her natural modesty so far as to ask him for his handkerchief as a memento of the visit. Throughout that tour, Amity, the hand-maiden of Commerce, was always threatening to crowd her mistress out of the picture.

That she did not altogether succeed, however, is witnessed among other things by the contract which was signed for a new tube railway, an undertaking which was to cost £10,000,000, and the material of which was to be bought in England.

For all that, the hectic circumstances of that earlier tour did not favour a complete fulfilment of every ambition. Business and hospitality, both at high pressure

combined to impose a severe strain on the Prince's health.
As often as not, he retired to bed at dawn or later, and
lack of sleep resulted in nerviness. He returned home
with the feeling of having done no more than lay the
foundations of trade relations between England and the
Argentine, and with every intention of returning as soon
as possible to consolidate his achievement. Not until
1931 was he able to carry out his wish. In the early part of
that year he started for the Argentine again, this time with
the Duke of Kent (then Prince George) as companion.
The immediate purpose was to open the British Empire
Exhibition at Buenos Aires, an exhibition which proved
to be one of the finest achievements of its kind in our
time. That it was planned and opened at all, was chiefly
due to the *rapprochement* between the business men of the
two countries which followed from the Prince's earlier
tour ; and, most decidedly, its outstanding success was
due in large measure to the presence of the King's
eldest and youngest sons.

They travelled by way of Bermuda, Jamaica, Panama,
Havana, Bolivia, Peru and Chile. On 1 March, they
arrived at Buenos Aires, where they were welcomed by
the President, General Jose Uriburu. At the opening of
the Exhibition the President observed that the event
marked one hundred and twenty years of unbroken
friendship between England and the Argentine. The
Prince made his reply first in English, then in
Spanish.

But Buenos Aires was only one point of concentration
in that great business campaign. British manufacturers—of motor cars, of gramophones and of many
other items—had, in the Prince, an uncommonly
effective salesman, one who untiringly stressed the
superior merits of their goods at every opportunity during
a journey of 9000 miles. In order to do this the more
persuasively, he had taken pains to improve his Spanish
before leaving England. His accomplishment in this
language has been of valuable service to him, not only

during the tours of the Argentine, but also on the occasions when trade delegations from that Republic have come to England.

Any comprehensive survey of the last twenty years of the Prince's life will reveal the difficulty of choosing one summary phrase which shall be more representative than another. Whether " Big Business Leader," for instance, is a more or less appropriate description than " Ambassador to the Empire " must remain, for the time being, a matter of personal opinion. Certainly the aspect of the Prince's endeavours which is reflected by the second of these phrases, can hardly be too heavily underlined. In relation to Imperial issues his attitude has been in keeping with the ever-changing ideas and forms which have been a feature of the twentieth-century British Empire. To obtain a clear impression of those transformations and their extent, it is only necessary to read some of the speeches made by prominent politicians during the past thirty years or so. Refer to some of the speeches of Mr. Joseph Chamberlain in which, as Colonial Secretary in Mr. Balfour's Government, he brought forward the policy of preferential tariffs in favour of the Colonies. Or to the vigorous, but always elegant, replies of Lord Oxford (then Mr. Asquith) in defence of the Free Trade position.

Here, for illustration, is a passage from a speech he delivered in October, 1903 : " Mr. Chamberlain says and says truly that the Colonies ought not to be treated as an appendage to Great Britain. I agree, and neither ought Great Britain to be treated as an appendage to the Colonies. After all—we must put in a word now and again for poor little England—after all, this United Kingdom still remains the greatest asset of the British Empire, with its forty-two millions of people, with its traditions of free government, with its indomitable enterprise, with its well-tried commercial and maritime prowess." Eight years later the same speaker was discussing the two common formulæ for the solution of the Imperial problem, one, a strong central government, the other, the method of gradual disintegration.

"After seventy years' experience of Imperial evolution," he remarked, "it may be said with confidence that to-day neither of these theories commands the faintest support either at home or in any part of our self-governing Empire. We were saved from their adoption—some people would say by the favour of providence or (to adopt a more flattering hypothesis) by the political instinct of our people. And just in proportion as centralisation was seen to be increasingly absurd, so had disintegration been felt to be increasingly impossible. Whether in the United Kingdom, or in any one of the great communities which you represent, we each of us are, and we each of us intend to remain, master in our own household. It is the *articulus stantis aut cadentis Imperii.*"

These words were spoken just before the period at which this study of the Prince's career begins. They indicate the speaker's belief that self-government among the units of the British Empire will ultimately bring a more stable unity than could ever be secured by a centralised system. And since that time the process of sanctioning independence has been gradually changing the whole face of the Empire. We now see the Dominions as free nations and, so convinced of its right-mindedness are some observers that, unflinchingly, they are seeking to apply the same political principle to India. It is more than possible that India, like Ireland, will have all the appearance of being an intractable exception; that her people will not respond in the expected way to this benevolent bestowal of freedom; that they may regard it, as many regarded the M.C.C.'s messages to Australia on the subject of leg-theory bowling, as a way of climbing down from the perch. But that will not alter the fact that the whole trend of Imperial politics during the past quarter of a century has been towards independence, not as a result of slackness or a patronising spirit or

Central Press Photo

The Prince of Wales and Prince George (now Duke of Kent) in South America

self-righteousness, but because of a new valuation of freedom and its influence.

So it has come to pass that the symbolism of the Crown in relation to Imperial unity shines with a new light. Not by accident, but by clear design, did the King base his Christmas Day speech in 1934 upon the metaphor of the family. Immediately before the speech, the efficiency of the British Broadcasting Corporation had enabled listeners in all parts of the world to hear greetings from Ottawa, the Isle of Arran, South Africa (the songs of boys on a wine farm near Capetown), from an Indian officer at Landi Khotal at the head of the Khyber Pass (unhappily, the least clear of all the messages), from Southern Rhodesia, a dairy farmer in New Zealand, a toll-keeper at the mouth of the Mersey Tunnel, and, immediately following him, another on Sydney Bridge, from one of a railway track gang in Western Australia, a Tasmanian fisherman (who, with a delightfully un-exalted air, reminded his audience that there was not much difference being a fisherman in Tasmania and being one anywhere else), a Pensioner at Chelsea Hospital, and finally, in a Cotswold shepherd's voice which rang most truly, from the heart of England herself. With those friendly voices giving direct evidence, the King's reference to the Empire's unity as being the spirit of one family, was made the more vivid and forceful. He spoke of it as a spirit knowing no barriers of space, and through the medium of broadcasting an added significance was given to the words. Of himself the King spoke as the head of this great family, and as such he urged his listeners to show compassion to those who were without health or work. The address gave rise to admiring comment and discussion everywhere in the Empire.

One writer[1] was especially wise and helpful in his observations. " Of course," he wrote, " the title of father is often given to the founder of a nation or a line of kings ; and it sits as naturally on the head of the clan

---

[1] " Scrutator " of the London *Sunday Times*.

or race as on those who direct the practice of a common religious faith. But this idea of Kingship as a political fatherhood of many peoples of diverse race and colour, of all creeds, in all climes, and at all stages of development, is new and, so far as one can recall, has never been fully expressed before the King's Speech on Christmas Day. That this should have impressed everyone by its manner, and hardly anyone by the originality of its governing idea, shows how unconscious we can be of our own distinction in history. We are too fond of making ourselves out to be dull, unimaginative people, whose practical instinct makes us distrustful of every general idea. The truth is that in politics we are a very original people and fonder than most of pressing an idea to its logical conclusion. There never has been a great political unity, either in the ancient or the modern world, at all comparable to what we loosely and inaccurately call the British Empire; and because of this uniqueness, the King had to fall back on a metaphor of fatherhood which in this association is also unique."

It is perhaps not altogether surprising that we are looking at the Imperial idea with new eyes, or rather that by penetration we have arrived at a new plane of meaning. With Noel Coward and others we have had our good laugh at mad dogs and Englishmen and all types representing our race as thickheaded and uncomprehending in the capacity of rulers or administrators among foreign peoples. Having enjoyed and exhausted the joke, we see that, after all, it did depend upon caricature and not altogether upon the truth. If the joke had been wholly or almost wholly true, foreign nations would have been justified in their expectation of a rapid break-up of the Imperial system. But it was not true— (and therefore was so much the better jest). The uniqueness of that system is now being recognised in a world which is sick under the burden of tyranny. It is being admired. It is seen to rest upon the constant application of an unambiguous political principle. Some go so far as to see it as the gradual realisation of a kind of vision. To such as these the idea of the King as head of a dispersed and widely varied family is a most natural conception, and one that is increasingly strengthened as a result of the gradual dissolving of formal obligations. They hold that this transcendant conception of Kingship gains power with the falling away of legalities.

Only by bearing this conception in mind can we discern the complete significance of the Prince's Empire missions. They were undertaken in a spirit of enquiry as well as in a spirit of adventure. The Prince knew well that as he passed from district to district he would be faced with a variety of problems, and that everywhere he would be required to take into consideration the organic changes which were happening in the Empire's constitution. His primary object was to stress the reality of Empire citizenship, which was a far from easy task, seeing that no name has ever been invented to represent that type of citizenship—and it is difficult to conceive the existence of anything which has no name. A foreign observer might reasonably assume that all members of a British Commonwealth of Nations would be called British, and then would be puzzled to find that newspapers in the Dominions commonly refer to the British House of Commons or the British Prime Minister. After that, he would be still further perplexed to read of British justice in relation to Imperial affairs.

In a bank in British Malaya a *Times* correspondent once read the notice : " No receipt is valid unless signed by a member of the British staff," which was obviously intended to make a distinction between the British and Asiatic members of the staff. Yet the latter were, in the technical sense, British subjects. It is clear then that " British " would be an ambiguous appellation, and to adopt it as a description of Empire citizenship would not win the approval of those subjects who do not claim Great Britain as the country of their origin. Here again

the symbolism of the Crown seems to offer a way out·
A descriptive name derived from that unifying idea
would admirably meet the case. To invent a satisfactory name of this kind is not a very simple matter,
but without one we cannot expect consciousness of
Imperial citizenship to be roused and kept awake.

The remarkable interest and enthusiasm which the
King's Christmas Day message of 1934 stirred in all
parts of the Empire were obviously dependent in large
measure upon the King's own personality. But
undoubtedly other contributory factors were the Prince's
widely and thoroughly planned Empire mission and the
subsequent tours of his brothers. And if the Prince
has played an important part in directing diverse Imperial
interests and sentiments to that focal point which is
the Crown, his role has been hardly less important in
attracting the interest and, in some important instances,
the affection of foreign nations. Thus it was that
innumerable people who were not the King's subjects
listened to that message, and on a day when peace and
good-will are most blessed in men's thoughts. To the
people of the United States especially the speech was of
great interest, a fact which recalls the outstanding
popularity of the Prince whenever he has visited that
country. Two nation-wide systems in the United States
were used to distribute the King's message and all over
the country the reception was clear. The significance of
this was well put in a paragraph from a leading article
in *The Times* : " Of the many influences drawing Americans and British closer together not the least of recent
years has been the growing regard felt in the United
States for the British Royal Family and for the King
personally, a regard which found striking expression
on the occasion of the Duke of Kent's marriage, and
which has now been manifested anew by the American
reception of the King's message and the comments
which have been made upon it. Indeed in most parts
of the world a similar interest has been shown. The

message was instinct throughout with that spirit of good-will by the help of which alone the nations can hope to reconcile their differences and achieve a real peace."

No more fitting prelude to the King's Silver Jubilee can be imagined than that message ; for it was a simply worded summary of all that the King has most cared for during his reign and has striven to attain. His example has been always a steadying influence ; his counsel, always sensible. No man has done more to help England endure the succession of crises which have made the last twenty-five years the severest ordeal in her history. Ten thrones have fallen during that quarter of a century, and there is no sign that their passing is lamented by the nations which have decided against them. But the anti-monarchy wave had spent its force before it broke upon England's shores. While other peoples were casting tradition away, the English, always odd and contrary, discovered an enhanced meaning in theirs. But without the personal influence of the King and Queen, and, in this context we may be permitted to add, of their eldest son, the Monarchy would not have won the high esteem in which it is now held. In these personalities the British have found clear reflections of their own normal characteristics. The Jubilee celebrations will enable them, wherever in the world they may be, to express a loyalty which is the stronger and deeper for being often inarticulate, and at the same time to reassert a faith in their inner being and constitution as a people.

To the confirmation of that faith and loyalty the Prince has contributed after his own highly individual manner. He has worked out for himself a way of fitting together tradition and a world of rapid progress. There was a time when to the superficial observer he appeared to be favouring modernity at the expense of tradition. Since then his judgment, even if it has not been infallible in every small detail, has been proved to be sound in general principle. His career has not been built up without criticism. Some have inclined to the opinion that his democratic manner has involved a loss of dignity. Instances of this opinion have been recorded at various stages of this study. Almost always they show such criticism to have been based on a false view of dignity, the very view, in fact, to which the Prince has always beendeterminedly opposed.

In earlier days, impatience with that attitude led him perhaps to make an exaggerated bid for freedom on some occasions. Faults of that kind, however, do but serve to endear him the more to those who have realised his problems and have admired the spirit in which he has approached them. Wherever he has travelled, into whatsoever circumstances of life he has enquired, he has insisted on the personal touch. It has been an obsession. The remarkable thing is that he should have retained the power of applying it and making it effectual. He cannot but be aware of the strength of his personal appeal; on the other hand he is also aware of the dangers which are the constant attendants of every public personality. Even the personality of a film-star calls for wise stewardship if its drawing-power is to be maintained—a fact which is known to some but of which others are woefully ignorant. How much wiser must the stewardship be in the case of a so popular Prince of Wales!

One of the most pointed and most deserved tributes ever paid to the Prince came from a man of Labour sympathies, the Acting-Premier of Queensland, who described him as " a new link between the British peoples." The point of the remark is that the unifying influence which the Prince brought during his Empire tours was felt to be a new force. The newness lay not so much in the tours themselves, for there had been Royal visits to the Empire before these, as in the man-to-man spirit which informed them from beginning to end. It was a spirit which was especially needed in that after-

War phase of disillusion, and because it was utterly spontaneous, its influence spread far beyond the people the Prince met and the lands he visited. In everything he did and said that spontaneity could be felt.

" I feel no stranger," he told the people of New Zealand in his first speech there, " but one of yourselves, among my own kith and kin. How could I in this great British Dominion feel anything but at home ? " And in all his utterances there was that happy personal touch, as, for example, in one of his earliest Empire addresses to a large audience in Toronto where he said : " The Dominions are no longer Colonies, they are sister nations of the British nation . . . and their international importance will steadily increase. Yet they all desire to remain within the British Empire whose unity is shown by common allegiance to the King. That is the reason why, if I may be personal for a moment, I do not regard myself as belonging primarily to Great Britain and only in a lesser way to Canada and the other Dominions. On the contrary I regard myself as belonging to Great Britain and to Canada in exactly the same way. This also means that when I go down to the United States next week, I shall regard myself as going there not only as an Englishman and as a Britisher, but also as a Canadian and as a representative of the whole Empire."

The idea of Empire citizenship could not have been more simply or more clearly put. The address was given fifteen years ago, yet it would be equally applicable to present-day relationships. How much the idea is in need of emphasis with regard to Australia can be gathered from a leading article which appeared in the Adelaide *Advertiser* towards the end of 1934. It referred to the recurrence of misunderstandings which were calculated to foster bad feeling and to spoil the intimate friendship existing between England and Australia ; and then warned readers of the perils involved in being for ever at cross-purposes. " We cannot afford these needless bickerings," the article continues, " and the people of Great Britain, in common with Australia, should be ready to realise that breeding bad blood between those who are, if possible, something more than kin is in the highest degree indefensible."

After references to the question of Lancashire cotton goods, the meat disputes and cricket controversies, there follow these questions and suggestions : " How much has been done officially to present both sides of the meat question for the information of the people as a whole ? Has the British public been fully and frankly informed, or the Australian public either, from Government sources of the realities of the situation ? If all the facts were adequately realised it might still be difficult to solve the problem, but the attempt would not be accompanied and possibly defeated by a needless feeling of irritation. The British public, for instance, would be little inclined to listen to sweeping condemnations of our tariff policy if fully cognisant of the extent of the adjustments made by Mr. Lyons's Government in the face of extraordinary difficulties. To preserve the priceless sentiment of mutual affection in all its natural force, in spite of economic stresses and party political ambitions, is a fitting task for statesmen at both ends of the earth."

This appeal reveals the good-will and reasonableness which we can still count on finding in Australians, and at the same time the grave dangers which are threatening to undermine those feelings in both countries. It is a mistake to take for granted that the natural sentiment of mutual affection between England and her " sister nations " will continue without care and cultivation. Being natural and not supernatural, the sentiment must be conscientiously tended lest it wither and die and its place be taken by the weeds of bitterness and hatred which, once sown, flourish exceedingly, needing no careful cultivation. On more than a few occasions during his tours the Prince found signs of these waste-

The King and the Prince at the Trooping of the Colour

ful growths. It was not to be expected that he would entirely clear the ground of their straggling roots in the limited time at his disposal ; but it is certain that friend-ship's flowering had never been more fair than during his Empire itineraries.

CHAPTER 14

OPEN-MINDED BACHELOR

Is the Prince a marrying man ? Rumours which have been a source
of annoyance. The English Royal family of to-day and of a
century ago. The Duke of Kent's marriage. The Prince and
the succession.

IT needs no great acuteness on the reader's part to
remark that the most difficult of all the questions
relating to the Prince has been avoided in previous
chapters. Indeed, the reader may well have been
thinking that the author's intention is to cheat him (to
cheat her, let us rather say) of what everybody desires
most to know about the Prince. " Is he a marrying
man ? " is the question which, in some form or other,
has been asked more frequently than any other about
him. A colloquial form, such as the one here chosen,
probably gives the most accurate expression of the
general curiosity. And perhaps it is advisable, for the
sake of any remote or foreign readers who may be
unacquainted with the idiom, to explain what is meant
by " a marrying man." The man whom we, perhaps a
little confusingly, describe as a marrying one, is not a
clergyman, as might easily be supposed ; nor is he one
who is for ever getting married. Really, the phrase is
very eloquent when once the meaning has been caught.
A marrying man is one who, whether bachelor or
widower, keeps an open mind on the subject of marriage ;
takes no vow to have done with womankind ; is not
puffed up with the idea of the self-sufficiency of his
own sex ; is not, as widower or bachelor, confirmed.

Now, with that definition in mind, the question need
no longer be regarded as awkward. The answer is

clear : without a doubt, the Prince of Wales is a marrying man. And on the heels of that enunciation, another
follows, as a kind of rider, namely, that hitherto the
Prince has not married because he has not met the woman
he would like to make his wife.

The subject was considered important enough for the
publication of a pamphlet in 1922. The writer of this
extraordinary essay took it upon himself to offer the
Prince some advice in the matter. " As the Prince of
Wales is now in his 28th year," he wrote, " the question
of his marriage is one that for many urgent reasons is
ripe for settlement. Already it has been fully and freely
discussed in all parts of the Empire, for it is not merely
a matter of supreme importance to himself and his
Royal parents ; it also affects the well-being and happiness of many millions of his future subjects." The writer
then looked round Europe and reluctantly admitted
that there was a dearth of eligible ladies in other Courts.
But he was not to be denied. He had his own suggestion
to make. With something approaching second sight
and with quite disarming boldness he brought it forward :
" There is one solution of the difficulty that would be
immensely popular with the British people and would
give pleasure and satisfaction wherever the English
tongue is known. The English people desire above all
things that the Prince of Wales should marry an English
lady, and believe that among the ranks of our aristocracy
one might be found who would worthily uphold the
august dignity of a future Queen of England."

In this matter of marriage the Prince has contended
with some of his greatest problems ; for his position as
heir to the Throne, and the publicity which attends his
daily life, have helped to make a question which for every
man is in any case difficult enough, even more complicated. However independent a man's judgment may
be, the constant pressure of public opinion cannot but
be felt as a factor in the situation. More than that, its
influence may have the effect of setting up an unconscious

resistance to forces which peradventure are pulling in the right direction. A man who, because he is in the public eye, is continually hearing rumours concerning his most intimate thoughts and desires, may conceivably arm himself against the possibility of their proving true. He may hope, by silently opposing the rumours, to end them. That is a possibility which, in the Prince's case, should never be overlooked.

During his early tours, that is to say at the most sensitive phase of his manhood, a tumult of rumours was the daily accompaniment of his life, rumours that were partly interrogation, partly good-humoured intrusion, partly exaction. It will be recalled that when the Prince was a guest of the Italian Royal Family during the War, public opinion both in Italy and in England, decided to marry him to the Princess Yolanda of Savoy. His visits to America were the cue for yet another flight of imagination; the gossip-columns were all set for an impending engagement. If it is possible to think of a human being dying a thousand deaths, it should be comparatively easy to think of the Prince enduring a thousand marriages.

The strain of public rumour and speculation has been considerably eased during the Prince's recent career. In this he has had the co-operation of the English Press. It has been generally agreed to let lie the topic of his marriage until the best of reasons for its revival occurs. With the ruthless methods of some sections of American journalism in mind, we can be grateful, for his sake, that such respite has been granted by Fleet Street, and perhaps we shall be justified in regarding it as a return for the tact and courtesy which the Prince has unfailingly shown towards journalists. After all, there was every likelihood of the topic being given a renewed and spirited lease of life by the marriage of the Duke of Kent and Princess Marina. The Prince as best man to his brother! To the picture-minded, story-gathering journalist, how short a step it is from that to the idea of the Prince's brother as best man to him ! Perhaps the Prince was spared that fate as a result of the heavy programme which he carried out during the days immediately following his brother's marriage. Certainly it helped to switch public attention from romantic to more drably realistic things. It also served to remind people that as long as the Prince was so actively occupied by his interests in social and industrial progress, it was highly improbable that they would be hearing of the culmination of any private interest.

The possibility of the Prince submitting to " a marriage of convenience " has never at any time been a serious one. At the present time, when we look upon the ruins of so many monarchies, it can hardly be said to exist. The ways of international diplomacy have changed. In a world full of suspicion, of bluff, of tentative friendships and alliances, the nations no longer look to royal marriages as a way of re-arranging the balance of power. Not that the principle of alliance through marriage is any more fallible than that of alliance by treaty. The point here is that, in the present state of affairs, the Prince will never be required to assent to a loveless, parade-marriage.

That the House of Windsor inspires as much affection and loyalty as ever in an out-of-joint world, is due to many qualities. Not the least of these is flexibility. The House has retained the dignity of its tradition without falling out of step with these quick-march times. When the Duke of York married outside the prescribed circle, the departure from custom was most heartily welcomed by English people. So, too, when Princess Patricia was married to a commoner. These marriages were eagerly taken to be signs that the Royal Family were in sympathy with current tendencies ; that the human element was of more consequence to them than pomp and circumstance. Enough has been related in these pages to show how little the Prince thinks of the Victorian conception of royalty. It is in him that we see how far the pendulum-swing has carried us in our notions of what a member of the Royal Family should be and should do.

An incident occurs to the writer here, one that has not previously been cited. In a sense it is quite insignificant. Yet it can be viewed as epitomising the Prince's character, and especially his impulsive sympathy. It happened at a ball a few years ago. During the evening the Prince noticed a girl wearing a simple black frock and sitting alone. She seemed to be out of it ; so he went to her and asked for a dance, and afterwards spent some time with her in conversation. He discovered she was a nursery governess in the house, and was then the more delighted he had rescued her from a lonely evening. It is that kind of incident which is so difficult to set down without suggesting a patronising air on the one hand or, on the other, an attempt to give a modern twist to " Cinderella." To relate it at all at once gives the false impression that it was in the nature of an enactment.

At the beginning of his manhood, there were, of course, occasions when the Prince could be said to be on the look-out for opportunities to express goodwill to all sorts and conditions. But with experience he has matured both in judgment and in the technique of public appearance.

In this book are many examples of his judgment, especially as regards the fitting moment and as regards the fitting thing to do and say at that moment. The technique itself can only be appreciated by direct observation. Only those who have watched the Prince on any public or semi-public occasion can fully realise with what command and balance he carries out his programme and its added improvisations. As in all techniques, whether in art, entertainment, science or everyday living, it is " timing " which is the most important element in the art of public appearance. And it is that very element which eludes the narrator's grasp when he attempts to describe an incidental episode in any such performance.

That is the reason why so many anecdotes relating to the deeds of famous public figures give the impression that the incident was a prepared enactment. Between the lines it seems that we are reading the stage instructions. Yet those public men who have command of their particular technique, have no difficulty in carrying off a spontaneous " scene." Only the spontaneity can rarely be reproduced in a verbal account of the scene.

If the reader suspects that the motive for this digression is to put him off the scent at the very moment when there was promise of good hunting, he is mistaken. Let him rather see in it a warning. The reader, after all, will frequently be one who has never set eyes on the Prince ; one who composes his portrait of the Prince wholly from anecdote and report. He, especially, must be on guard against the composition in his own mind of an utterly unreal person. When he reads an account of an incident (such as the one which has just been recounted), he will do well to give the Prince credit for the normal thoughts and emotions of a normal person. For the spontaneity of that and many another invitation to the dance was the result partly of the acquired technique of a man of the world, but partly also of quick and simple sympathy.

The essential difference between the English Royal Family of the present and that of a century and less ago is revealed in what is now and what was then considered expedient. Even if simple sympathy was felt by the Victorian Royalty, it was not—certainly not—deemed desirable to express it save through the most devious channels and under cover of the most forbidding formalities. So much so that we are at liberty to wonder whether the sympathy towards ordinary people was so simple after all and whether, if it existed at all in the first place, it was not gradually smothered under the weight of its own expression.

Queen Victoria, even in her bursts of freest gaiety, was never forgetful of the narrow circle she must describe and move in. There was such a burst at the time when her eldest daughter made her début; but even then—and it was a period of restored peace and high spirits—she observed the rule that she must only waltz with Royal partners; and in this she had the support (if support was needed) of Lord Melbourne. It is true that English country dances allowed her more latitude without countenancing any excessive familiarity. Indeed their grave, calculated merriment was the very thing to show exactly how far she meant to go. So she cultivated these, rehearsed them with her ladies and gentlemen and then brought them to the new ballroom at Buckingham Palace.

Look on this picture and then on that of the Prince dancing with the nursery governess. Or try, if possible, to make a composite picture; imagine, that is, the Prince Consort sitting up for his Queen till the small hours; watching her execute dance after dance in the last desperate attempt to recall her youth; stifling an occasional yawn; and suddenly catching sight of his descendant dancing with what he would so justly describe as a total stranger. Imagine, too, that as the couple came into his view, the music, suffering a change, had become a jaunty, rakish dance-tune of the late 1920's. Macduff's cry of horror at the discovery of the murdered Duncan, would do less than justice to the Prince Consort's feelings in the awkward position in which we have placed him.

The contrast between the two Royal Families, that of (say) 1856 and that of the period 1920–1935, has a direct bearing on our theme of the Prince as a marrying man. In that earlier period even religious differences were sometimes overcome in favour of alliances with the Crowns of Europe. (For example, one of the House of Coburg became a Catholic in order to marry the Queen of Portugal.) And even when such differences were not overcome, the possibility of an alliance by royal marriage was always important enough to be debated seriously.

A question of this kind arose when Queen Victoria's cousin, the charming Princess Mary of Cambridge, was sought in marriage by the King of Sardinia, the Princess being a Protestant, the King, a Catholic. The Princess refused him ; and the Queen's opinion was that she was right in doing so. The upshot of the matter was the confirmed view that no member of the English Royal Family ought to renounce the Protestant faith for a Catholic crown. But the very fact that the question was debated at all and that the Queen's opinion was so firmly stated, indicates the attraction which these royal alliances held.

Time, the great healer, has changed all that. The last thing English people expect of the Prince of Wales is that he should marry for politics' sake. So romantic has been their conception of him in the past that most people probably expect him to avoid such a marriage. Those rumours of an Italian marriage were perhaps begotten by a desire for its fulfilment. If so, they represented a conception of the Prince which was based upon old-world ideas. In the light of his post-War career, the conception has been radically changed. Even those who fain would have retained it, have been compelled to admit that it does not tally with the facts.

There is no gainsaying that the announcement of the Prince of Wales's engagement would give rise to something like a tidal wave of popular approval and enthusiasm. To be convinced of that, it is only necessary to recall the extraordinary popularity of the Duke of Kent's marriage. There were those who asserted that the rejoicing which attended that event was a journalistic fabrication, that the mass of English people were comparatively unmoved. There is but slender evidence for the assertion. If, in certain details, a united Fleet Street guided popular opinion during the weeks preceding the wedding-day, it is equally true that canny editors were responding to an overwhelming demand from their readers. After a long, dark period of depression, the event came as an opportunity to reassert a spirit of faith and hopefulness. It was to be a day of general blessing. In London for a few nights there were such scenes as had not been witnessed since the Armistice. Yet how different from those! Instead of exhibiting that pathetic release of hysteria, of joy that had not yet ceased to be pain, the crowds in Bond Street walked from end to end in a mood of restrained wonder. To that narrow thoroughfare a cosmopolitan London throng had been drawn " to see the decorations," and once again it was possible to hear the beating of that sentimental heart. It was the occasion for another " Cockaigne " overture ; only the new music would be less flamboyant than the old.

The Duke of Kent's marriage brought one fact into an especially clear light, namely that the Royal Family were holding the affection of English people as securely as ever they did. The Prince has played a great part in maintaining that hold. There will always be those who make a reservation of judgment here, who entertain the belief that the part he has played will be incomplete so long as he remains a bachelor. If enquiry were made it would probably be discovered that the belief for the most part rests on a misconception. Many people still have at the back of their minds the idea that any unmarried Prince of Wales, who had a younger brother with a wife and children, would not ascend the Throne ; that the Duke of York, in fact, will be the next King in the present position of things. Other people repeat the notion, until it becomes a firm conviction, that the Prince will never, never marry. These are mistaken ideas. The second has already been corrected here. As for the first, it is enough to state that in the normal course of events the Prince of Wales, married or unmarried, will succeed to the Throne of England.

It behoves us now to bring this chapter to an end. Not without design has it been made the briefest episode in the book. In a study where the subject, whoever he may be, is still living, and in an episode which concerns the most private of all his affairs, author and reader alike should agree to stand at a respectful distance ; also to stand there for a strictly limited time, lest they outstay a welcome which, in any case, they have probably invented for themselves.

CHAPTER 15

PERSONALITY AND ATTRIBUTES

(AND SOME THOUGHTS ON THE SUBJECT OF PUBLICITY)

A note on the public and private characters of the famous. Key-
note of the Prince's character : sympathy with the under-dog.
Accomplishments. Language studies. Interest in radio,
gramophone, films and aviation. Tastes in literature, in music.
The Prince's voice and speech-delivery. The Prince and
publicity. Counsel to a future biographer.

TO point out that every public figure has had the
task of developing and establishing two separate
characters, is merely to state a platitude. Perhaps, however, it will be considered something more
than a platitude to assert that if there be any serious
inconsistency between the published and the private
characters, between the façade and the life of the building,
it is almost invariably the public's fault. For in the
majority of cases that façade has been erected by the
spectators themselves. Or rather, they choose to see in
it qualities and embellishments and a design of which,
in many cases, it gives but a shadowy suggestion. The
assertion cries out for examples. No examples shall be
given. Not that they do not come to mind fast enough.
Not that some of them do not present a rich harvest
to the student of public gullibility. But to reap that
harvest is not our present purpose. It will wait for
another occasion and, be sure of it, will not diminish in
the meantime.

The peculiar problem which confronts the spectator
who would learn something of the character of the Prince
of Wales, is that there is little apparent difference between
its public and private aspects. He will ask : is there a

catch here ? Or, is the apparent coincidence a true one ? They are questions which can be more shortly asked than answered. But a beginning can be made if the spectator will agree that a clue to the Prince's character can be found in the kind of work he has undertaken in order to do the State some service. For in making that choice there was room for a certain amount of free will. It was the path of social service that he decided to take, knowing that his chief interests lay there, and believing that his abilities would there have greatest scope. In the light of what he has accomplished in twenty years, the wisdom of that decision cannot be doubted. But had the service been undertaken with less than a whole heart, the accomplishment would have been so much the less impressive.

In one thing the public and private aspects of his character are in accord, each to each and in every part, namely, his constant sympathy with the under-dog. That is proclaimed in every branch of his work, whether for ex-service men, for the National Council of Social Service, for slum-dwellers, for the unemployed or for Toc H.[1] No other of his qualities is so deeply rooted in his very nature. Something of it was obviously show-ing in the twelve-year-old boy whom Lord Esher met, and so acutely described in his *Journals and Letters*. No one gossiped quite so well about his period as Lord Esher. This is what he wrote on one of the occasions when he was a guest of King Edward at Windsor : " We had a very lively tea last night. The kids were in high spirits, and Prince Edward as composed and clever as ever. He develops every day fresh qualities, and is a most charming boy ; very direct, dignified and clever. His memory is remarkable ; but the look of *weltschmerz* in his eyes I cannot trace to any ancestor of the House of Hanover.[2]

[1] See footnote, page 252.
[2] To Lord Esher we also owe the recording of this illuminating incident relating to the boyhood of the present Prince of Wales

That look of *weltschmerz* has not been altogether lost,
even if in a boy it must always be more fetching than in
a man. There are recent photographs of the Prince
which show very clearly what Lord Esher meant. The
look does not belie him. The sensitiveness that can be
perceived there is indeed an essential part of his make-up,
and if in the past it has accounted for his shyness and
some of his nervous mannerisms, it has also been the
soil in which the roots of his major achievements have
been embedded. The other qualities which Lord Esher
noted in the twelve-year-old boy are equally apparent
in the man of forty. When the Prince was first facing
the ordeal of public appearance and the more severe
ordeal of public speaking, the composure of his boyhood
deserted him for a time. Absent-minded preoccupation
with tie and cuffs betrayed a temporary lack of self-
confidence, especially during his speeches. But in recent
years he has regained the mastery, and has become so
much the practised speaker that many of his addresses
are now given extempore.

As for his boyhood's charm, directness, dignity and
cleverness, they have not been clouded by the intervening
years. Cleverness of the obvious kind—the cleverness
that has now become so common that we summarily
dismiss it with the word " brilliance "—that has never
belonged to the Prince. The dazzling performance, the
dubiously witty word, the smart reply, the flash in the
pan, these are not to be numbered among his accomplishments. Those who concentrate on such passing
incidents or who, having no matches or squibs of their
own, delight in admiring other people's brief displays,
will find little in common with the Prince, and little to
excite them in his career. As likely as not they would vote

and Duke of York : the two brothers were looking at a book of
photographs ; they found there one of the elder boy and, under-
neath, the words " Our future King " ; when the younger boy
pointed to the caption, his brother pushed away his finger and
quickly turned the page.

it dull, though it is a word that they should be the last to use. The Prince's cleverness appears in a more level and sustained attainment, in his campaigns for social and industrial improvement, in the ordering of his busy life, in his business abilities (to which even Americans have paid tribute), in his judgment of when to appear in the public eye and when to withdraw, and, above all, in his capacity for hard work.

The last-named attribute has been prominent throughout the Prince's career. An instance is the period during which he was learning Spanish. Under the tuition of Dr. Antonio Pastor, he studied the language with systematic thoroughness. The lessons were sometimes continued until the early hours of the morning. At other times the Prince and his tutor would dine together, while the conversation, in Spanish, would be devoted to history and points of grammar. Telephone conversations with Dr. Pastor were carried on in Spanish. In short, every opportunity was taken to become proficient in the language. Dr. Pastor's opinion of his pupil was that he had a remarkable power of concentration. He had known others to work hard at Spanish with smaller results. He has spoken well, too, of the Prince's sense of rhythm, which is so important in the study of any language. Also of his outstanding memory. With Dr. Pastor's help, for example, the Prince had prepared a speech in Spanish for a certain occasion. When the Prince arrived he saw that the company lacked those persons for whom the speech had been specially composed. So he improvised another. When he next saw Dr. Pastor, he, being anxious to know if the right things had been said, repeated the address word for word.

Of foreign languages the Prince speaks Spanish best—better than French, for example. He speaks it with the Argentine accent, a fact which may be either the result of his visits to South America or the result of plan and intention in preparing for those tours. In Dr. Pastor's opinion Spanish spoken with an Argentine accent is comparable to English spoken by educated Americans, and is no more objectionable.[1] In any case, that Argentine accent has often served the Prince's purpose.

Several of the Prince's minor accomplishments have fallen into place in the foregoing pages—his talent for telling stories whether English or Scots or American, his varying attainments in games and sports, his essays as an instrumental soloist, more especially as a piper. There is hardly any need to insist that the Prince is no high-brow. His tastes in music show him to belong to that large group which radio's benevolent despotism has brought into such great prominence, the group called ordinary listeners. Similarly, his tastes in literature are those of the ordinary reader. He finds relaxation in listening to gramophone records, particularly of new dance-tunes, and in adventure stories and detective and mystery fiction. In leisure hours, in brief, he resorts to that kind of entertainment which is called light.

Among the attributes which show the Prince to be essentially a man of his time, his easy adaptability immediately comes to mind. The early part of his manhood was a time of continually changing conditions. One technique after another arrived to be studied and mastered. Radio, the gramophone, the films and aviation, each of these made new demands and presented fresh problems. In each of these spheres the Prince gave a lead. At an early date he became acquainted with the awe-inspiring interior of a broadcasting studio and, as a result of many appeals on behalf of charities and societies, he has gradually made a friend of the unfriendly-looking microphone. Gradually, that is to say, he has acquired that technique of speaking which is peculiar

[1] That, of course, hardly represents an English point of view. How unimportant the question of American accent is regarded in Spain is seen in the fact that many Americans are employed there to teach English.

Watching the Schneider Trophy Race.

to broadcasting.[1]   Before making a gramophone record
he devotes much time and trouble to rehearsing.   In
1924 he recorded for the Gramophone Company a talk
on Sportsmanship.   This was the result of a successful
record which had been made of an Empire Day message
from the King and Queen to the children of the Empire.
It was thought that a similar record of a speech by the
Prince would greatly assist Earl Haig's fund for ex-
service men.   When the decision had been made and the
Prince's consent had been obtained, a recording apparatus
was fixed up in his study in York House.   The Prince
consulted the recording experts as to the best manner of
delivery.   They advised him to speak as if it were an
after-dinner occasion.   (The vogue for intimacy had not
yet begun.)   Even with the bland assurance of the
experts that everything would be all right, the Prince
would not embark upon the new adventure until he had
declaimed the speech several times and prepared his
points of emphasis.

One of the best records of the Prince's speaking-voice
is that which was made at the *Daily Express* Remembrance
Festival in the Albert Hall on Armistice Night, 1927.
This record, which had the advantage of the electrical

[1] Some idea of the Prince's early experience in this sphere can
be formed from the following list of his broadcast engagements
from August, 1926 to September, 1927 :

1926, August 4.	The Annual Meeting of the British Association at Oxford.
October 13.	Official welcome to the Prince at City Hall, Hull, and the Prince's reply.
1927, June 1.	The Prince made an appeal from the B.B.C., Savoy Hill, for the National Playing Fields Association.
June 7.	Opening of new wing at University College, Exeter, by the Prince.
June 28.	Speech by the Prince at the opening of the New Miners' Convalescent Home, Blackpool.
July 14.	The Prince opened the Scottish War Memorial at Edinburgh Castle.
August 7.	Speech by the Prince relayed from Canada.

process, was greatly in demand, and, as with the earlier record, the profits were handed over to Earl Haig's fund. It is of particular interest in conveying an all-but-immediate impression of the Prince's popularity among members of the British Legion. The record opens with a great roar of cheering, punctuated here and there by an individual greeting, now from a man's voice, now from a woman's. Then, in the distance, a few voices are heard singing " For he's a jolly good fellow." The first phrase has hardly ended before the whole audience has taken up the song. Then, after a silence, the Prince asks them all to sit down, and begins his address.

Whatever the occasion may be, the most distinctive quality of any speech by the Prince is the natural manner of his delivery. This speech to the British Legion is an admirable case in point. There is no rhetoric; no affectation of pronunciation; no flight of fancy. The speaking is so natural indeed that the dropped ends of some of the phrases give the manner of a communication from one man to another rather than from one to thousands. On the other hand the environment of the Albert Hall is felt in the dividing of the phrases and the pause after each division. A clipped word here and there is part of the Prince's natural manner. An echo of the hunting-field is in that manner, not only in the diction but also in the intonation. The echo can be caught in the vowel-sounds of words like *to-day*, *agree* and *time*. Yet on the whole, it can be said that the Prince, no less than his father, speaks the kind of English which is not associated with any separate class or set of people. In the particular and in the general sense, his is King's English. His voice is of a light quality and for the most part is pitched in the higher register, although he sometimes brings tones of the lower compass into play with good effect, as, for instance, in the recorded Albert Hall speech, at the end of the phrase, " he is no less our comrade and our friend to-day."

As a speaker he can conveniently be described as

" light baritone " (although he himself would hesitate to claim that distinction as a singer). He favours short sentences and plain statements. The majority of his sentences have a similar rhythmic basis—strong, widely separated points of stress and with defined pauses at the outset, then as the end of the sentence comes into sight, a quick sprint for home. He makes attention easy ; for, not only are his sentences clear-cut, not only is his language homely but also the plan of his speeches makes a virtue of brevity. In the last respect, his addresses are examples to all who, because they forget or do not know that the public speaker is a privileged person, are disposed to mock the time between the banquet's end and midnight with much windiness.

When he is reading prose or verse the Prince speaks with the same natural air as when he is delivering his own speeches. At the Festival of Empire Remembrance of 1934, he read Laurence Binyon's " To the Fallen." More than 8,000 members of the British Legion had come together in the Albert Hall, and in the semi-darkness they listened to those commemorative lines, spoken with a careful clarity, but in no sense recited. It was one of those scenes which number so many in the Prince's life ; yet it remains a separate, singular experience in the spectator's memory.

In this consideration of the Prince as a man of his time, there remains to be noted his great interest in the film industry. If he can be regarded as a performer in relation to radio and the gramophone, he can no less be regarded as such in connection with the films. His appearances on the screen have been numerous and in a variety of roles and settings. An exceptionally interesting composite film could be made of these appearances, if only an editor with imagination would devote some time to their proper arrangement. Unfortunately, the Prince has hitherto lacked good production in this respect. The existing composite film of his activities is a dull compilation, having no design and doing no justice to the panorama of his enterprise and experience. In return for the support which it has invariably received from the Prince, the least the film industry can do is to build up a chronicle of his manhood in relation to a background of national and imperial life, to build it up imaginatively that it may be both a tribute and an enlightenment.

The Prince has been a good friend to British films. In early days one of his speeches contained these words : " It is well worth the British nation's while to take the film industry seriously and to develop it to its utmost as a national industry." Since then he has attended first night after first night, welcoming every sign of development and every incident pointing to England's future as an important film-producing country. Moreover, the Prince has played a part in making the first night of a film as brilliant a social event as the first night of a play. At least such an event must be supposed to be brilliant when crowds in the street attempt to rush the cinema, as they did when the Prince attended a *première* at the Tivoli in the Strand on 30 November, 1934. Many who had come from the provinces for the wedding of the Duke of Kent and Princess Marina availed themselves of an outside chance of seeing the Prince that night. They took up their positions outside the cinema long before the performance was due to start. When the Prince's car arrived, it could hardly make way through the throng. Then, when the Prince entered the foyer between a guard of honour in uniforms of the period of the film, the crowd rushed after him and the guard of honour was discovered for what it was, a very feeble, flimsy affair, and no guard at all. Moreover, the crowd waited till the performance was over and repeated the scene ; but with less success, for meanwhile a reinforcement of police had arrived.

It must not be thought, however, that this so very social aspect of a film's first night is all. Profits derived from these occasions are often devoted to hospitals and charities. As a result of that particular *première*, for example, a sum of more than £7,500 was raised for the Reconstruction Fund of the Hospital for Sick Children, Great Ormond Street. The fact is recorded here to draw the reader's attention to the incidents attendant upon the Prince's consent to be present on such occasions. And this, in turn, is closely related to the matter we are now considering in detail, namely, his personality and attributes.

Aviation is another branch of twentieth-century progress to which the Prince has always been drawn. By temperament he is an air-traveller. Ever since his Oxford days when he was hearing of Graham-White's experiments in a hydroplane, his interest in flying has been a live one. He did not at first obtain his wish to fly, and when an opportunity came to experience a flight in a Zeppelin, bad weather at the last minute brought disappointment. But it was not long after when he was allowed to go cruising for half an hour in an English airship. Not all who have sought that experience have returned to earth with that same zeal wherewith they rose. The Prince descended with zeal increased. From that time he has been in the forefront of those who prefer to go by air. No one outside professional aviation[1] has done more to encourage that state of peculiar elation which we call air-mindedness.

From the qualities we have so far enumerated, then, two can be said to be high-lights in the whole view of the Prince's personality : his compassionate regard for unfortunate people (of which the outward sign is that look which is remarked in Lord Esher's *Journals*, and which has stayed with him since childhood) and his eagerly progressive mentality. We need search for no other than these to account for the vigour and wholeheartedness of his social service. With these in mind the " incidents " of his English and Empire journeys, the " human " incidents, lose all appearance of being in any

[1] Always excepting Lord Rothermere.

way remarkable. In the context of the Prince's day-to-day life they call for no special emphasis.

The Southern English have a habit of stressing the human side of members of the Royal Family as if it were the exceptional side; a habit of describing the Royal Family as if its members were displaying great condescension in not being condescending. It is our way of showing respect. In this we are open to criticism; for undoubtedly it is a way of make-believe. Watch the crowd at the Wimbledon centre court when the King and Queen are present. It is near enough to realise that the King and Queen are kindly human beings. It has plenty of evidence of that fact if the match is an exciting one. Yet for the most part it persists in taking an unreal view, a view in which the geniality of the King and Queen becomes a matter for continual surprise instead of one to be always assumed. In this respect, the attitude of the Northern English and of the people of the Dominions and Colonies is more complimentary by far. It is the honest-to-goodness, no-nonsense attitude which, however roughly it may sometimes be expressed, rests upon a more solid, because less sentimental, regard.

The Prince is better pleased by that attitude than by any other. But he still meets people who are unaware of his preference, or, if they are aware of it, are shy of approaching him on a strictly human basis. Here is an instance. The Prince has no greater aversion than publicity on private occasions. The majority of London theatre managers know it well, and allow him to visit their theatres without calling attention to his presence. But there are others. On one occasion the Prince, having telephoned for seats at a theatre, arrived a few minutes late that he might take his seat unobserved. He found that the manager had delayed the curtain-rise until his arrival, and as he entered the whole audience stood. Soon after the play had begun, he left the theatre as a protest. (But a few nights later he visited the play again and afterwards congratulated the leading actor on his performance.) Other similar instances are numerous and instructive enough to make a small book of cautionary tales. The tale of the railway superintendent gives perhaps the best warning of all. He was an efficient but nervous man, and had been invited to travel with the Prince over the particular section of line which he controlled. It was too much for him. Each time he was addressed, and before each of his replies, he stood and stiffly bowed, at least as stiffly as the swaying train permitted. He made the Prince as nervous as himself, and when he rose for the tenth bow, the Prince implored: " For heaven's sake, sit down. You'll be spilling your drink if you go on like that."

No view of the Prince's personality will be in perspective which does not recognise the natural ease of his manner towards everyone he meets. This, as much as anything, has accounted for the charm which people of all classes and races have found in him. Such charm as his does not depend in the least upon publicity. There is no need to remark that publicity enters into the Prince's life, that, indeed, it is a department requiring the most careful organisation and supervision. He would not be a twentieth-century Prince if he disdained to avail himself of the benefits of newspaper circulation, of radio and of the films. The point is, his charm works its end upon the public's senses, in spite of publicity's influence. For it will not have escaped the observant reader's notice that this will-o'-the-wisp called Charm has become so much rarer since we have started the vogue of advertising personality. Personality has now become a synthetic product, consisting of a good word for this skin lotion, a compliment to that cigarette, and a round of applause for so-and-so's tablets for this and that and everything. Personality is so easily manufactured: " all you have to do " is to send a photograph and sign the form. But Charm? Whither has Charm fled? Does she find advertisement shy-making? Without a doubt, she does, and rightly does. But not all publicity is blatant advertisement. The way of dignity is still open to those who prefer that way ; and in this super-advertising world, no better example of that way can be shown than that along which the Prince's publicity is conducted.

It must not be supposed that every item about the Prince which finds its way into the columns of a newspaper, appears with his consent. Gossip-writers must live, or so, for want of contrary evidence, we must suppose. And it is because of that melancholy fact that we encounter from time to time such an announcement as this : " The Prince of Wales sometimes wears glasses nowadays[1] when reading. Yesterday, when he attended the annual meeting of the presidents of the League of Mercy at the Mansion House, he was seen to be wearing tortoiseshell-rimmed spectacles to read the agenda paper and his notes. The Prince has never before been seen wearing glasses in public. The general opinion of those present was that they suited him very well. It seems he has been wearing them for very small print, but otherwise his eyesight, it was stated last night, is excellent." Or, again, such an item as this : " In a frolic with an Alsatian dog at Fort Belvedere, the Prince of Wales's Berkshire residence, the Prince's favourite Pekingese was bitten and almost lost one of her eyes. The dog was taken to a Reading veterinary surgeon and has now recovered. While the dog was convalescing, the Prince paid it several visits." Or this : " The Prince of Wales will be the next captain of the Worplesdon Golf Club, in succession to Mr. J. Murray, whose term of office expires in a few weeks. The Prince has been a member of the Worplesdon Club for many years." Or again that item (which is a kind of recurring decimal in the gossip accounts) announcing that the Prince was expected, or looked in for a moment, or stayed quite a while at the Embassy Club.

It is not that such announcements are not of interest to all sorts and conditions of people who follow the

[1] December, 1934.

At Mildenhall before the England-Australia Air Race

Prince's daily life. It is not that they do not throw side-lights upon his state of health, his affection for his dogs (which must certainly not be overlooked in an estimate of his character), his enthusiasm for golf, his relaxations and so forth. Rather should criticism be made of the way in which these items are presented by some editors, and of the want of discrimination shown in the choice of what should be prominent and what should be less prominent. Here, for example, is a paragraph which is obviously of some importance as a piece of informative news : " The Prince of Wales has cancelled his proposed visit to the Scilly Isles during his three-days' tour of the Duchy this week. The exceptionally rough weather now being experienced off the coast of Cornwall is the reason for the cancellation. The Prince is to leave London by train to-morrow night for Cornwall, where he will visit the Duchy oyster farm on the Halford River, inspect building developments at Newquay and visit his Home Farm at Stoke Climsland, near Tavistock. It is under-stood that the Prince will probably visit the Scillies later in the year." But in one important newspaper, having a large circulation in Cornwall, the information was deemed of less importance than the news that America had started a craze for jig-saw puzzles. It was even assumed that Cornish readers were far more interested in the fact that the Prince had been skating the day before on Virginia Water.

Examples of the haphazard manner in which some editors present news of the Prince are to be seen almost every day. (And, of course, only those editors who are favourably disposed are being considered here.) An instance was the report which appeared in one journal of the Prince's speech in the House of Lords at a meeting of King Edward's Hospital Fund for London (December 11, 1934). The address contained this passage : " The problem of road accidents embarrasses hospitals in two ways. The injured occupy beds which are badly needed for other purposes, and they cause heavy expense to hospital funds which are contributed for those other purposes. The number of road accidents has increased to such an extent that sometimes, especially in outlying hospitals near the big highways, they may overflow all the accident beds, with the result that, if the hospital is full, urgent local cases of the kind for which the hospital is intended, may have to be sent elsewhere." Now, to any editor who habitually regards the Prince's public activities as news, this was obviously an occasion of some importance. The problem of safe road-travel is, next to that of keeping the peace, the most acutely urgent of our time. (But from the majority of English journals published in the last months of 1934, a foreign visitor would have gathered that it was rather less urgent than the problems raised by the beacon called Belisha.) Here was the Prince commenting on that problem in relation to our over-crowded hospitals, and giving the general statement of the problem in plain terms. Yet in the journal in question (one, incidentally, that is by no means averse to reported speeches) the address was briefly quoted and cursorily dismissed.

Fortunately there are a few English newspapers whose editors are aware of a responsibility in presenting the Prince to their readers. But those others—those whose editors are hedged round about with strident advertisements—are concerned not so much with giving space as with saving it. " Space " is engraved upon their hearts. Whatever the subject may be, they never allow a reported speech to appear, except in a mutilated form. Their purpose is better served by a gossiping paragraph. They believe in what they call the personal touch. A speech, they argue, gives their readers no idea of what the Prince is " really like," whereas a glimpse of him at a night club is a revelation. A revelation! Is there anything more artificial in journalism than gossip writing? Is there anything more ignorant or more grossly misleading?

Do readers truly believe that their gay informer was

in St. James's Square (where he saw an enormous box being carried into her ladyship's car : it contained—you'll never guess—little pots of caviare for the servants on her country estate) ; in Grosvenor House for the farewell dinner to his lordship (always known as Piggy), just off to Vladivostok ; at the Grange where the hostess has been having such a busy time preparing for her step-daughter's marriage ; in Paris for the first night of *Et ses boys ;* in Berlin for the last act of *Siegfried ;* at the Seven Sisters Ball where he met his lordship (known to his friends as Tips), and danced with her ladyship to the strains of Mozart's celebrated minuet (you know the one, of course ?) ; at Standoff's poetry reading where he ran straight into Godiva Maypole and her adopted son—do they truly believe that he did all these things on the same day and night, or did them at all ? And if they do not believe one word of this frothy nonsense, why do they support the newspapers which so freely serve it to them ? Why do they allow editors to pass off as a lordly dish, so painfully obvious a fake ?

No answers to these questions are to be expected. They are among the minor mysteries of life. The purpose of raising them here is to put special emphasis upon a particular point in connection with the Prince's publicity. It is this : editors should agree together to save the Prince from the more fatuous manner of gossip-writing. No good ever came of a form of journalism which is nothing less than a system of mischievous busybodying. Often, because incidents and details have been turned and twisted, the result has been harmful. Not out of snobbery, but out of a desire to retain a grain or two of dignity in journalism, many English people—a referendum would probably show them to be in the majority—would welcome a rule forbidding reference to members of the Royal Family in columns which are specifically devoted to tattle. The Prince, for example, provides newspapers with unfailingly interesting matter in the course of his official engagements. Editors whose unending quest is to show their readers what the Prince is " really like," cannot do better than print a verbatim report of some of his speeches. Something of his personality is almost invariably reflected in them, even on the most formal occasions. His considered opinions, his outlook, his reforming ideas, his energetic spirit, his loyalty, all these can be caught in reading the more outstanding of his speeches.

Ordinary people who go about their daily business in an ordinary way, are always curious to learn what famous people are " really like." (The very fact that the two words must be enclosed in quotation marks gives some indication of the strain which is put upon them by the intensity of this contemporary quest. A new word is wanted. For the quest is being pursued in every branch of life. In literature, for example, it is clearly apparent in the biographical inquests which are being held on the characters of all the famous figures of history, and especially of more recent history. Exposures occur almost weekly. Then, these in turn are contradicted and a wholly new valuation is made. Until at length we begin to wonder if we shall ever know what these famous ones were " really like," and, indeed, if we shall ever know what our famous contemporaries, what our closest friends, what we ourselves are *really* like.) It is this curiosity among ordinary people that present-day journalism has set out to exploit. The exploitation has gone so far that the supply of available facts is hopelessly inadequate. To meet the demand, invention and fantasy are freely drawn upon.

Sooner or later the next stage will be a general disgust among these ordinary readers. It is for this reason that Newspaper Street should establish the rule suggested above, namely to mention no members of the Royal Family in any feature which can be described as gossip. Already the harm done by such features is incalculable. If they do not actually account for, at least they encourage, the acrimonious contempt for Society, in its restricted sense, that is indiscriminately felt by large numbers and groups of people everywhere in Great Britain and the Empire. That contempt and loathing have been slowly increasing throughout the years of this century. Hardly a more forceful expression of them can be found than in the writings of Alice James. There speaks the true democrat of America. Condescension from man to man was to her the unforgivable, incomprehensible sin. How angry she became when journalistic fuss was made over a royal marriage or over a Prince being kind to a fainting sentry! If these anomalies had been merely ludicrous, they would not have mattered to her so much. But they were open denials of Man's true nature. They were sacrilege.

Here is a passage in which the heat of her swiftly spreading wrath can be felt : " A monarchy to which they (the English) bow down in its tinsel capacity only, denying to it a manly movement of any sort! A boneless Church, broadening itself out, up-to-date ; the hysterical legislation over a dog with a broken leg, whilst society is engaged in making bags of 4000 pheasants or gloating over foxes torn to pieces by a pack of hounds ; the docility with which the classes enslave themselves to respectability or non-respectability, as the ' good form ' of the present day may be ; the ' sense of their betters ' in the masses ; the passivity with which the working man allows himself to be patted and legislated out of all independence ; then the profound irreconcilable in-the-bone-and-sinew conviction that the outlying regions are their preserves."

Anger so righteous and so sweeping as this is not easily understood by the normal Englishman. Yet there are thousands who share it and would give vent to it in a similar manner, if not in stronger terms ; and they are the very people whose fires of indignation are fed by loose, shamming, gay-life journalism. For this is the type of writing which insists on that tinsel aspect of royality to which Alice James refers ; and as for manliness, in any shape or form, it is studiously excluded from the picture. Yet there has never been a time when royalty's trivial side has been so completely forgotten as during King George's reign ; nor a time when its virility has been more pronounced. It has been a period demanding high ideals of service and sustained endeavours.

By the King and by his eldest son (to name only one of his family) the urgent needs of fellow-men have always been remembered. They have responded to the urgency of the call not only in times of sharp crisis, but through the harassed intervening years. They have done much to bring the idea of kingship into line with the idea of priesthood. The point was remarked at the beginning of this study, and since then the reader has had some evidence of its truth so far as the Prince is concerned. Both as heir to the Throne and as the King's first ambassador, he has played an increasingly difficult part with staunch fidelity. He has worked outside the circumscribed fields of diplomacy, and has helped to bring reforms which never could have been achieved within those areas. Direct in speech and vigorous in action, he has been a leader in many diverse movements. He has shown, too, that a human personality is compatible with the functions of a King's son, just as it is with those of the priesthood. And in all this, his peculiar problem has been to fit in his highly individual self with the context of contemporary life and its swiftly changing ideas.

An analysis of that individuality in its private aspect is outside the scheme of this book. Nor would it be a desirable thing to dissect in public a character who lives, moves and has his being among us, and, by all the laws, has still to pass through modifying phases. It is enough here to remark that the problem mentioned above has not been an easy one, for the Prince's character has a far from simple constitution. The well-defined features of quick sympathy, alertness, plain expression and honest fellowship are high-lights among qualities more subtle and elusive.

The future biographer of the Prince will need to be a psychologist of clear vision and outstanding ability. It is more than possible that misunderstanding will flourish fashionably for a time ; that a Lytton Strachey will again go just too far, and that it will be necessary to effect a balance between his extremity on the one hand and uncritical leniency on the other. But whatever the ultimate judgment, we can be certain that those high-lights of the Prince's public character will remain undimmed ; also that his humble-mindedness—such as emerged when, looking back over the years of his manhood, he confessed that he had had his failures—that this in him will not easily be forgotten. Nor will his genial sense of humour be overlooked in any just appraisement of his disposition, for humour among the English is of such great importance that many who have it not—no, not a shadow of it—will falsely assume it to win favour of their fellows. The Prince's humour, though not smart, is genuine. How genuine and incidentally, how scornful of smartness, can be judged from the impromptu talk he once gave to the boys at Rugby School.

" Those of us who think that the public school system is a very fine one," he said, " and those of you who have the good fortune to be educated under that system, will agree with me, I think, that we have sufficient sense of humour to take with a grain of salt Wellington's remark that the battle of Waterloo was won on the playing-fields of Eton. We have also, I think, got enough sense of humour to allow us to laugh at the somewhat ribald joke of the old school tie without having any of our illusions shattered at all." Could any words be more faithfully representative of normal English humour than those ? There speaks the Englishman who laughs at his own oddities, and, having done so, feels justified in holding on to them more tenaciously than ever.

In the nature of things this must remain an incomplete

biographical study. But if the author lacks certain advantages which the future biographer will be able to command, nonetheless he has had other advantages which will be denied to that other. For to be alive with his subject, to be in touch with his thoughts and interests, to feel the force of the currents of opinion and vogue which are running through the years of his life, this is much gain to the biographer. Therefore to that student of a later time, the present writer ventures to offer this counsel : if he would discover the true relation of the Prince of Wales to the times in which he lived and to the people of that period, let him study the humanitarian movements which the Prince has led and supported ; let him also apply himself to an examination of the Prince's addresses against their historical background. However fascinating he may find the task of unravelling the Prince's intimate character, he must take care not to be led into the mists of psycho-analysis, lest the finished portrait be clouded beyond recognition. If he would complete a portrait in which the little complexities have fallen into place and in which the features are clearly limned, let him concentrate chiefly upon the solid achievements of the Prince's life. And if he would lucidly show which motives were subservient and which were dominant, let him recall the outstanding examples among the Prince's public utterances and appeals, for it is often in these that his personality is resolved and made manifest.

In case this book, by any outside chance, should fall into that future biographer's hands, the author is making sure that he will be able to refer to one at least of those appeals. It was a message sent at the end of 1934 to those who had assembled for the Toc H[1] birthday festival in Leicester. Because it is so clear and vivid an

---

[1] The Morse form of T.H., the initials of Talbot House, Poperinghe, behind Ypres. During the war Talbot House was Everyman's Club. Since then the aim of the organisation has been to maintain and strengthen the original spirit of fellowship.

The King's First Ambassador

expression of the Prince's spirit of public service, it has been chosen as the final cadence of this study of his manhood.

" I have a task for you to begin this year," the Prince wrote. " Our immediate problems are still great enough, but there are at any rate some signs that the clouds are lifting. The time is coming when Toc H will be able to apply what it has learnt to the tasks of the future as well as of the present. A time is coming for the brave building of all that is best in the life of our people into a commonwealth. The long trench warfare against immediate difficulties will draw to an end, sooner perhaps than we think. For the advance, when it comes, Toc H must be ready. So I bid you think hard, this year, against the practical background of your Toc H life, what is to be the practical contribution of our movement to the future.

" And I would suggest this. The tasks that are ahead of us require not only a friendly heart and a serving hand, but an understanding mind. The business of Toc H is not to frame policies but to furnish a steady supply of men of character and wide outlook to the nation's needs in every sphere. All problems at bottom are human problems. I have often called on Toc H to serve. I call on it now to serve with its mind as well as its hand. Do not slacken your allegiance to the first two points of the Toc H Compass, Fellowship and Service, but bring them into relation with the third, Fairmindedness. Understanding comes not from the heart only but the head. To think fairly it is necessary to think straight. So I bid you rise to the increasing responsibility which Toc H ought now to face. From now onwards work as hard as ever, but, above all, think where Toc H is going, and what is going to be its contribution to the constructive tasks that lie before us.

" ' Tubby,'[1] as you all know, has been touring in

[1] The Rev. P. B. Clayton, one of the two founders of Toc H. The other was the Rev. Neville Talbot.

South Africa and the Rhodesias, and, as a result of a strenuous and exhausting campaign, he has made it possible for Toc H there to provide itself with an adequate wholetime staff. One of these has already arrived to see Toc H at home before beginning his work. While we rejoice at the success of ' Tubby's ' tour, we must all remember, before laying new burdens on him, how hard he has worked himself in 1934.

" I learn that in many cases Toc H has been studying housing and that in addition to playing its part in the general rousing of public opinion, it has found, as one always does when one studies a thing carefully, the special ways in which it can best help. Many problems confront the slum dweller moved to a new house. In some Scottish towns where the old box-bed prevails, the move entails the cost of new bedsteads. Toc H in one such place has tackled this problem. In other cases furniture has to be renewed; in others again people need friendly help in setting their new house to rights, or in overcoming the loneliness of new and strange surroundings.

" In such ways as these Toc H is bringing friendship to bear and so helping to ensure that new houses become real homes. As the back of the slum problem is broken this work again becomes more necessary than ever. It, too, must go on. This year I am not going to ask you to tackle any special new problem. Hold on to these and the other jobs you are doing for the training of youth and the helping of the unfortunate, but see that your service with each year's added experience grows in quality and effectiveness."

APPENDIX A

The Line of Succession.

1. The Prince of Wales.
2. Duke of York.
3. Princess Elizabeth.
4. Princess Margaret Rose.
5. Duke of Gloucester.
6. Duke of Kent.
7. The Princess Royal.
8. Viscount Lascelles.
9. Hon. Gerald Lascelles.
10. Princess Arthur of Connaught.

THE HOUSE OF WINDSOR

QUEEN VICTORIA = Prince Albert of Saxe-Coburg and Gotha, Prince Consort, b. 1819, d. 1861.
b. 1819, acceded 1837, m. 1840, d. 1901.

KING EDWARD VII = Princess Alexandra of Denmark, b. 1841, acceded 1901, d. 1910. m. 1863, d. 1925.

Victoria, Princess Royal, = Frederick III, German Emperor, m. 1858, d. 1901. d. 1888.

Wilhelm II, German Emperor.

Alfred, Duke of Edinburgh, b. 1844, d. 1900. = Grand Duchess Marie of Russia, m. 1874, d. 1920.

Arthur, Duke of Connaught, b. 1850. = Princess Louise Marguerite of Prussia, m. 1879, d. 1917.

Leopold, Duke of Albany, b. 1853, d. 1884. = Princess Helen of Waldeck-Pyrmont, m. 1882, d. 1922.

Alice, = Louis, Grand Duke of Hesse, m. 1862, d. 1878.

Helena, = Prince Christian of Schleswig-Holstein, m. 1866, d. 1917.

Louise, = Duke of Argyll, m. 1871, d. 1914.

Beatrice, = Prince Henry of Battenberg, m. 1885, d. 1896.

Alfred, b. 1874, d. unm. 1899.

Marie, = King Ferdinand of Rumania, m. 1893.

Victoria = m. (1st) 1894 Grand Duke Ernest of Hesse m. (2nd) 1905 Grand Duke Cyril of Russia.

Alexandra, = Duchess of Fife, m. 1913.

Arthur, b. 1883. Earl of Macduff, b. 1914.

Margaret, = Gustavus Adolphus, Crown Prince of Sweden, m. 1905, d. 1920.

Patricia, = Hon. Alexander Robert Ramsay, m. 1919.

Beatrice, = King Alfonso of Spain, m. 1909.

KING GEORGE V = Princess Mary of Teck, b. 1865, acceded 1910. m. 1893.

Louise, Princess Royal, m. 1889, d. 1931. = Duke of Fife, d. 1912.

Alexandra = Duke of Fife, m. 1896.

Ernest, Prince of Hohenlohe-Langenburg.

Victoria.

Maud, = Haakon VII, King of Norway, m. 1896.

Albert Victor, Duke of Clarence, b. 1864, d. unm. 1892.

EDWARD, Prince of Wales, b. 1894.

Albert, Duke of York, b. 1895. = Lady Elizabeth Bowes-Lyon, m. 1923.

Alexander, died in infancy.

Henry, Duke of Gloucester, b. 1900.

George, Duke of Kent, b. 1902. = Princess Marina of Greece, m. 1934.

John, b. 1905, d. 1919.

Mary, Princess Royal, m. 1922. = Earl of Harewood.

256

APPENDIX B

A SELECTION FROM THE PRINCE'S SPEECHES

" It is no exaggeration to say that future historians will look to the Prince's speeches to learn the best that can be said of the industrial, social and commercial life of his day and generation."—THE ARCHBISHOP OF CANTERBURY.

The United States and Canada—Washington, 11 November, 1919.

I regard it as a great honour to have been invited to pay this visit to the United States. I wish, indeed, that the President, whose visit to England last year I am so happy to be able to return on behalf of my father the King, had been with us here to-night. I have followed his illness with the deepest concern, and I associate myself most earnestly with the hope of his fellow-countrymen that he may soon be restored to health.

Your President is revered far beyond this country's shores, and the great world is as deeply affected as his own people by his absence from active political life. I was happy to hear a better report of President Wilson at the White House this afternoon, and hope to see him before I leave Washington.

This is Armistice Day, and it is indeed a happy coincidence to have been invited to-night to meet the representatives of so many countries which were gallantly allied in the great struggle, and so gloriously associated in the victory. I am particularly glad to be able to meet His Excellency the French Ambassador, M. Jusserand, pre-eminent amongst the diplomatic representatives accredited to this great capital, just as his country was conspicuous amongst the Allies.

As you know, I have recently been travelling in Canada, and I am the richer, since that three months' journey, by a wonderful experience. I come here, therefore, not only as an Englishman and as a representative of the British Empire, but also as a Canadian who is as intimately and personally

257

concerned as you yourselves in the life of this North American Continent. The British Empire is held together by the common aims and united sentiment of five sister-nations, all devoted to the same cause of democratic self-government.

Canada shares with the United States the splendid territories of this rich continent. She is divided from you by no physical barrier, no military line, no frontier other than a boundary guaranteed by international law and goodwill. North of that frontier we cherish our British institutions, our British form of freedom, our British allegiance to the King. South of it you cherish equally the institutions into which the American citizen is born. The forms are different, but the aim of both systems of Government is the same.

It seems to me that this example of nations dwelling side by side in a spirit of political tolerance, and human liberty, is entirely incomparable with the militarism which threatened Europe in the Great War, and is a living example of the great principles for which we gave our best in that terrible ordeal.

As a representative here of the British Empire, and also—I hope I may say—as a friend and great admirer of the American people, I reflect, with pride, that our common victory was a victory for the ideal to which we, with our institutions, and you with yours, have given practical shape upon this continent for a hundred years.

Commonwealth Banquet, Sydney, 16 *June,* 1920.

. . . When I replied to this toast at a similar gathering in Melbourne I had only just landed in Australia and so was hardly justified in saying very much. But after three weeks I am in a position to express something of what I feel about the Commonwealth. I have had a wonderful time in Victoria, but this is my first day in the capital of New South Wales, the mother-State of the Commonwealth, and I feel behind the Prime Minister's eloquent greeting the cordial welcome that this great city, Sydney, the oldest and largest in Australia, has given me to-day.

We have with us here to-night His Excellency your Governor-General, whom I wish to congratulate on his distinguished tenure of his high post during the last six years. I also congratulate the Commonwealth on the appointment of

APPENDICES

Lord Forster as the new Governor-General, who, I feel confident, like his able predecessor, will do credit to his great office. We have also with us this evening two out of your three War Prime Ministers, Mr. Hughes and Sir Joseph Cook. The only absentee is my friend Mr. Fisher, your High Commissioner in London, who was one of my hosts at a luncheon on Australia day. These were the men who expressed Australia's policy during the War. But throughout the Empire British policy was dictated by the peoples and by their spirit. Now I was able to realise the spirit of Australians, long before I came to the Commonwealth, by my close association with your gallant troops in Egypt, in Flanders, and in Belgium. I have been travelling in the Empire ever since peace was signed, and the more I travel, the more I feel what a privilege it was to see and to live with the men of the Empire at the front. The Service men of the Empire expressed two things. Firstly, they expressed the spirit of their own nations, and there was no finer body of men than those which Australia sent to represent her in the various theatres of war. But they also expressed the unity of sentiment and belief which made all the peoples of the British Empire stand together against Central Europe's challenge to freedom and right. It is very difficult to do justice to the devotion and vigour with which men of British blood fought, and to the manner in which they fought. Mere words sound pompous, and are always inadequate. But it was these men on active service who gave me my first real initiation into the spirit of the Empire, and I owe them much for that alone. I shall never forget the splendid impression which they conveyed of the force and the unity which have made the British Commonwealth of nations so living and invincible a power.

As I have said before, I have been travelling a great deal in the Empire lately. I have been seeing its people for myself. I have learnt that the British determination which won the War has everywhere been handed down by pioneer ancestors, who by sheer grit, and through their vision and judgment, have built up our British institutions in times of peace. It is quite true that the wisdom of great statesmen and the ability of great commanders have served the Empire—have saved the Empire—in ways for which we can never be too grateful. But the life of the Empire, its character and its destiny, have been made, are made, and always will be made, by its peoples, who have conducted their own affairs. When I think of Australia I am reminded of a fine saying used, I think, by the first Prime Minister of the Commonwealth, Sir Edmund Barton, whose recent loss in common with that of another great Australian Prime Minister, Mr. Deakin, I greatly deplore. Sir Edmund Barton expressed Australia's aspirations in one sentence : " A continent for a nation and a nation for a continent." I can now see with what faith and force the Australian people have taken that ideal to their hearts. You are determined that this nation shall be pure of race, and that all citizens of your Commonwealth shall have an equal chance. You have also proved in the last five years that you do not follow this ideal in selfish isolation ; you are prepared to give of your best for the King, for the Empire, and for the worldwide cause of liberty and justice. I am quite sure of one thing, that as Australia stands by the Empire, so will the Empire stand by Australia for all time.

There is another part of my experience in coming to Australia that I should like to mention. Before the War we, the nations of the British Empire, were naturally all very busy with our own affairs, and it took Germany's challenge in 1914 to make us realise how solid and indivisible we are. Our enemies had failed entirely to allow for this. They may have expected to find themselves up against a few battalions from the Dominions, but they certainly did not count on several Army Corps, and the whole-hearted participation of the Dominions was one of the factors that upset their war plans, and brought about their ultimate defeat. During my travels I have realised how deeply the roots of our common civilisation are set. It is the continuity of British methods and ideals which is their strongest point. On my way to Australia I passed sea after sea and island after island, bearing the record of our race, and calling to mind such names as Grenville, Drake, Cook and Flinders ; and when I reached New Zealand and, finally, this great Continent, I felt that I had come upon the realisation of long centuries of continuous British vision and enterprise. I am sure that no nation of the Empire can properly understand itself, or the links which bind it to other British peoples, unless it follows British history a long way back into the past.

APPENDICES

The Durbar, Delhi, 16 *February*, 1922.

. . . It is a pleasure to me to receive this welcome at Delhi, which has become the Capital of India by my father's command, and to meet to-day the representatives of those bodies which were brought into being by Royal Proclamation last year, and which were inaugurated on behalf of His Imperial Majesty by my uncle the Duke of Connaught.

It was to have been my privilege to perform those ceremonies; but circumstances prevented my taking part in them; and it is with all the greater pleasure that I at last realise deferred hopes in meeting you here to-day.

Among the members of the Chamber of Princes I shall, I know, renew many old friendships this afternoon, and form new ones. No greater proofs were needed than those furnished by our past relations, and the recent splendid efforts of the Indian Princes in the Great War, to show that at all times, whether in the days of peace or the hours of trial, the Crown can rely on the fidelity and unswerving support of the Indian Princes; but, in addition, Your Highnesses, during my tour in India, have in the most unmistakable manner impressed on me, at every stage of my journey, the great depth and strength of the tradition of loyalty in the Indian States. If I, on my part, have in a measure been able to convey to Your Highnesses the gratitude of my House for those feelings and to convince you of the confidence, trust, and esteem which His Imperial Majesty reposes in your Order, I am satisfied.

I know the high hopes which His Imperial Majesty entertains for your Chamber. May the history of the Chamber be a tale of a wider part played by your Order in the development of India, of an ever-strengthening bond of union between the Ruling Princes and the Empire, and of the steady advancement of the well-being and prosperity of the peoples of this land.

With you, Gentlemen, who are members of the Imperial Legislatures, I feel I may also claim a special tie. I come before you to-day as one who is anxious to ripen and perfect an acquaintance which has already been pleasantly begun. I have had the honour of meeting a number of the members of the Council of State and Legislative Assembly during my tour in the Provinces. My visits to the Legislative Councils in the Provinces and my talks with the members of these bodies, who look to you for example and inspiration, have taught me something of the problems lying before the Provincial Legislative Councils, and the central bodies on which you serve as representatives of the peoples of India.

In my journey through India nothing has struck me with greater force than the vastness of your task. In the aftermath of war, legislative bodies all over the world are passing through a difficult time. Even our British Parliament, with centuries of tradition and experience behind it, with all its store of gathered strength and achievement, and its firm foundation in the confidence of the people, has not found these new problems simple of solution, or these new needs easy of adjustment.

I realise how infinitely more difficult is the task before India's Imperial Legislatures which were only created last year. The vast extent of your field of labour, the complexity of interests, and the diversity of the peoples and creeds of this great country, would render your responsibilities specially onerous in any case. The journey along an untrodden road towards a new goal would, taken by itself, be no easy adventure, but in addition to these perplexities, you have the formidable burden of the new difficulties which are taxing the powers of highly trained and experienced Legislative bodies in other countries.

Gentlemen, I have heard with appreciation of the ability and sense of responsibility which characterise the debates of the Imperial Legislatures. I have been pleased to learn of the energy and patience with which you have begun your work. I sympathise with and admire—and I know that the British nation sympathises with and admires—the courage with which you are facing your work. You may count on me, as one who knows your difficulties, rightly to appraise the results, which, by the help of Providence, your good intentions and fortitude will secure. That you may be rightly guided to secure the well-being and prosperity of the peoples of India, whose interests you represent, is my earnest prayer.

World Power Conference, Wembley, 30 June, 1924.

It is with great pleasure that, as President of the British Empire Exhibition, I now welcome the delegates who are assembled in session to discuss the many vital problems connected with the first World Power Conference. I feel this to be an occasion of great importance, for it may prove the beginning of a series of conferences, whereby the combined knowledge and judgment of the world may be devoted to the solution of the many difficulties confronting, not only science and research, but also economic progress throughout the world. We have become accustomed to the idea of an international clearing-house for many things, and in the League of Nations, with its Labour Office and International Court of Justice, have seen international co-operation at work in political and labour questions and in law ; but the deeper questions connected with industrial progress and equipment, with natural resources, with the conservation of energy and of fuel, with standardisation in design and manufacture, have hitherto, I believe, been examined by each country in isolation, with results that are apparent to everyone. In this effort to create for industry, and especially power, what the League of Nations intends for politics, lies, I think, the true significance of the World Power Conference, and in the belief that something more fundamental than merely technical discussions will result, I extend a cordial welcome to the distinguished representatives here to-day.

The study of power, if we consider only the technical aspect, is still in a comparatively elementary state ; no effort has hitherto been made to find out on what foundations our present industrial structure is built, and what part power plays in this structure. It is difficult to conceive any modern industry where power in some shape or form does not play a part. Power, whether in the form of steam, gas, oil, water or electricity, is the one great instrument in the possession of man by which he is capable of extracting from nature everything of value that nature can offer, and of converting this natural wealth into something of immediate use. As one expert says : " The social structure itself is in a sense bound up with the effective use of power for industrial purposes, and there are many reasons to support the view that the weakness of the social structure in an industrial State is due to inefficient or inadequate utilisation of power."

You are all familiar with the main objects of the World Power Conference, and have each in your own degree contributed to our knowledge of certain aspects, so that it is unnecessary for me to discuss the matter in detail; but there is one consideration which has specially appealed to me. You each represent the views of the main countries of the world on certain questions relating to power. Though your individual views may not necessarily coincide, the mere fact of discussion, in an atmosphere of cordial appreciation, must do much to tighten those personal contacts which form the inspiring motive of progress in every great activity connected with the modern industrial State, in finance as well as in science and in research. All three, finance, science and research, are universal, but the utilisation of the results derived from those three activities is not universal, and in this disparity lies one of the greatest obstacles to progress. We should find inspiration in the vision of over thirty countries here contributing, each in its highest capacity, to the discussion of one subject of more than merely temporary importance. You are at grips with fundamentals, and from your deliberations will result the first enunciation of a policy applied internationally, which may contribute very largely to the harmony and economic progress of the world.

You have before you, in the reports submitted to the World Power Conference, the raw material for a survey of the power resources of the world; you can now explore many countries which have hitherto been veiled in mystery, and assess at their true value the possibilities of an immense industrial development in many of them; you may from this material erect the structure which will go beyond the confines of one country, or group of countries, and include all those parts of the world where man can hope to prosper. International co-operation may emerge from the realm of the ideal, into the realm of practical utilisation, as the result of your deliberations, and I sincerely trust that full success will attend them.

Farmers' Union, Leicester, 25 February, 1925.

The toast which I am going to ask you to drink is " Prosperity to Leicestershire Agriculture and to Fox-hunting." It seems almost a case of bringing coals to Newcastle, for all fox-hunters are united in wishing prosperity to the farmers, whose goodwill makes the sport possible, and I think all my friends who farm in Leicestershire will have no hesitation in wishing long life to fox-hunting in their county—a county which for so many years has been identified with the finest sport in the world.

The Minister of Agriculture is sitting within a few yards of me, and, as I look round the room, I see the critical eyes of more than one M.F.H. fixed on me. In the presence of so many experts I am not going to lecture you on either farming or fox-hunting. We have all been told, when we were young, never to try to "teach our grandmothers to suck eggs," and it is a very sound maxim.

But at this gathering, which is so representative both of Leicestershire farming and Leicestershire hunting-men, I do want to say this : that I am very grateful to all those connected with the county who, during the past two seasons, have made it possible for me to enjoy such wonderful sport ; to those farmers whose land I have ridden over, and to those responsible for the many packs of hounds in the neighbourhood. It has been the greatest possible boon for me to be able to come down here and to enjoy, in the very heart of England, the best and healthiest of English sports. When I leave this country at the end of March it will be with the recollection fresh in my mind of many good days in the open air, many fine hunts, and many pleasant friendships formed in the hunting field. For this I can assure you I am very grateful, and I hope sincerely that all of us here may enjoy many more such runs together.

We shall only do so if the relations between fox-hunting and Leicestershire agriculture remain as friendly in the future as they have been in the past. It is in the belief that they will do so that I ask you to drink this toast—" Prosperity to Leicestershire Agriculture and Fox-hunting."

Dinner given by Joint Houses of Parliament, Capetown, 2 May, 1925.

I find it hard to put into words my appreciation of the welcome you extend to me on my arrival in South Africa on behalf of the Parliament of the Union. I appreciate its cordiality all the more because it comes to me in the name of all parties, in the name of representatives of distant constituencies scattered throughout this great land, whose local interests may perhaps force them to face their own problems in their own particular way, but who are all animated by the spirit of free government and conscious of one single purpose, the welfare of the Union of South Africa.

Many of these places I hope to visit in the next few months, and I need not assure you, gentlemen, how greatly I am looking forward to my tour.

At this early stage I am hardly competent to make any remarks about South Africa. Indeed, I was—though I am no longer—rather alarmed at the thought of having to address this distinguished gathering so soon after my arrival; but you have already made me feel that I am no stranger here, and if the wonderful welcome that I have received, not only here to-night, but ever since I landed in Capetown, is a foretaste of what awaits me throughout my tour I can assure you that I shall feel very much at home, and that I shall leave these shores, at the end of July, with feelings of regret, but with a deep and lasting affection.

During the last five years it has been my privilege to visit all the great Dominions. I have reached South Africa a little late perhaps, but I am genuinely delighted to be here. Some of you may question why I have not visited South Africa sooner. The answer to that is not one for me to give, but when your High Commissioner entertained me at luncheon just before I left London it was plainly pointed out to me that I had reserved the best till the last.

The visits which I have already made to the other Dominions have helped me to realise the great development in the constitutional status of the various self-governing parts of the British Commonwealth which has taken place since the War. That development was strikingly marked by the separate signature of the Peace Treaties by the Representatives of the Dominions and by their inclusion as members of the League of Nations. Anyone who has followed the history of the period since 1919 will realise that development is going on all the time, and that the full conception of what is meant by a Brotherhood of free nations such as ours is still being worked out.

I realise that the welcome which you extend to me is in recognition of the fact that I come to you as the King's eldest son, as Heir to a Throne under which the members of that

APPENDICES

Commonwealth are free to develop, each on its own lines, but all to work together as one. No Government can represent all parties and all nations within the Empire, but my travels have taught me this, that the Throne is regarded as standing for a heritage of common aims and ideals, shared equally by all sections, parties and nations within that Empire.

As I have made mention of the League of Nations, I would like to refer to the important position which your Government holds in the League as exercising the mandate for the great territory now known as South-West Africa. That mandate, as you know, was conferred to be exercised on behalf of the King by the Government of the Union. Unfortunately, time will not permit of my visiting South-West Africa and seeing the work which has been accomplished there since the War, but I shall always watch with interest the progress of the territory under the administration for which your Government has accepted responsibility. Although I cannot visit South-West Africa, it is my hope that the tour, which has been planned with such care and foresight, will enable me to see as much as possible of all sections of the community, thus helping me to an increased knowledge of the Union, its life, its problems and its boundless possibilities.

Understanding can only be achieved by the frequent exchange of visits between members of the nations of the Empire. I am very glad that the delegates of the Empire Parliamentary Association were able to come to South Africa last year. The valuable results which follow from personal interchanges of ideas cannot be overestimated. Perhaps I might quote the words used by the King in his reply to the address from the last Imperial Conference in 1923, where he refers to the immense value of such meetings : " First comes the spread of mutual knowledge of the conditions obtaining in all parts of the Empire, then the increase of good feeling that springs naturally from such knowledge, and lastly the hearty desire to co-operate in strengthening the bonds which unite us, so that, however distracted the world may be, the British Commonwealth shall stand steadfast and undismayed."

If my visit to South Africa serves in any degree to add to our mutual knowledge and co-operation I shall be content. . . .

THE KING'S FIRST AMBASSADOR

President's Banquet, Buenos Aires, 17 *August,* 1925.

It gives me the greatest pleasure to take this the first public opportunity of expressing to Your Excellency, and through you to the Argentine nation, the sincere gratification with which the King received your cordial invitation that I should visit the Argentine Republic. For my part, not only do I feel profoundly grateful for the opportunity which has thus been afforded me of becoming acquainted with a land which, to us in England, is associated with adventure, progress and vast material resources, but also I rejoice to think that your invitation has been inspired by the ties of traditional friendship and mutual interests which link together our two nations.

Your Excellency has welcomed me to the Argentine in expressive words for which I thank you most heartily, convinced as I am by my reception to-day that they interpret the real feeling of the Argentine people. From the moment of landing on your shores I have received such a warm-hearted welcome from the citizens of Buenos Aires as will always remain in my memory, one for which no words can adequately express my appreciation. I now understand the reality of the traditional Argentine greeting to a friend, " Esta en su casa."

I consider myself fortunate, while the vivid experiences of my tour through South Africa are still fresh in my mind, to be enabled to pay a similar visit to the southern part of the American continent—both new lands with different problems to solve, but both working confidently for human progress and civilisation. This note in Your Excellency's speech of the confidence of the Argentines in the future is particularly refreshing and stimulating in these times of vague apprehensions and disturbed economic conditions. It provides a message which I will take from the New to the Old World. Your confidence is obviously justified, based as it is on liberty and goodwill to all men, the ideal of the Argentine nation.

Your Excellency has described, in words which will find a response of gratitude in every British heart, the services which it has been the privilege of the British to render in relation to the formation and growth of the Argentine Republic. For my part, I am struck with the lavish return which the progress of Argentina has made to the economic welfare of Great Britain. She has contributed bounteously to our food supplies and raw materials, has offered a field of investment for British capital and enterprise, has given countless opportunities for the exercise of the pioneering spirit of our men of business, and lastly has provided homes and livelihoods for the thousands of our fellow-citizens who have been attracted to this land of equal opportunity.

To these strong ties of reciprocal material benefits Your Excellency has added an appreciation of the spiritual influences which British customs may have had on Argentine life. I like to think, as an Englishman and a lover of sport, that the remarkable enthusiasm for athletic sports which has spread throughout the Republic within the last ten years is destined to have a great effect upon the character of the Argentine race. We British are firmly convinced of the beneficial influence of sport, and I venture to predict that it may lead to more intimate understanding and sympathy between future generations of Argentine and British.

This year has seen the celebration of the centenary of the Treaty of Amity and Commerce between the United Provinces of the River Plate and His Britannic Majesty. The signature and ratification of this Treaty, in the year 1825, inaugurated relations of friendship and commercial intercourse between our respective countries which have continued uninterruptedly through the course of a hundred years—surely a notable episode in the history of any two nations—relations which we all hope will be prolonged to the next and succeeding centuries. It is the happiest coincidence which has enabled me to visit your hospitable land in the year of the commemoration of the centenary of the Anglo-Argentine Treaty, to bring to the Argentine nation on that occasion the cordial greetings of the King and of the British people, and to assure you that the confidence of the British, which accompanied your early struggles to nationhood, is assured to you undiminished in the great destinies which await you.

The King and Queen still retain the happiest memories of Your Excellency's visit to London in 1922, and desire me to convey to you and to Madame Alvear their heartiest greetings, their wishes for your health and happiness, and for the welfare of the nation which you so worthily represent.

THE KING'S FIRST AMBASSADOR

At the Albert Hall, 27 *January,* 1932.

I find my task to-night in addressing this great gathering anything but an easy one, but we start on common ground, for we are all, young and old, seriously perplexed by the many problems that confront us and are all equally anxious to do what we can to help our country in a time of need. I do not pretend for one moment to be able to offer any concrete solution of our difficulties. I propose merely to speak in general terms with the hope of suggesting to you some lines of thought which you can carry away to-night.

I believe there exists in many minds a feeling that while our troubles are largely due to outside causes, they are not due to these alone—that while political and economic changes may be effective to avert financial disaster, they cannot in themselves ensure a true and sound growth of our national life. There is, too, I think, a certain doubt whether the social progress of recent years has not perhaps been rather superficial —a feeling that, just as many a fine-looking house may conceal a load of mortgage or hire-purchase debt, so the better material conditions that have been won may not represent any very solid gain.

Now if financial sacrifice is required people will face it, as they are doing without a murmur to-day ; if reorganisation of industry is demanded, people will seek to carry it through. But they will have no real confidence that these measures alone will secure what is best in life. They are looking for a positive aim, and that aim is, I think, to be found in the realisation that each man must, and can, work out his own salvation in common service. Whatever the coming years may hold of hardship and difficulty, we can win through triumphantly if only we will recognise that the future lies in our own hands. By all means let the State do all for us that it can, but it cannot do much more than give us conditions in which our individual task is made easier, and neither the State nor anyone else can relieve us of that task.

For this reason you should not think of social service purely as State action—such as education, public health, insurance, old age pensions, and so on—nor only as the wonderful voluntary work which is being done in connection with countless good causes throughout the country. Let us think of it rather as kindliness between man and man, as mutual understanding, as all those acts of unselfish devotion that can be done, and indeed are being done every day, by thousands of people without one thought of material gain or personal advancement.

No country in the world has developed its social services to the extent that we have, or devotes so much money to their provision and efficient performance. But we cannot ignore the fact that the present financial stringency may have to result in some curtailment—that the high level will fall unless we can make good by an increased individual effort. Then, too, the wide provision of State social services has perhaps lessened in some of us the sense of the need, the duty, of personal service, and has encouraged a tendency to take all these things for granted—encouraged a readiness to receive without at the same time inculcating that readiness to give which is the only justification for the privileges of citizenship. We must realise that the amenities of life, like its essentials, are best secured by the personal effort and individual contributions of every member of the community, and are not a sort of heaven-sent manna to be garnered and enjoyed without effort, service, or obligation.

There is an enormous call at the present time for personal service—a call that is increasing. Almost every good cause needs the time and personal effort which each one of you can give, and there is some place, however small, where your services can be of real use and worth. So do not stand aside and leave it to others, for the opportunities are at your threshold, in every town and village, wherever you may happen to live. The tasks are there, and every one of us can play a part, for the race is not necessarily to the swift nor the battle to the strong.

I know, of course, that many of the elder section in this great gathering are already devoting much of their spare time to voluntary service, but I have to-night a wider audience— the vast audience listening-in beyond this hall. There are many who, in these times, have to work harder for a living, whose day's toil is more exacting and who have less leisure to give. But every member of the elder generation can be a partner in a joint enterprise—in the promotion of youth's opportunity—to see that every boy and girl in this country should have a fair chance. Let each one of us ask of himself what he is doing, or is prepared to do, to give them that chance.

We meet in a time of national anxiety, but let us also say, taking strength from the past, that it is a time of national opportunity, when the traditions we inherit should be more than equal to the need. Emerson wrote, a good many years ago, that he found the Englishman to be him of all men who stands firmest in his shoes ; and I am sure that is true of the rising generation of to-day.

It was not your fault that there was a war. It is not your fault that there is now a world crisis. But do not congratulate yourselves just because in these things you are blameless. Better to realise that you alone are the ones to repair wrongs, to do those things that have been left undone. And it is not going to be easy.

There is a danger that some people are, so to speak, getting too used to the present critical situation. They read of it daily in the newspapers, find it all very complicated, but feel that, somehow, sooner or later, things will all come right again. It is no use waiting for that doubtful thing—a good time coming. We have got to fight to keep England " a bulwark for the cause of men," to keep our great heritage in trust for those that come after. It has been said that the most hopeless hour in national history has always been the most hopeful, because it is precisely the moment which calls forth the best and the bravest in the soul of our nation.

We have before us to-day a world sick with fearful doubt, weary with repeated disappointments, a world of troubled nations whose vital need is courageous faith in each other. It is an era of potential plenty, when confidence should be supreme, yet we see in almost every land widespread distress and perplexity. The War-time generation still doubts, is still seeing through a glass darkly, and here lies youth's opportunity. For you have it in your power to confront every obstacle with boldness and originality, with the faith which means to triumph, and to encourage and invigorate those who may be older than you in years and experience.

Youth cannot long remain a spectator of life : it will only be a short time before the work of the world will be placed on your shoulders to carry. Many tasks wait for your help :

knowledge to be discovered, open spaces to be peopled, natural resources to be developed, sickness to be conquered, and wrongs to be righted. With these high quests before you, you will realise that the mere acquisition of material things is not in itself the fulfilment of an individual or a national purpose, and is as little compared with the satisfaction derived from your own effort, especially when that effort advances human welfare and happiness.

I want you to understand that we are not just facing a few months of " grin and bear it," but that we must get into training for a long period of work—hard work and effort sustained despite possible discouragements. You must be prepared, as others have been before, to enlist " for the duration," without asking how much may in the long run be required of you.

You cannot hope to influence directly the trend of international affairs, but close at hand is a domestic problem, vast and baffling if looked at in the mass, though easier to help when broken up into individual pieces. It is made up of men and women, boys and girls. I am, as you will have guessed, thinking of unemployment. I am thinking now neither in terms of economics nor of politics, but of each member of the unemployed population as a single, separate personality, beset by depression, labouring under a sense of frustration and futility—a blank wall in front of him which he can neither climb over nor scramble round. My appeal here is not to statesmen, nor even to philanthropists, but to all those who are in work to play the part of neighbour and friend to the man out of work. That is the open road of duty and a short cut to happiness all round. There is no central machinery here in London that can provide a substitute for the good neighbour.

The enemy to-day is depression and apathy. Let us attack them with two of our old-fashioned characteristics—good sense and good humour. I believe there are groups of the unemployed here and there, dead sick of prolonged idleness, who are themselves feeling out towards ways of giving their unhired labour in co-operative effort for the help of others in need. It is up to us to back such attempts with every possible support. Get together wherever this burden lies heaviest, face up to the most urgent local need, and see if the community on the spot cannot make its own self-directed contribution towards this vast problem. So far as is humanly possible let us break it up into little pieces and refuse to be browbeaten into paralysis by its size. I am talking, I repeat, neither on the economic nor on the political plane, but on the humane plane of simple friendship in those places where the clouds are darkest, where the pits are closed or the furnaces damped down. What matter if some trifling blunder is committed here or some project fails there. The very attempt of the community to achieve some social betterment for the sake of the workless in their midst will lift the general level of hope and make easier every national solution by statesmen and economists.

Of much that I have spoken to you to-night we Englishmen find it difficult to put into words. But the things of which I have been speaking are present in many minds to-day up and down the country, and we want the subconscious thoughts to become concrete, and to take concrete form in action and life.

The world passed into a new age with the end of the Great War. Never was a new age born in greater agony, nor in a more difficult environment for healthy and normal growth. What we make of it as a democracy is of vital concern not only to ourselves, but to the whole world. So far as my part is concerned, many paths in life are closed to me : much that I would like to do I cannot. But I have tried to bring more closely together the people of the Empire, the English-speaking peoples, and to further our interests abroad. I have had my failures, I know ; but in these years, with few precedents to guide us, to have no failure is to have attempted nothing.

Let me make it quite clear that I am not asking anyone to launch yet another organisation. Far from it. The message that I have tried to give you is a threefold one. First, for a fresh response to national service ; for a greater spirit of un-selfish and adventurous helpfulness in the midst of problems which our ablest men find difficult to unravel. The second point is that the opportunity for service is at our door—in our own village, in our own town. And my third and last point is this : That depression and apathy are the Devil's own ; they are not English, so away with them !

Many great audiences have filled this hall, many great

causes have been pleaded from this platform. But never, I am confident, has there been such a gathering, of both young and old, eager to help in the service of their fellow-men. Let us make ourselves fit for that service and dedicate ourselves to it to-night.

At the Livery Dinner of the Worshipful Company of Stationers and Newspaper Makers, 15 November, 1934.

In my capacity as Master I want to thank the Archbishop of Canterbury for the very notable and very interesting speech which he has just made. As one who has listened to a great many after-dinner speeches I would personally like to congratulate him, and to express my thanks for his very kind references to myself.

It is a pleasure to welcome here so many distinguished representatives of foreign and friendly countries. I think that if the Archbishop of Canterbury had been brought up as a diplomat he would have told a white lie this evening, and instead of saying that he had overheard me talk Spanish to the Brazilian Ambassador he would have said that he had overheard me talk Portuguese. The Livery Companies of the City have always been renowned for their hospitality, and if happily this is not extended nowadays in quite the lavish style, not only as regards the food, but as regards the list of speeches, which prevailed in the past, an occasion like this to-night gives us an opportunity to repay to Their Excellencies the hospitality, both official and private, which so many of us, and I speak from experience, have so often enjoyed on our travels abroad.

Though we are not calling on them to speak, I feel sure that Their Excellencies have been fully primed by efficient secretaries as to the nature and the function of this Worshipful Company. I would remind them that we were founded early in the fifteenth century for the protection of the manufacturers and vendors of books, and that quite lately by a happy amalgamation we now concern ourselves with the protection of newspaper makers as well.

You may rightly ask, what is the nature and extent of the protection demanded nowadays by publishers and Press ? I sometimes feel that the boot should be on the other foot, and that it is the public who needs protection against the flood of printed matter that is daily and hourly poured upon its defenceless head. One has only to pick up any newspaper at any hour of the day or night, or turn the pages of any publisher's list, to realise that of the making of many books there is still no end, and the weekly output of printed matter from Fleet Street involves one in figures as regards weight and mileage that are astronomical in their proportions.

Protection, indeed! Has there ever been a freer trade? I sometimes wonder what happens to all these thousands of books, what happens to these tons of newsprint. I have always been the first to encourage a " growing industry," and even if some of the books remain unread, if some of the newspapers are returned unsold, at any rate binders, printers, and many others must have been employed in their production, which in these days is all to the good.

Seriously speaking, we have little to complain of. With all this uncontrolled spate of printed matter one might be inclined to favour the idea of " restriction of production," an economic theory of which we hear a certain amount these days, but restriction of any kind in regard to a genuine expression of opinion, however extreme, is, I am glad to say, entirely contrary to our belief and to our traditions. We should be thankful that in this country we enjoy freedom of opinion, freedom of discussion in our books as well as in our speech, and that we can point with pride to a free Press.

This company has in the course of a long and varied history done much, both on the technical and the benevolent side, for the craft with which it is identified. I am very proud to be your Master, and I am fortunate, too, in having now as my deputy one whose name is associated with the best traditions of Fleet Street, whose experience will, I know, be of the greatest value in the councils of this company. Mr. Blumenfeld, I feel sure, needs no introduction to Your Excellencies. Though chiefly known to us as a newspaper maker, the publication not long ago of his entertaining memoirs gives him double right to his place here as a " manufacturer of books." He is, as I have said, Deputy Master, which means that he is going to do all the work, and I am sure you will agree that it could not be in more capable hands.

I thank you once again, My Lord Archbishop, on behalf of the Company for having proposed the last toast, and assure our distinguished guests how very pleased we are to have had them with us to-night.

Centenary Dinner of the Royal Institute of British Architects, 22 November, 1934.

. . . I ask you to carry the principle of mass production over to architecture and the building trades. I am convinced that in no other way will it be possible to raise the living conditions of the great majority of our people. They should have better conditions, and they can have them by these means. I am sure that the principles of mass production can be applied to housing, and I am equally sure that you can do it, and that you will be able to overcome any barriers of prejudice that may exist.

The meanness of our narrow, twisting streets is the major cause of two great evils—the congestion of transportation on the one hand, and our lack of civic pride on the other. You could develop the idea of widening the streets and raising the height of buildings so that they could be spaced at greater distances from each other, which would tend to greater openness and less congestion. I feel very strongly about this. We could make areas which no vehicles except fire engines or the trucks that collect refuse could enter, so that you would get an area with houses farther apart. In other words, we should take a bigger and more generous outlook on the planning of our cities, following the trend of our times, which is to have less of the limited group of individuals and more of the national point of view.

Modern science has produced and improved all those various architectures and devices which make for greater help and comfort in the home. And our great industrial and commercial concerns, like the motor-car manufacturers and the great multiple stores, have shown how, by mass production, amenities of life can be produced attractively at low costs, whereas formerly they were only for the well-to-do. Perhaps, the same principles can be applied to housing. You may at first find it difficult in designing a building to keep it good to look at from the outside and yet give the housewife the

comfort that she is entitled to inside. I think this difficulty
lies in the fact that as artists you have been devoting your
time to the consideration of the abstract ideal, which is good
in itself when you are considering only the individual client.
You must give consideration to another—a greater and more
important—ideal, designed and working for the great majority
of our people, instead of studying the needs of the minority,
which is ever dwindling. You all know how concerned I am
for the living conditions of the great masses of our people,
and how anxious I am to see them improved as quickly as
possible. My visits to the distressed areas and the slums of
great cities have impressed on me the urgent necessity for
rebuilding these areas. The housing of the great industrial
groups in our country has not been too well considered in
the past, and in your study of this problem I would ask you
to include along the same lines the schools and buildings in
which they are reared as children and the hospitals in which
they are treated when they are sick.

In other words, the problem is the planning and arrangements of our towns and cities. To-day we are not the race
of individuals which we were in Victorian and Edwardian
times. We are now living—mostly because of the results of
the World War—in a world which is more collective in principle than individualistic. Wealth is more evenly distributed
throughout the country than it has ever been, and the interest
of professional men, in common with the interest of commercial men, is being directed to a greater consideration of
the mass of the people, and their requirements, than it is to
the individual client or more selective group we commonly
call Society.

*Opening of the Royal Academy Exhibition of British Art in
    Industry, January 4, 1935.*

. . . This exhibition is a new departure. Most winters
the Royal Academy shows us art treasures of the past; this
year it is showing British modern arts and crafts and giving
expression to the thought and ideas of to-day. The exhibition
is backed by the prestige of two great societies, and its object
is to prove that the British manufacturer, in co-operation with
British artists and designers, can produce in all branches of

industry articles which combine artistic form and utility with sound craftsmanship.

There is no need to dwell on the achievements or the deficiencies of the past. We have always been able to produce some very good things, but with the fierce competition in the world to-day we need to explore every means of producing better and more attractive things. I think that this exhibition will give the public an idea of what can be produced to-day, and I think that the results are decidedly encouraging. Naturally, there will be criticism. Some manufacturers whose wares or whose exhibits have been rejected by the Selection Board will complain and criticise. I personally am very much relieved to think I was not on that committee. And then the public—as is always the public's right—will criticise some of the exhibits. But if those criticisms are well founded they will serve the useful purpose of drawing attention to any deficiencies, and, knowing our manufacturers, they will hasten to make good these deficiencies.

Unlike the previous winter exhibitions of the Royal Academy, this one does not aim at providing æsthetic enjoyment for the select few. Its object, put simply, is to show the public many attractive and, in frequent cases, inexpensive articles which British industry can produce for them to enjoy in their daily life. But the public will have to show a real and genuine interest in the improvement of industrial products—improvement of the design as well as of utility and attractiveness—to make it worth while for the manufacturers to go on producing those articles. Only by showing this interest will the public be able to obtain in the future the classes of articles which they will see in the galleries. It is by the attendances at Burlington House these next few weeks that the manufacturers will measure the success of the exhibition and be correspondingly encouraged or disheartened.

Here I should like to thank the Press for the generous support they have already given us in this great venture. They have realised that the exhibition has been organised without any idea of gain, but for the good of British industry as a whole and the British public as consumers. We who are so closely identified with the exhibition ask the newspapers to continue their valuable support, and we shall be most grateful to them if they will do so.

(In conclusion the Prince paid tribute to the Royal Academy and the Royal Society of Arts for their part in bringing the exhibition into being.)

A Send-off Dinner to Empire Press Union Delegates, 17 *January*, 1935.

The Prince, who presided, toasted the Fifth Imperial Press Conference. He began by remarking that at the first of those conferences the Earl of Rosebery made what was regarded as one of his best speeches, and added : " I am one of a younger generation who never had the opportunity of hearing Lord Rosebery. In that speech he reminded his audience that there had been many important conferences before that—conferences at which Prime Ministers and statesmen of the Empire had met and consulted on great matters of Imperial policy. Lord Rosebery admitted the deepest respect for Prime Ministers and Ministers, but he said that, whatever their splendour when in the ascendant, they were essentially transient bodies, whereas good newspapers were—or should be—eternal. The power of great newspapers in guiding and embodying public opinion was immeasurably greater than that of any statesman could ever be."

Referring to Major Astor and Mr. J. H. Thomas, the Dominions Secretary, the Prince went on : " As I am sitting between a newspaper proprietor and a statesman I am hardly in a position to give an opinion on the matter. I am only quoting the words of a former Prime Minister. The success of that first Imperial Press Conference was so great that it was decided to hold a second one, but owing to the War the second one was not held until 1920, when the delegates met at Ottawa. The third was held at Melbourne, again under the leadership of the late Lord Burnham, and five years ago it met in London, under the able presidency of Major Astor. That year, 1930, was an important year. The Empire Chambers of Commerce were in session, and a very important Imperial Conference was taking place, and I feel that that Press conference gave the delegates an opportunity of studying in this capital aspects of Imperial problems outside their own particular and personal ones.

To-morrow you are leaving for the fifth of these great

conferences. I think the United Kingdom delegation is very fortunate in again having Major Astor as its leader. I, personally, know nobody who can better combine a charming personality and sound judgment with a very great deal of experience.

The Press of the Empire has a great tradition in its support of the King and his peoples, quite apart from any personal affiliations. ' The power of the Press ' is a saying with which we are all familiar, and it is a saying that is becoming truer every day. Your power, and the power of your newspapers, is immense, and it is no exaggeration to say that you can mould public thought and opinion to almost any shape you please. So we are confident, those of us who are looking with expectant eyes to this Conference, that it will result in an even truer moulding of opinion, and in giving a clearer conception throughout the world of British enterprise, British commerce, and British ideals, and what this great Commonwealth of Nations stands for. I also think the Empire Press Union made a wise provision in holding this Conference at the important centres of the Empire, and because it has flourished for twenty-five years it is a very happy coincidence that you should be going to South Africa this year, where they are celebrating the twenty-fifth anniversary of the Union as we know it to-day. I have tested South African hospitality, and so I know from personal experience how generous they can be, not only in South Africa, but also in the two Rhodesias. I cannot prophesy the trend of gold shares during your stay, or whether some of you, while on the Rand, will try to share in this prosperity, but those who go will return richer for the knowledge of the wonderful country, and for the contacts you will establish during a conference with your colleagues from other parts of the Empire. You will meet two very important and interesting men—General Hertzog and General Smuts—to whose clear vision and wise statesmanship South Africa owes recent developments.

We of the Company of Stationers and Newspaper Makers wish you all a very pleasant and enjoyable trip, success in your deliberations, and a safe return."

THE KING'S FIRST AMBASSADOR

Appeal at St. James's Palace for "King George's Jubilee Trust,"
  1 *March,* 1935.

I can think of no cause that would make such a national appeal as the cause of the younger generation. We have all been young ourselves, and I have ascertained that nothing else would give the King and Queen such pleasure as the devotion of a national thank-offering to the welfare of the rising generation.

I shall invite subscriptions to be sent to me here. Many will no doubt contribute direct, but I want to make it easy for every one to contribute who desires to do so—pennies as well as pounds. So I invite you to help me by opening local subscription lists for the fund.

I propose later to form a committee to help me in framing exact proposals for submission to the King. But I can tell you now the general lines of what I have in mind. I have realised from my own first-hand experience the wonderful progress which has been made in the King's reign by the health services over which so many of you preside. But in common with you all, I am concerned for boys and girls after they have left school, during that difficult time up to the age of eighteen.

Young people need three things to fit them for life—discipline, friends and recreation. These three gifts are in our power. They will help youth to master the means of making life worth while. Whether in or out of employment the boy or girl who is facing life for the first time needs some provision for a fruitful leisure.

I am told that there are more than half a million boys alone between fourteen and eighteen, drifting into manhood without an outlet or without an opening for their natural high spirits and ambitions ; many indeed without the space for the essential boons of recreation and exercise.

Such organisations as clubs, Scouts, Guides, and many others, are helping boys and girls to grow up with just those qualities that make a nation great ; those ideas of mutual service and physical, mental and spiritual fitness.

We do not want to aim at uniformity or to limit freedom of idea and action. I do not want to start a new organisation, but I should like the Trust to assist in the local extension of these existing movements throughout the country. The Trust could help these bodies to equip leaders. It could

APPENDICES

help them to increase facilities for physical recreation and games ; for the practice of hobbies, the pursuit of interests, and the cultivation of abilities which, in so many boys and girls, only await their outlet ; and for the extension of camping and other forms of healthy holidays.

I ask you to join with me in doing all that is possible to make this Jubilee not only a time of thanksgiving for the past twenty-five years, but the beginning of a future in which, to ever greater extent, the rising generation will be given a better chance.

INDEX

INDEX

C

Cairo, 180, 205
Calcutta, 83
Calcutta, H.M.S., 194
Calgary, 99
California, 66
Cambridge, Lady May, 194
Cambridge, Princess Mary of, 229
Canada, 52 *et seq.*, 74, 96 *et seq.*, 164, 165, 167, 219, 237 *n.*
Canterbury, Archbishop of, 143, 152 *et seq.*
Capetown, 166 *et seq.*, 193, 194, 213
Carlyle, Mr., 97, 98, 99
Carnarvon, 24
Chalmers, Mr. Patrick, 191 *n.*, 201 *n.*
Chamberlain, Mr. Joseph, 211
Chartered Insurance Institute, 26
Chelsea Hospital, 213
Cheops, Pyramid of, 181
Chile, 176, 210
Chumah, 182, 183
Clarkson, Mr. Willie, 166
Clayton, Rev. P. B., 253, 254
Clement Hill, 184
Clyde, 50
Coblenz, 47
Cockaigne Overture, 230
Cockneys, 92 *et seq.*
Coke of Norfolk, 94
Colman, George, 26
Cologne, 47, 107
Colombo, 88
Compton Place House, 106
Coolidge, President, 164
Cora, 149
Cornwall, Duchy of, 49 *et seq.*, 89 *et seq.*, 100, 121, 245
Cotswold Shepherd, 213
Covent Garden, 100
Coward, Noel, 214
Craven Lodge, 121
Cridlan, Mr., 156, 157
Crossing the Line, 67, 182
Cunningham-Reid, 107
Curlew, H.M.S., 174

D

Daily Express Remembrance Festival, 237
Daresbury, Lord, 156
Dar-es-Salaam, 192, 193, 194
Dartmoor, 91
Dartmouth College, 63
Degomme, 111
Delamere, Lady, 184

Delamere, Lord, 184, 199 *n.*
Delhi, 84
Depressed Areas Bill, 131
Devon, 92
Dickman, General, 47
Dodoma, 191, 192
Dorset, 92
Dover, 43, 206
Drury Lane, 119
Dufferin, R.I.M.S., 83
Dundee, 162
Dundee (S.A.), 170
Durham, 129, 161

E

East Africa, 121, 180 *et seq.*
East Anglia, 50
Ecclesiastical Commissioners, 143
Edinburgh, 162, 237 *n.*
Edward VII, 30, 31, 101, 113, 156, 172, 233
Egypt, 40
Embassy Club, 244
Empire Exhibition, 160, 162 *et seq.*
Empress of France, 161
Entebbe, 184
Enterprise, 192
E. P. Ranch, 97 *et seq.*, 160, 164, 179, 207
Escombe, 129, 131
Esher, Lord, 233 *et seq.*, 241
Evergreen, 156, 157
Exeter, 237 *n.*
Exhibition of 1851, 160, 173

F

Falmouth, 91
Farnborough, 106
Fiji, 67, 69
Finch-Hatton, 195 *et seq.*
Fishmongers' Company, 48
Flanders, 50, 89
Fleet Street, 153, 175, 224, 229, 248
Fletcher of Saltoun, 81
Fort Belvedere, 107, 244
Framwellgate Moor, 131
French, Sir John, 34, 38, 41
Friedrichshafen, 107
Fuad, King, 180, 205

G

General Strike, 177
Germany, 106

INDEX

INDEX

INDEX

INDEX

Hutchinson's

IMPORTANT NEW BOOKS FOR THE SPRING OF 1935

+++++++++++++

BOOKS OF HISTORICAL IMPORTANCE

Napoleon's Letters to Marie Louise

With a Preface by PHILIP GUEDALLA.

" *P*robably *not for a hundred years has there been such an important contribution to history.*" *In these words the famous
French historian M. de la Roncière has assessed the value
of these recently discovered Napoleonic letters which we are now privileged
to present to the English reading public.*

*These letters, numbering over three hundred, have never before been
printed. The originals, which were purchased recently in the London
sale-room on behalf of the French Government at a price of £15,000,
have been edited in the Bibliothèque Nationale in Paris.*

*They provide, in a number of ways, a new picture of Napoleon
himself and of the historical events of his last years of power. The first
letter, written to his future Empress in February, 1810, shows Napoleon
attempting by flattery to overcome Marie Louise's political prejudices
against their marriage.*

*More than a third of the collection relates to his seemingly successful
but ultimately ruinous campaign in Russia in 1812. The grandeur of
Moscow and the disaster of its burning are described by the conqueror
himself, and he gives a personal account of the retreat.*

*In one of his letters, which was intercepted by Blücher, Napoleon
gave away the secret of his plans for the French campaign of 1814 and
enabled the Prussian general to march without fear of molestation upon
Paris.*

*" As a historian," to quote again from the words of M. de la
Roncière, " these letters have given me the thrill of my life. Historians
of the past bewailed their loss, fallen into the hands of no one knew who.
Now that they have been found we shall have to revise many of our notions
of the Napoleonic epoch."*

*Important as they may be to the historian, it is to the general public
that these letters will make their wide appeal. " They tell," writes M.
de la Roncière, " one of the most passionate love stories of the age. They
are thrilling in the intensity of emotion they convey. . . . The victorious
general, before whom the world trembled, became the anxious, tender
lover."* *Illustrated,* 10s. 6d.

Twenty-Five Years

A Popular, Concise and Pictorial Story of the Life and Times of the Nation during the twenty-five years' reign of Their Majesties the King and Queen.

During this year we are to celebrate the Jubilee of our King. The celebrations will be on a scale never before equalled and the Empire will unite in thankfulness and gratitude for the services which King George has contributed, not only to his own Empire, but to the other nations of the world.

To the success of this historic occasion we are publishing this record of the past twenty-five momentous years which, under the brilliant editorship of Sir Philip Gibbs, must achieve a pre-eminence amongst other publications of its kind.

Intimate, revealing, containing many illuminating stories, this book covers the life story of the King. It is written in chronological order and all the outstanding events are dealt with.

Within the covers of this book an era in our history passes for review. We travel with the King in distant parts of his Empire ; we watch him, through the medium of the 500 dramatic photographs, play his great part in the shaping of our history ; we see him with other members of his family indulging in his favourite sports and we become aware of a loyalty and an admiration given to few kings in history.

" Twenty-Five Years " is the Jubilee book which will find a welcome in countless homes all over the Empire.

With over 500 photographs, 3s. 6d.

512 pages, Demy 8vo.

Edited by

SIR PHILIP GIBBS

The Turning Point
Three Critical Years, 1904–1906

*M*aurice Paléologue is perhaps the most brilliant of that brilliant band of French ambassadors who, by their untiring devotion to the State, created for themselves an unequalled reputation in post-War Europe.

In this valuable and important volume M. Paléologue gives us that portion of his own journal relating to the years 1904–1906 : a period of uneasiness and menace, in which French diplomacy, under the direction of Delcassé, had to face situations as complicated as they were delicate. In the course of these three years the picture of the world tragedy which burst forth in 1914 assumed shape. Here, in this book, are the French-English, French-Italian agreements which, ten years later, were to bear fruit as indispensable alliances. Here also are revealed the incessant provocations of William II which finished by stiffening resistance and uniting most of the entire world against Germany : the Machiavellian game of the Kaiser with his cousin, Nicholas II, to launch Russia in the disastrous adventure of the Russo-Japanese War : the symptoms of the stupendous cataclysm which, in 1917, was to wreck the majestic edifice of Czarism. *Illustrated, 18s.*

by
MAURICE PALÉOLOGUE
Author of *An Ambassador's Memoirs* (6th Imp.), *The Romantic Diplomat*
Translated from the French by F. APPLEBY HOLT

Espionage !
The story of the Political Secret Service of the English Crown from 1300 to 1900

*H*ere is a book of extraordinary interest and fascination describing the development of the Secret Service through six hundred years of history.

Tracing the development of Secret Investigation from medieval times, it shows how the present C.I.D. developed from the ancient system. *Illustrated, 18s.*

by
M. G. RICHINGS

BOOKS OF HISTORICAL IMPORTANCE

The Brooke Letters

Being the Letters of Sir James Brooke, first Rajah of Sarawak, to Miss Angela Burdett-Coutts

The story of how James Brooke became the first white Rajah of Sarawak is like a tale taken from romance. After the Sultan of Brunei had surrendered his sovereignty over this portion of his territory in Borneo, Brooke had a long struggle to free Sarawak from the ravages of pirates and head-hunters, and a no less bitter struggle to secure the British Government's recognition of his Raj.

One of the firmest friends and champions was Miss Angela (afterwards the Baroness) Burdett-Coutts. They met in 1847, saw each other constantly when the Rajah was in England, and wrote frequent letters when they were apart. From this correspondence, none of which has been published hitherto, Mr. Rutter has made a judicious selection, and his knowledge of Borneo affairs has enabled him to string it upon a thread of well-informed commentary and explanation.

Illustrated, 18s.

Edited by
OWEN RUTTER
Author of *British North Borneo*, *The pagans of North Borneo*, etc.
Foreword by H. H. The Ranee Margaret of Sarawak

========================= ⊡⊡ =========================

The Murder of the Romanovs

The completion of Russia's five-year plan and the measure of success which went with it have rather had the effect of drawing a veil over the Revolution and the fall of the Romanovs. But here is a book which, though devoid of cheap sensation, is a true and authoritative account of the " fantastic medieval drama," as Kerensky terms the Revolution. The author of the Introduction was the first Minister of Justice of the Provisional Government, and in this capacity had to direct the work of a commission which investigated the Rasputin affair.

As an important contribution to one of the greatest tragedies of history it is unique, and it will be read and studied. *Illustrated, 18s.*

by
CAPTAIN PAUL BULYGIN
Formerly in command of the Personal Guard of the Dowager Empress
Foreword by Sir Bernard Pares
Introduction by A. F. Kerensky
Translated from the Russian by G. Kerensky

The King's First Ambassador

A Biographical Study of H.R.H. THE PRINCE OF WALES

Since his coming-of-age, the Prince of Wales has set himself the task of carrying out a definite programme in connection with social reforms and endeavour in this country, and yet another programme for encouraging goodwill and co-operation among the peoples of the British Empire. The purpose of Mr. Basil Maine's study is to follow the Prince along the many adventurous paths he has taken in carrying out that programme, and frankly to appraise his achievement and his character. Mr. Maine has undertaken this work as a result of a spontaneous admiration for the Prince's spirit and accomplishment. His book has none of the ephemeral quality which pervades so many publications about royal personages. As the author says : " The Prince of Wales deserves a better fate in literature than to be presented as a uniformed effigy in a waxwork show. His work has been of real importance ; yet, in spite of the affection which he has inspired through-out the world, the true nature of it is rarely understood."

The publishers believe that this book will promote a more complete understanding and will explain the secret of a popularity more stable than that of any other figure of our time. They are confident that it will meet a real need throughout the Empire, especially in this Jubilee Year.

Before embarking on his study, Mr. Basil Maine discussed the project at length with Sir Godfrey Thomas, the Prince's Private Secretary, who encouraged him to complete it. Mr. Maine is well-known as an essayist, critic, novelist and orator. In 1933, reviewers throughout Europe and America were unanimous in acclaiming his biography of Sir Edward Elgar as a brilliant achievement. Illustrated, 7s. 6d.

by

BASIL MAINE

Front Everywhere

"*In this book,*" writes the author, "*I describe how I joined the 'Daily Mail' in* 1913 *and served it during the Great War in* 1914 *and* 1915. *Before crossing the doorstep of Carmelite House I had been but once in my life in a newspaper office—and that office indeed was not so much a newspaper office as the Liberal Consulate in Fleet Street. Within eleven months I had become a war correspondent, a transition surely as violent for the public as for myself. Some sort of explanation is due from me.*" *Mr. Jeffries' words give an indication of the character of "Front Everywhere." His book is full of great contrasts. The farcical charm of his entry into journalism is told in it alongside a cold narrative of a line of waggons from the front dripping blood on the Middlekirki road. "I Encounter Carbons and Commerce," "The General Sings," "I Witness Exodus" are among the chapter headings. Acrid rejoinders to the critics of the Popular Press accompany remarks such as "scoops are the necessities, not the accomplishments of newspaper work."*   *Illustrated,* 18s.

by
J. M. N. JEFFRIES
The famous Special Correspondent

□□

Triple Challenge

*I*n *the trenchant fearlessness of this autobiography, in the honest sincerity of its author's opinions, and in the very human story which it reveals, lies a worth not often to be found in the reminiscences of comparatively unknown men. Its author is a Harley Street doctor. At the age of forty-one he was confronted by the War. For a year he served in the battle-cruisers, but then, for the remainder of the War, was transferred to the Army, where he served with the Scots Guards and R.F.A. He has been an uncompromising champion of the doctor's privilege of professional secrecy and of the public's right to health-giving knowledge. At the conclusion of the War he entered politics, and he reveals here the many scandals which he discovered.*

Dr. Bayly discourses in his book on many subjects. From the width of his experiences he brings to them a refreshing sanity which will make his book of great interest and value to many readers. *Illustrated,* 18s.

by
DR. HUGH WANSEY BAYLY, M.C.

Turn Over the Page

Every Londoner and every Englishman is proud of the Royal parks and gardens. He points out their glories to visiting foreigners and awaits their delighted exclamations with peculiar gratification.

It is to Sir Lionel Earle, for so long Permanent Secretary at the Office of Works, that we owe much of their beauty. His career, in many spheres, has been long and distinguished; he has met great men and women, played an important part in the fulfilment of great events, and has now recorded, in a delightful and vivid volume, the story of his activities. Illustrated, 9s. 6d.

by

SIR LIONEL EARLE, G.C.V.O., K.C.B., C.M.G.

Reminiscences of Fifty Years

Few men have lived a more active or a more varied life than Sir Max Pemberton. His novels, of which there are nearly sixty, have thrilled millions and his recent biography of Sir Henry Royce, the famous engineer, was widely read. He was a pioneer in both cycling and motoring; he has known some of the greatest cricketers, footballers and oarsmen of our time.

Associated, then, with many branches of activity during the last fifty years, Sir Max has compiled a quite unique volume of reminiscences full of amusing anecdotes and experiences. Illustrated, 18s.

by

SIR MAX PEMBERTON

Hindenburg

This biography written by his nephew is a vivid and detailed portrait of a very great man whose stoical calm in the most fierce crises, whose philosophical and patriotic reaction to the changed conditions of republican Germany, whose indignant and effective challenge to the investigating committee of the Reichstag, whose dignified and unbiased conduct as President of the Reich aroused world-wide admiration Illustrated, 18s.

by

MAJOR GERT VON HINDENBURG

Strange Street

In 1920 *a young Canadian officer who had duly spent his gratuity and was looking for a civil career, turned up in London and joined Lord Beaverbrook as a leader-writer on the " Daily Express." His name was Beverley Baxter and his journalistic experience exactly nothing. How he was fired after his first leading article, how he became a reporter, then Literary Editor, then Editor on the " Sunday Express," and finally Editor-in-Chief of the " Daily Express." . . . How he became the most controversial editorial figure in Fleet Street, how he fared as junior partner in the famous combination of " Max and Bax," how he carried the " Daily Express " to two millions a day and then resigned, how he played his cards behind the scenes, how he tore up a £77,000 contract given him by William Harrison, and how he saw the making and breaking of the great contemporary figures of post-war England. . . . Beverley Baxter tells it all in this thrilling story of his own life.*

Illustrated, 18s.

by
BEVERLEY BAXTER

□□

Author-biography

This exhilarating book is dedicated to " All who have ink in their veins and whose hearts beat the faster because of it," but it will be read by the widest public. For it is the story of a boy with the itch to write who, in face of stern opposition and without an atom of influence, fought his way into Fleet Street and into the ranks of rising novelists before he was thirty. He begged Lord Northcliffe to take him as an office boy at nothing a week, but this and other desperate and impudent plans failed. Mr. Hunt at last sought dozens of different jobs, finally secured a safe-for-life-and-a-pension post, threw it up after three years to write—and failed again.

This brave, exciting, and always humorous book tells how Mr. Hunt at last graduated through free-lancing, trade-paper editorship, publishing, novel-writing, and now, an acknowledged expert, he is Fiction Editor of the " Daily Mail " and " Evening News," and an authority on fiction.

Illustrated, 18s.

by
CECIL HUNT
Author of *Late Dawning*, etc.

Reminiscences of an Octogenarian, 1847-1934

*The father of four distinguished sons, including Evoe of " Punch "
and Father Ronald, Dr. Knox in this diverting and brilliant
volume looks back from the age of 87 over a life crowded with
activity and interest. From a clerical home where plain living and hard
work are the order of the day, we pass through the gates of St. Paul's
School to Oxford and are taken behind the scenes of transition of Oxford
from something like a Church Seminary to a Secular University, from
compulsory attendance at Chapel to compulsory roll-calls ! From Oxford
we move to a country parish, which for forty years has been under a
tractarian régime, thence to the intensely modern problem of Aston, a
parish of 42,000. From Birmingham, in the most exciting days of its
history, where the author combines the offices of Rector, Archdeacon,
Bishop Suffragan and Chairman of the School Board, to Manchester.
We stand with the crowds on Blackpool shore, march with the Lancashire
lads in demonstration against Birrell's Bill and witness the departure of
those same lads to the battlefields of France and Gallipoli.*

Illustrated, 18s.

by
THE RIGHT REVD. E. A. KNOX, D.D. (OXON), HON. D.D. (ABERDEEN)
Formerly Bishop of Manchester

ロロ

An Autobiography

*No racing motorist has won more trophies and honours than Sir
Malcolm Campbell, holder of the world's speed record. No
racing motorist has ever held that record more often. And yet,
strange as it may seem, this man, who stands to-day with so many
adventures to his credit, is many years past the age at which most racing
motorists are supposed to have reached the peak of their career.*

*Sir Malcolm has packed his life with adventure—flying, hunting for
pirate treasure, motor racing and yachting. He has explored most of the
civilized and uncivilized world, and has escaped death on land and sea
probably more often than any man alive.* *Illustrated,* 9s. 6d.

by
SIR MALCOLM CAMPBELL

Dollfuss and His Times

This is the life story of the heroic "little Chancellor" of Austria, the "Millimetternich," as he was familiarly called by the League of Nations, together with a survey of Austrian history from his birth to his death by murder on July 25th of last year. Picturesque details and anecdotes of his life, accounts of peasant customs and descriptions of pageants are interwoven with dry political facts, but the times described were throughout so turbulent and fraught with adventure that the interest in the fortunes of the hero of the story and of his country never flags. *Illustrated*, 18s.

by
J. D. GREGORY

Prince Bülow, Man and Statesman

With the exception of Bismarck, no German Chancellor has been the subject of so much literature as Prince von Bülow. The present study, from what Bülow himself described as the "skilled hand" of Dr. Münz, is, however, authoritative and unique inasmuch as it was prepared with the direct approval of its subject, to whom the greater part was submitted personally.

The author repeatedly spent considerable periods of time in the intimacy of the Bülow family circle, where he had every opportunity to observe and talk with Bülow and his many important visitors. *Illustrated*, 18s.

by
SIGMUND MÜNZ
Author of *Edward VII at Marienbad*

Clouds That Flee

"Clouds That Flee" is a very charming and a very individual book dealing with its author's school days at Eton, London social life in the "nineties," service with the Horse Gunners in India and elsewhere, and continues his career through the Great War.

The life of a young officer serving during Edward VII's reign is portrayed. As the war of 1914 approaches clouds mar the blue horizon; brushes with the War Office are dealt with in detail and there is an unforgettable description of the Somme and Loos battles from the viewpoint of an artillery officer. *Illustrated*, 18s.

by
COLONEL MONTAGUE COOKE, D S.O.

Ventures and Visions

*C*aptain Garro Jones has written a powerful living story of experience before he is forty. He is known to the public only as a young Liberal M.P. who in 1924–1929 assailed the administration with tremendous verve and persistence. His career, however, is unique in its variety. His doings must be listed to be realized : cavalry trooper ; machine-gun commander ; air pilot in Europe and U.S.A. ; private secretary in three government departments (including that of the last Chief Secretary) ; barrister-at-law ; sea fisherman ; travelling bank clerk ; daily newspaper editor and leader-writer ; company director and manufacturing executive !   *Illustrated, 18s.*

by
CAPTAIN GARRO JONES

Horses, Jockeys and Crooks

*S*tories of the Turf, its personalities and its incidents, its compelling associations, are ever welcome. The author of this volume, who admits that he began " going racing "—by accident—in his perambulator days, has collected his memories of thirty years' " going racing " as a journalist. This is the authentic record by a writer whose authority is unimpeachable.   *Illustrated, 12s. 6d.*

by
ARTHUR J. SARL
Larry Lynx of *The People*
With an introduction by THE RT. HON. THE EARL OF LONSDALE, K.G.

It Was Such Fun

A member of the well-known family of Farquharson of Invercauld, the author of this witty and delightful volume was brought up at Langton, one of the most beautiful houses in Dorset. At the age of eighteen she married Mr. Hwfa Williams and was immediately plunged into the greatest and most brilliant society of her time in and on the continent. Her husband was a keen racing man and was one of the most intimate friends of King Edward, and this record of an active life, passing in review nearly sixty years, is a fascinating commentary in which hosts of celebrities appear.   *Illustrated, 18s.*

by
MRS. HWFA WILLIAMS

Queen Anne

One of the most brilliant critics of our day ; gifted not only with rare critical acumen but also with a witty and pungent pen, Mr. Straus' excursion into a fascinating period of our history is an event of importance.

Mr. Straus in this book is more concerned with the romance and drama of Anne's reign than he is with its historic importance through the years, and he has written a brilliant and entertaining study likely to be widely read and as widely discussed.   Illustrated, 18s.

by
RALPH STRAUS

□□

Christina of Sweden

During her life Christina of Sweden held the stage of Europe and after her death her name was on every tongue. Was she "un monstre au moral," an heroic murderess, as Walpole suggests, or a brilliant and gracious queen ? With such material at his disposal Alfred Neumann, with an international reputation as one of the most brilliant writers of our day, presents a living study of that brilliant queen who, uncurbed by reason, dominated by a capricious will, loving power and ambition, embraced the Catholic faith and voluntarily resigned the sceptre.   Illustrated, 18s.

by
ALFRED NEUMANN
Author of *The Rebels, The Patriot, The New Cæsar*, etc.

□□

George, Prince and Regent

George, Prince of Wales, afterwards George IV, is the member of our Royal Family who has suffered most at the hands of the historians and other writers—among whom Thackeray is the most prominent. Mr. Sergeant, inspired by mistrust of the possibility of so black a picture being true to life, has examined George in his earlier, though long, period as Prince, and here has made an honest attempt to present him as a personality that was something more than the "waistcoat"—or lots of waistcoats—to which Thackeray reduces him.   Illustrated, 18s.

by
PHILIP SERGEANT
Author of *A Century of British Chess, The Life of Anne Boleyn*, etc.

Rachel The Immortal:

Queen of the Stage ; Grande Amoureuse ; *Street Urchin and Grand Lady*

A full, frank, and impartial biography of Rachel, the world's greatest actress, has been written by Mr. Bernard Falk. Many letters which have not yet appeared in any written "life" of the great actress are introduced, together with a vast amount of fresh material, the whole combining to make a volume of fascinating interest.

Rachel is shown not only as Queen of the Paris stage, but as " la grande amoureuse," the cheeky street urchin and the great lady whom kings and queens, dukes and duchesses were glad to welcome.

The book, which has occupied two years of the author's time, will, in addition to numerous photographic illustrations, contain twelve special plates drawn by Frank C. Papé, one of the most notable book illustrators of the day. Illustrated, 18s.

by
BERNARD FALK
Author of *He Laughed in Fleet Street, The Naked Lady.*

□□

Sir Anthony Hope Hawkins

One of the most distinguished and experienced biographers of the day, Sir Charles Mallet, has chosen wisely in giving us this fully documented and brilliantly informed life of a novelist who, in his lifetime, achieved much more than a reputation as the author of some of the finest novels in our language. Illustrated, 18s.

by
SIR CHARLES MALLET, J.P.
Author of *Herbert Gladstone, Lord Cave,* etc.

□□

Six Portraits

With the skilled novelist's appreciation of the dramatic and an unerring penetration into character, Miss Clarke has succeeded here in giving memorable portraits of some of the greatest women of literature. Her selection will arouse controversy, and she includes Madame de Staël; Jane Austen ; George Eliot ; Jane Carlyle ; Mrs. Oliphant ; Mrs. Craigie (John Oliver Hobbes) and Katherine Mansfield. Illustrated, 18s.

by
ISABEL C. CLARKE
Author of *A Tragic Friendship,* etc.

Lady Beaconsfield

*O*f the long line of Prime Ministers which England has had, none stands out more dominantly, more romantically, than Disraeli— "My Dizzy," as Lady Beaconsfield called him.

In this most charming and illuminating of biographies Mr. Baily tells the story of a very great lady but for whom it is doubtful if Disraeli would ever have had his great political career.

"Lady Beaconsfield," says Mr. Baily, "was a great heroine of a great love story, and not only a great love story, but a great unselfish love story."

When they were both very old, and ill in separate rooms in the house at Grosvenor Gate, Disraeli used to write letters to Mary Anne, as everyone called her, from his sick bed, and in one of these he said: Grosvenor Gate has now become a hospital, but I'd rather be in hospital with you than in a palace with anybody else."

A charming story which typifies a charming book. Poignant, amusing, revealing, this altogether delightful biography is the most brilliant of Mr. Baily's accomplishments.   *Illustrated*, 18s.

by
F. E. BAILY
Author of *Twenty-Nine Years' Hard Labour*, etc.

□□

The Magnificent Montez

*H*orace Wyndham, in his new book, "The Magnificent Montez," selects a new subject and treats it in a new fashion. His subject is the glamorous career of Lola Montez, a flashing, vivid personality who began life as a coryphée, continued it as a courtesan, and ended it as a convert.

A woman of fascination and charm, of rare beauty and intelligence, and of loves and liaisons by the score, Lola Montez made history in two hemispheres. She ruled a kingdom ; she stood on the steps of a throne ; she experienced poverty and riches, staggering successes and abject failures. She sang in the gutter, and she danced in opera houses.

With the ball at her feet, Lola Montez suddenly renounced the world and its pomp and vanities ; and, becoming "converted" she directed her energies to the "saving of souls," and ended her meteoric career as a British Pelagian in New York.   *Illustrated*, 18s.

by
HORACE WYNDHAM
Author of *Ginger, Limelight*, etc.

The Black Tents of Arabia

From the complexities and distractions of modern civilisation this strange and romantic book transports its readers to the peaceful and yet perilous life of the Arabian desert and its Bedouins.

Carle Raswan is one of the few men who have penetrated the unexplored desert of Northern Arabia. He lived with the warlike Bedouins, not as a foreigner, but as one marked by the rite of blood-brotherhood with their Sheiks. He shared in the migration of over 30,000 people, hundreds of tents and thousands of camels seeking water and grazing land, experiencing with them the eternal struggle against hunger and drought. The romance, the adventure, the friendship, the courage of nomad life were revealed to him. His book, which is gripping in the simplicity of its style and the splendour of its many unique photographs, tells of life in saddle and tent, of racing camels and war horses, falcons, panthers and forays and of the love of beautiful Tuema for her brave Faris.

Illustrated, 18s.

by

CARLE R. RASWAN

⊓⊓

African Log

" African Log" is based upon the log which Shaw Desmond kept day by day during four months' journeyings in Africa, South, East and North, after he had stepped off his sailing ship from five months at sea in going round the Horn, as recorded in his now famous " Windjammer : The Book of the Horn."

His book does not profess to be an exhaustive or even deep work upon Africa and her problems. It is simply a mirror held up, day by day, to the African scene, the impressions being set down as they came flashing from the African furnace. In this mirror held up to Black and White, Dutch and English, to civilized centres in South Africa as to the more or less primitive Zulu and other communities, problems of vital import not only to the future of the Dark Continent but to that of the White world outside are indicated. Problems of politics ; of sex ; of witchcraft ; and especially problems of Colour, including the possible results to the future of the impact of White civilization on Black.

Illustrated, 18s.

by

SHAW DESMOND

Author of *Windjammer*, etc.

Loafing Round the Globe

Translated from the German by GERALD GRIFFIN

It is the ambition of most of us to loaf round the world. To the majority of us it is an ambition which can never be fulfilled and we have to be content with the stories of those, like Richard Katz, who managed it and be thankful that they have been blessed with the gift of writing.

Wherever he went Katz took with him the keenest observation and always he saw that which was interesting, amusing and important. His impressions are those of an expert and he tells his story racily and vividly so that from this picture emerges a very complete picture of the world to-day, with all its strangeness, its complexities and its customs.

Illustrated, 18s.

by
RICHARD KATZ

□□

On Horseback Through Hungary

But why on horseback, one might ask, when there are motor cars and comfortable trains in Hungary, and luxurious steamers on the blue Danube? Mr. Langlet says : " A long-distance ride, in the saddle, is the best way of becoming thoroughly acquainted with a foreign country. From the air you catch only a bird's-eye view, a fleeting glimpse of the landscape. On the other hand, trains and motor cars on the road rush too quickly past the picturesque scenery. *Illustrated,* 15s.

by
VALDEMAR LANGLET

□□

Professor John's Adventures

A number of books have been written on war imprisonment in various lands, but none other, we think, on a prisoner's fate in exile in Siberia. Words must fail in any description of this incredible human document in which P. C. Ettighoffer narrates the story of " Professor John."

" Professor John " was no adventurer, but was pitchforked into experiences wellnigh incredible by the force of circumstances.

Illustrated, 12s. 6d.

by
P. C. ETTIGHOFFER

Author of *The Island of the Doomed*

Steps Towards Indian Home Rule

In the course of a distinguished career, and with a particularly wide experience of Indian administration and affairs, Lord Zetland has acquired recognized authority to deal with the problem of Indian Home Rule which, above all others, is now engaging the people of this country.

Lord Zetland was on the Viceroy's staff as far back as 1900 ; he was a member of the Royal Commission on the Public Services in India, and from 1917 to 1922 was Governor of Bengal. He is President of the India Society and was a member of both the India Round Table Conference in 1930 and of the Parliamentary Joint Select Committee on India in 1933.

To this important book he thus brings a mind fully acquainted with every aspect of the problem ; able to delve into its many intricacies and form judgments of immense value to men and women anxious for the truth and unable, amidst so much and so fierce a controversy, to find it.

5s.

by

THE MOST HON. MARQUIS OF ZETLAND, G.C.S.I., G.C.I.E., F.B.A.

Anti-Semitism Past and Present

A distinguished diplomat, a linguist able to speak twenty-six languages, a traveller and a scholar, Count Condenhove-Kalergi all but completed this important and pertinent book before his recent death. It has now been concluded by his son and is published as one of the most striking, if not the most striking, contribution to the most discussed and controversial topic of our day.

Count Condenhove-Kalergi belonged to no political party, but was liberal in his views and above all a friend of truth and an enemy of injustice. With a quite unbiased mind and with the training of a scholar he approached this subject and studied it to its depths. His researches led him to many conclusions and discusses here all the causes of the wave of anti-Semitism now sweeping so many parts of the world. Men and women of all points of view should read this book. Its importance is obvious and it leads one to a fresh and helpful approach to the dangerous subject it so lucidly explains.

15s.

by

COUNT HEINRICH V. CONDENHOVE-KALERGI

Challenge

*T*his is Colonel Hutchison's challenge to the existing order—a political
creed and a philosophy.

        Readers of " Meteor," " Footslogger," and " Warrior " will
know that the author has something to say, and that he says it frankly.
His is the creative mind. He writes with clarity and with purpose.
And his are the convictions of a faith. Great Britain is at the cross
roads. "Challenge" is a signpost, its author already marching along
a road on whose horizon he perceives national prosperity and happiness
. . . and, more than that, a new world leadership. This road is neither
Fascism nor Communism. " Challenge " may mark the beginning of a
new political epoch.   8s. 6d.

by

GRAHAM SETON HUTCHISON, D.S.O., M.C.

Author of *Meteor, Footslogger* (5th Imp.), *Warrior* (2nd Imp.), *Arya*, etc.

□□

The Way of the Dictators

The Drama of the World Dictatorships

*S*trong Men have smashed their way to power since the war—Mussolini,
  Hitler, Mustapha Kemal, Stalin, Pilsudski. Everywhere they and
  hard-eyed youth have put liberty " on the spot." Everywhere—but
not in England, and one of the questions this important book asks is :
Shall we in this country ultimately find ourselves in the grip of a Dictator-
ship, whether Fascist or Socialist ? Who are these Strong Men in
Europe and America ? How did they rise to power ? Can they last ?
What is their secret history ? This book answers these questions
authoritatively. For the first time the stories of all the Dictators of the
world appear in one volume—their private lives and public selves,
the dramas, terrors, and triumphs of their rule.

        Mr. Lewis Broad holds no brief for or against. In this vivid,
biting, illuminating book he gathers the evidence on which every reader can
judge for himself.

by

C. LEWIS BROAD

A Falcon on St. Paul's

*M*r. *Wentworth Day, in addition to being the biographer of Sir Malcolm Campbell and Kaye Don, is one of the most brilliant and knowledgeable writers of the day on all branches of sport and natural history.*

The title of this book so chosen on account of the peregrine falcon which, within the last ten years, nested in the dome of Saint Paul's Cathedral, is symbolic of the everlasting natural history and sporting history of London.

Mr. Day develops his theme that every Londoner is at heart a countryman, and that within the very heart of the metropolis are dramas of nature, and material for the study of nature, denied even to many who dwell in the depth of rural England. He paints in his book a picture for the Londoner of his own rural heritage, and brings to light a multitude of surprising facts. Who knows, for instance, that snipe were shot in Vauxhall Marshes a hundred and fifty years ago? That a duck from Iceland nests yearly in Richmond Park? That in the same locality are foxes and herons and great crested grebes? That a stag was hunted down Tottenham Court Road before the War? That badgers have been dug from their earths within four miles of Piccadilly Circus?

Illustrated with photographs of unique interest, this fascinating and brilliantly written book brings to the Londoner that breath of fresh air for which he so often pines. Illustrated, 10s. 6d.

by
J. WENTWORTH DAY

□□

The Glory of the Dog

*E*ver since his very early childhood Mr. Sheard has been not only passion-ately fond of dogs, but immensely interested in them and in their history. He has read every book on the subject he has managed to secure, and now, from an entirely new and original angle, he presents his own most fascinating study.

From most other dog books it differs in that it touches the fringe of the dog's understanding and of his mental life in relation to ourselves. It emphasizes our responsibility towards him, and, from a wealth of legends from the mythology of ancient people, describes how dogs talk to one another and to their masters. Illustrated, 3s. 6d.

by
WILFRED SHEARD

Cricket with the Lid Off

In this book A. W. Carr, whose recent resignation from the captaincy of the Nottinghamshire team caused so much discussion, lays bare the whole disgraceful series of controversies which in recent years have done so much harm to cricket. Mr. Carr has no axe to grind ; he loves cricket for the game it is and from that all-important, yet so frequently ignored, aspect, he deals trenchantly and fearlessly with the problems raised. " Cricket with the Lid Off " is a sensational book, and through its very sensation and through its utter sincerity it may prove to be the very " medicine " for which the game is waiting. 6s.

by

A. W. CARR

A Message to the Neurotic World

Throughout this book Dr. Francis Volgyesi, deals with the vast material which the " highly strung " child of the twentieth century must know in order to be able to rid himself of " nervousness," this modern ill of our Age, or—if he does not suffer from it as yet—to avoid catching it. Dr. Volgyesi's excellent book is, as it were, a Bible of adaptability, self-discipline and love, the three factors which alone can cure the neurotic sufferer of his tormenting disease. 12s. 6d.

by

DR. FRANCIS VOLGYESI

Can You Write English ?

Among all handbooks on the writing of English, this one is unique in an important particular. Mr. Williamson's immediate interest is not academic but practical. His primary concern is not that of the grammarian but with executive writing. Whereas other handbooks on the subject lay down principles and proceed to adduce imaginary instances of deviation from them, Mr. Williamson begins with actual errors which journalists have made and adduces principles which will be corrective. 3s. 6d.

by

KENNEDY WILLIAMSON, M.A.
Editor *The Writer*
Author of *Can You Write Short Stories ?*

" *Me* " *in the Kitchen*

A collection of suggestions for the housewife who likes good food and wants to make every shilling do its duty

Here are no wearying lists beginning: " Take eight eggs and two pounds of butter," but recipes that are simple and attractive and are " talked " not hurled, at you. " Vulgar dishes " are Naomi Jacob's speciality, and she tells how to cook a kipper, how to make a Welsh rarebit, how to put up a good lunch basket for the children to take to school, how to entertain three friends to luncheon when the housekeeping purse is at its thinnest, and how to use up that " cold joint." 5s.

by

NAOMI JACOB

Author of *Me—a chronicle about other people*, *The Loaded Stick* (15th thous.), *Four Generations* (14th thous.), etc.

□□

Queer People

Few writers are better qualified for such a book as this than Dr. Dearden. He is an expert upon " queer " people and in his clear-cut, amusing, and penetrating style he sums them up, discusses their motives, explains their idiosyncrasies, and recounts their exploits.

Here, in this book, one meets face to face such queer people as Dr. Cook of Polar fame ; Cagliostro ; Beau Brummell ; Wilhelm Voigt, the German criminal ; John Hatfield, the gentleman bigamist, and a host of others whose fame has spread through their very " queerness." 8s. 6d.

by

DR. HAROLD DEARDEN

Author of *Death Under the Microscope*, *Cases of Sir Bernard Spilsbury*, *Such Women are Dangerous*, etc.

1001 Great Wonders of the Universe

In this unique and wonderful book the Editors have attempted to depict, with the minimum of letterpress, the wonders and beauties of our earth and the universe about it. Such a selection must be controversial, but here will be found pictures of beautiful things you have heard about and others which will be new to you. Fascinating, instructive, and beautiful, this book is unique in its scope and unique in the value it offers. 3s. 6d.

Unsolved Crimes

In this unique and fascinating volume all the most famous writers of mystery and detective stories have combined with retired Scotland Yard detectives in the attempted elucidation of famous " unsolved" crimes.

Anthony Armstrong, Valentine Williams, Freeman Wills Croft, J. S. Fletcher, Anthony Berkeley, Francis Iles, Tennyson Jesse, Milward Kennedy, Dorothy L. Sayers, J. D. Beresford, Margaret Cole, Sydney Horler, Mrs. Belloc Lowndes, and many others contribute with Supt. Percy Savage, Supt. John Protheroe, Supt. George Cornish, Supt. Charles Cooper, and Chief Inspector James Berrett upon a series of crimes ranging from Trunk Crime No. 1 to the Murders of Jack the Ripper.

The outstanding unsolved murders of recent years are surveyed afresh and their clues discussed. In several cases facts hitherto unknown to the general public are disclosed. Illustrated, 18s.

by
DOROTHY L. SAYERS, etc.

Famous Trials

Uniform style with our famous " Century Omnibuses," this remarkable volume contains those two volumes, published in the first instance at a guinea each, entitled " Famous Trials of History " and " More Famous Trials." This volume contains all the original illustrations and is remarkable value for 3s. 6d. 41 illustrations, 3s. 6d.

A selection from the magnificent reviews which marked the original publication.

"*They are of the very stuff of which tragedy is made . . . richer in plot than the most ingenious novel, more dramatic in climax than any play, and the duel between judge and prisoner at the bar is often as dazzling as a clash of swords.*"—DAILY MAIL.

". . . *the drama lives again, the dead, both killed and killer come to life, and the rights and wrongs of Justice stand out through the glass of time in their true perspective.*"—SUNDAY EXPRESS.

"*The most astonishing thing about Lord Birkenhead's quite astonishingly brilliant book is his reversal of famous judgments . . . most entertaining reading.*"—DAILY GRAPHIC.

by the
FIRST EARL OF BIRKENHEAD.
LORD CHANCELLOR OF ENGLAND 1919-1922.

COLOUR BOOKS

A Book of Old Ballads

Compiled and introduced by BEVERLEY NICHOLS *and illustrated with* 16 *coloured plates and numerous black-and-white illustrations by* H. M. BROCK, R.I.
9*s.* 6*d.*, *and De Luxe Edition*, 19*s.* 6*d.* *Special limited edition of* 250 *copies signed by Beverley Nichols and H. M. Brock*,   42*s.*

Compiled by
BEVERLEY NICHOLS

▭▭

The Modern Rake's Progress

8*s.* 6*d. net.*
De Luxe Edition, 15*s.*
A Special Limited and Signed Edition, 25*s.*
Demy Quarto size, with 12 *three-coloured plates and printed throughout in two colours.*

by
LOW AND BEBECCA WEST

▭▭

Hounds

15*s.*
De Luxe Edition, 30*s.*
Special Limited Edition signed by Mr. Lloyd, 42*s.*

by
T. IVESTER LLOYD

▭▭

High Tide at London Bridge

"*Wonderful London To-day*" *was one of the most enthralling books ever written about London, and all those who enjoyed the glamour of its pages will welcome this new volume with its many beautiful illustrations by Frank Mason.*   21*s.*

by
JAMES A. JONES
Author of *Wonderful London To-day*
Illustrated in colour and in black-and-white by FRANK H. MASON, R.I.

▭▭

Hunting Sketches

15*s.*, 21*s. and* 30*s.*

by
ANTHONY TROLLOPE
With an Introduction by JAMES BOYDE, M.F.H., and drawings by ROBERT BALL

The History of Tom Jones

*In two volumes, boxed, 15s. the set. De Luxe Edition, 30s. the set.
A special Limited Edition, signed by W. R. S. Stott, 42s.*

by

HENRY FIELDING

With illustrations in colour and black-and-white by W. R. S. Stott

□□

The Country Wife

*A special Limited Edition of 1000 copies, signed by Steven Spurrier,
31s. 6d. net.*

by

WILLIAM WYCHERLEY

Decorated in colour and in black-and-white by Steven Spurrier, R.I.

□□

Fun Fair

A Book of Collected Drawings

*9s. 6d. net.   De Luxe Edition, 21s. net.
Special Limited Edition of 250 copies signed by Fougasse, 31s. 6d.*

by

FOUGASSE

□□

Absurdities

A Book of Collected Drawings

*6s. net.   De Luxe Edition, 12s. 6d.
Special Limited Edition of 250 copies signed by Heath Robinson, 25s.*

by

HEATH ROBINSON

□□

Considered Trifles

Uniform with *A Book of Drawings*

*6s. net.   De Luxe Edition, 12s. 6d.
Special Limited Edition signed by H. M. Bateman, 25s.*

by

H. M. BATEMAN